Biotechnology Law and Policy
Searching for a Balance

Biotechnology Law and Policy Searching for a Balance

Ida Madieha Abdul Ghani Azmi
Majdah Zawawi
Abdul Haseeb Ansari
Lim Heng Gee
Nik Ahmad Kamal Nik Mahmud
Noriah Ramli

MADHAV BOOKS
GURGAON (HARYANA)

First Published – 2011

ISBN: 978-93-80615-02-8

Published by

MADHAV BOOKS
F-2562, Palam Vihar
Gurgaon-122 017 (Haryana)
Phone : 0124-2365193, 9810373248

Contents

Foreword

The biotechnology initiatives around the world has resulted in a debate between the promises of improving the quality of human lives with the dangers that lurks behind the effects that comes from the use of the technology. In many countries, including Malaysia, biotechnology has been hailed as the bringer of wealth and the bearer of many possibilities. Hence, it is necessary to strike a balance between the benefits brought by the technology with the dangers that may possibly befall us with the correct law and regulation.

This book provides an analysis of two key areas of biotechnology, i.e. agriculture and medical biotechnology. It discusses in detail several pertinent issues including the patentability of biotechnological inventions, the legal framework of agricultural biotechnology around the world as well as in Malaysia. Aside from the legal aspects of biotechnology, the book also looks at the ethical implications of agricultural and medical biotechnology.

Written in a succinct manner, this book will be a useful guide for those who are involved in the biotechnology industry. Nevertheless, many will also find it useful especially for those who are interested in discovering the position of biotechnology and the issues that arise from researches done, products developed and commercialised.

It is hoped that this publication will be a catalyst for further research on any aspects of biotechnology in Malaysia and elsewhere.

Acknowledgements

This book culminates from a two and a half years research project from 2006-2009 under the fundamental research grant (FRGS) scheme managed by the Ministry of Higher Education. The authors are thankful of the Research management Centre for supporting this research by providing all the necessary assistance. The authors are also indebted to the many organizations in Malaysia for assisting in the case study including Biotech Corp, SIRIM, PORIM, Sarawak Biodiversity Centre, UKM Medical Molecular Biology Institute (UMBI), Human Genome Centre, Universiti Sains Malaysia Ministry of Agriculture, Ministry of Science and Ministry of Health.

Table of Cases

A

American Cyanamid v. Ethicon
[1979] RPC 215

B

Brenner, Commissioner of Patents v. Manson
383 U.S. 519; 148 U.S.P.Q. (BNA) 689

BRUKER/Non-invasive measurement
T385/86 [1988] EPOR 357

C

Ciba-Geigy/propagating material
[1984] OJ EPO 112

CYGNUS/Diagnostic method
T964 [2002] EPOR 26

D

Diagnostic Methods G1/04
[2006] EPOR 15

Du Pont/Appetite Supressant
[1987] EPOR 6

Dysmenorrhea/ Rorer
T 81/84, 19 IIC 803 (1988)

G

Genentech Inc.'s (Human Growth Hormone) Patent
[1989] RPC 613

Genentech Inc's Patent
[1989] RPC 147

General Tire and Rubber Co. v. Firestone Tyre
[1972] RPC 457

Georgetown University/Pericardial access
T35/99 [2001] EPOR 21
Gillette Safety Razor v. Anglo American Trading Co.
(1913) 30 RPC 465
Graham v John Deere Co of Kansas City
383 US 1
Greenpeace UK v. Plant Genetic Systems N.V.
24 IIC 618 (1993)

H

Harvard/Onco-mouse
[1990] EPOR 4
Harvard/Onco-mouse
[1990] EPOR 501
Harvard/Onco-mouse
[1991] EPOR 525
Harvard/Transgenic animal
(T315/03) 2005 EPOR 31
Humpherson v. Syer
(1887) 4 RPC 407

I

ICOS Corp/(Transmembrane Receptor)
[2002] OJ EPO 293
In Re Durden
763 F.2d 1406

K

Kirin-Amgen Inc v Hoechst Marion Roussel Ltd
[2005] RPC 9
KSR International Co v Teleflex Inc
127 S. Ct. 1727; 167 L. Ed. 2d 705

M

Max-Planck/BDP1 Phosphatase T870/04
[2006] EPOR 14
Merrell Dow Pharmaceuticals Inc and another v H.N. Norton & Co Ltd.
[1994] RPC 1 (Pat. Court); [1995] RPC 233 (CA), and [1996] RPC 76 (HL)

Monsanto v. Schmeiser
[2004] 1 SCR 902; 2004 SCC 34

N

Novartis AG G 1/98
[2000] OJ EPO 111; [1999] EPOR 123

O

Occidental Petroleum's Application
(1986) 16 IIC 216

P

Plant Genetic Systems/Glutamine Synthetase Inhibitors
(1993) 24 IIC 618
Plant Genetic Systems/Glutamine Synthetase Inhibitors
T356/93
[1995] EPOR 357 TBA
Pro-Mold & Tool Co v Great Lakes Plastics Inc
75 F 3d 1568

R

Re Dane K. Fisher and Ragunath v. Lalgudi
421 F.3d 1365
Re Dembiczak
175 F 3d 994
Re Deuel
51 F 3d 1552 (Fed Cir 1995)
Re Kotzab
217 F 3d 1365
Riddlesbarger Application
(1936) 53 RPC 57

S

Schering AG's Application
[1971] RPC 337
Schering's and Wyeth's Applications
[1985] RPC 545
Schneider (Europe) Ag and Schneider (USA) Inc v Scimed Life Systems, Inc
1995 U.S. App. LEXIS 9754; 39 USPQ 2D (BNA) 1596 (CAFC 1995)

Shell/Bloodflow T182/90
[1994] EPOR 320

T

Technograph v. Mills and Rockley
[1972] RPC 346

The Standard Oil Company v American Cyanamid Company
774 F.2d 448

U

Unilever Ltd (Davis's) Application
[1983] RPC 219

V

Valensi v British Radio Corp
[1973] RPC 337

W

Windsurfing International v. Tabur Marine
[1985] RPC 59

Z

Zymogenetics/Hematopoietic cytokine receptor T898/05
[2007] EPOR 2

Table of Statutes

Control and Licensing of Poultry Farming (Johore) Enactment 1997

Control and Licensing of Poultry Farming and Poultry Related Activities (Negeri Sembilan) Enactment 1996

Control of Drugs and Cosmetics Regulation 1984

Control of Pig Farming Activities (Selangor) Enactment 1991

Control of Rearing of Pig (Malacca) Enactment 1980

Control of Rearing of Pig (Perak) Enactment 1992

Control of Rearing of Pigs (Negeri Sembilan) Enactment 1981

Control of Rearing of Pigs (Pahang) Enactment 1998

Customs Act 1967 (Revised-1980)

Customs (Prohibition of Exports) Order 2008

Customs (Prohibition of Imports) Order 1998

Customs (Prohibition of Imports) Order 2008

Destruction of Disease Bearing Insects Act 1975

Environmental Quality Act 1974

Federal Animal Quarantine Station (Management and Maintenance) By-Laws 1984

Federal Constitution

Fisheries (Adoption) Enactment (Johore) 1989

Fisheries (Adoption) Enactment (Kelantan) 1986

Fisheries (Adoption) Enactment (Negeri Sembilan) 1989

Fisheries (Adoption) Enactment (Perlis) 1988

Fisheries Act 1985

Fish Marketing Regulations 1973

Food Act 1983

Food Act 1985

Food Regulations 1985

Human Tissues Act 1974

Lembaga Kemajuan Ikan Malaysia Act 1974

National Forestry Act 1984

Pesticides Act 1974

Patent Act 1977

Patents Act 1983

Pathology Laboratory Act 2007

Plant Quarantine Act 1976

Plant Quarantine Regulations 1981

Poisons Act 1952

Prevention and Control of Infectious Diseases Act 1988

Protection of Wild Life Act 1972

Protection on New Plant Varieties Act 2004

Radiation Protection (Basic Safety Standard) Regulation, 1988

Sale of Drugs Act 1952

Sale of Food and Drugs Ordinance 1952

Sarawak Biodiversity Centre (Amendments) Ordinance, 2003

Sarawak Biodiversity Centre Ordinance 1997

Sarawak Biodiversity Regulations 2004

Standards of Malaysia Act 1996

Trade Descriptions Act 1972

1

Biotechnology as the New Economic Driver

In 1998, Jeremy Rifkin wrote about how the new biotechnology will challenge our perceptions and value system. He spoke of how 'our definition of life and the meaning of existence is likely to be radically altered.' He also wrote about the advantages that biotechnology will present to humankind. This includes the increasing volumes of food, commercial applications of novel transgenic bacteria, viruses, plants and animals and other new commercial applications of biological resources.[1] As the potential benefits arising from biotechnology could be countless, it has been identified by many national governments as the new economic driver, including Malaysia.

Biotechnology is a set of technologies utilising the biological sciences. [2] At its most general, it can simply be defined as the application of biology to human needs. A more specific definition would be that "it is a set of technologies that use biological molecules and cells to make products, solve problems, and do research, based upon an understanding of cellular and molecular structure and processes".[3] Another description of biotechnology is that "it relates to the applied forms of biological science, and generally speaking refers to the technological use of organisms and organic processes to produce outcomes which have economic or industrial value."[4] The Convention on Biological Diversity defines 'biotechnology' as; "before any technological application that uses biological systems, living organisms, or derivatives thereof, to make or modify products or processes for after specific use".[5]

Traditional biotechnological processes include fermentation techniques and traditional plant and animal cross breeding. Modern biotechnology, however, has come to refer to the processes and products associated with manipulation of DNA, and the technologies resulting from gene sequencing. This is associated with "genetic engineering" which includes processes like "recombinant DNA technology" (also known as genetic modification, gene technology, or genetic manipulation), the techniques of joining or recombining DNA material to create new genetic combinations which then can be propagated to produce a desired new outcome.[6]

Another important international definition is found in the Bio-safety Protocol, which defines " 'modern biotechnology' as the application of: a. in vitro nucleic acid techniques, including recombinant deoxyribonucleic acid (DNA) and direct injection of nucleic acid into cells or organelles, or b. fusion of cells beyond the taxonomic family, that overcome natural physiological reproductive or recombination barriers and that are not techniques used in traditional breeding and selection."[7]

The technologies involved include monoclonal antibody technology, cell culture technology, genetic engineering technology, biosensor technology, antisense technology, DNA chip technology, tissue engineering, bio-processing technology and bioinformatics technology.

The possible end products of these technologies would include both products per se or they could relate to processes. Examples of products would include recombinant DNA, gene coding for specific protein or nucleotide sequence or promoter, plasmids, cell lines, tissue media, hybridomas, monoclonal antibodies and genetically engineered tissues and organs. Other products would include genetically engineered drugs and medicines produced by host cells, or even novel microorganisms or transgenic plants and animals. Related products would include DNA chips and diagnostic kits.

A wide range of processes would emerge from the above technologies, including gene transformation techniques, methods of expressing DNA, methods of purifying product, methods of attenuating virus, fermentation process, and somatic gene therapy, among others.

Despite the speed in which the technology moves, it now appears that many novel issues arising from new applications of biotechnology are not adequately addressed by existing regulatory framework for biotechnology. In fact, these technological advances will create significant challenges to national government's oversight. In many instances, the old traditional rules applicable to old technology have been extended to cover biotechnological processes and products.

Malaysia is taken as a case study only to illustrate the position of a gene rich developing country aiming to tap into her biological resources as a new economic driver. The Malaysian experience is unique as it is driven by a set of industrial policies introduced by the government contained in the Biotechnology Master Plan. This Master Plan consists of a three phase development programme (known as The Biotechnology Master Plan from 2006 to 2020). The first phase covers the period between 2005 and 2010 and is dedicated to capacity building; the second phase (2011 - 2015) focuses on the transformation of science to business; and the third phase (2016–2020) aims to develop Malaysian biotechnology to become a global business.

The National Biotechnology Policy which was launched in 2005 addresses vital aspects of biotechnology development such as priority areas, legal, safety, financial and other issues. It also spells out nine policy thrusts including the use of biotechnology to create and enhance value in agriculture, health care and industrial production. The Malaysian Biotechnology Corporation Bhd (BiotechCorp) was established the same year to spearhead the policy implementation in the sector.

The Eighth Plan Period was committed to laying the foundation for a competitive biotechnology industry. Under the Plan, the government has intensified its efforts on capacity building which includes human resource development, research and development (R&D) in biotechnology in priority areas and enhancement of technological infrastructure and facilities. Under this plan, the then Ministry of Science, Technology and Environment proposed to develop three national institutes within a Malaysian Biotechnology cluster known as Bio-Valley. It was formed to accelerate research and commercialisation of technologies critical to the development of Malaysia's regional and global competitiveness. Although the Bio-Valley project was short-lived, this was replaced by seven Biotechnology Cooperative Centres that have been established to help foster cooperation, improve coordination and reduce duplication in biotechnology research activities. The centers are located as follows:

- Molecular Biotechnology Cooperative Centre at both University Malaya (UM) and University Kebangsaan Malaysia (UKM).
- Plant Biotechnology Cooperative Centre at Malaysia Agriculture and Rural development Institute (MARDI).
- Animal Biotechnology Cooperative Centre at University Putra Malaysia.
- Medical Biotechnology Cooperative Centre at University Malaysia Sarawak.
- Environmental/Industrial Biotechnology at SIRIM Cooperative Centre.
- Biopharmacy Cooperative Centre at University Science Malaysia (USM).
- Food Biotechnology Coöperative Centre at UPM and MARDI.

In the area of human resources development, key initiatives such as.Biotechnology Entrepreneur Development framework, Malaysia's BeST, Global Bio-Entrepreneurship (qb3), Executive–in-Residence Mentorship, and Association of University Research Parks (AURP) have been employed by the BiotechCorp to enhance skills and talents. Already, Malaysian's BeST has produced its first set of graduates numbering two hundred and six (206) and about seventy percent (70%) of whom have obtained placements with some of the BioNexus companies. Twenty Malaysian senior personnel from research universities, government agencies, financial institutions and existing entrepreneurs have benefitted under the Global Bio-Entrepreneurship (qb3) which provided them with training in life sciences, entrepreneurship and venture financing.

The goals of biotechnology under the Ninth Malaysian Plan (9MP) are to harvest the potentials of biotechnology as a growing source of wealth creation and to enhance its application in various sectors of the economy. A sum of RM 2.1 billion is allocated to biotechnology under the 9MP and the BiotechCorp has already utilised RM300m of it to initiate commercialisation, technology acquisition, entrepreneur development and the development of an Intellectual Property (IP) framework. The following Table 1 contains the flash points of these efforts:

Incentives in the form of Bill of Guarantees and tax incentives have been offered by government to companies as a strategy to attract both foreign and local investments. However, only companies having Bio-Nexus status are qualified to enjoy the incentives. Bio-Nexus status is a recognition awarded by the Malaysian government, through Biotech Corp, to qualified companies that participate in and undertake value-added biotechnology businesses. A company is eligible for the award of Bio-Nexus status if it meets the following criteria:

(a) Establish a separate legal entity for Bio-Nexus qualifying business activities,

(b) Provides products or services based on life sciences, or substantially employs processes involving life sciences in its production or agricultural activities,

(c) Possesses research capability and conducts research in thrust areas,

(d) Employs significant percentage of knowledge workers in its total work force; and

(e) Complies with environmental and ethical laws and guidelines.

Table 1
Biotechnology (9MP)

Initiating Commercialisation	*Technology Acquisition*	*Entrepreneur Development*	*Development of Intellectual Property*
• Granted BioNexus Status to 42 companies • Attracted Investment capital and Funding (about RM3.5 billion]	• Acquired Nanotechnology Platform • Local & International Alliances • BioMaysia (2006 – 5,000 participants; 2007 - 7,800 participants) • BIO International Convention (USA) Philadelphia 2005, Chicago 2006, Boston 2007	• Biotech Entrepreneur Framework • Executive-in Residence Mentorship • Global Entrepreneurship Programme (qb3) • Biotech Entrepreneurship Special Training (BeST)	• IP Certification in Malaysia • International IP Benchmarking Study • Patent Examiner International Exchange Programme • Patent Examiner Outsourcing Programme

So far, forty two (42) companies have been awarded Bio-Nexus status and nineteen (19) of them are players in the field of health care biotechnology. The terms covered in the Bill of Guarantees are:

Table 2
Terms in Bill of Guarantees

- Freedom of ownership
- Freedom to source funds globally
- Unrestricted employment of knowledge workers
- Eligibility for competitive incentives and development programmes – tax incentives, grants and other assistance
- Provision of enabling environment that meets international accreditation standards
- Provision of an environment for intellectual property protection and enforcement comparable to international standards
- Access to a supportive information networking research centres of excellence
- Access to shared laboratories, facilities and services
- Biotech Corp as the dedicated agency empowered to act as one-stop-centre and provide fast track options for Government approvals and licences

The Biotechnology Policy demonstrates that Malaysia wishes to venture into biotechnological industries on a massive scale. However, the country lacks the necessary legal and regulatory framework.

This book intends to explore the legislative framework applicable to the agricultural and medical biotechnology industry in many countries. In agricultural biotechnology, bio-safety tops the list of concerns raised by consumers. It is not surprising that among the pioneer regulatory framework developed with agricultural biotechnology industry in mind is bio-safety law. Global standards on this could be found in Cartagena Protocol and the WTO Sanitary and Phyto-sanitary Measures Agreement (SPS Agreement). It is under the SPS Agreements that disputes arising from the exportation of GMO products are being resolved. This book, in its chapter two, explores all of these issues as well as the member country disputes that have been raised under the SPS Agreement.

Chapter two also contains a survey of the status of agricultural biotechnology in some of the major biotechnology producers in the world today. In some countries, GM crops are already at the stage of regulatory approval, whilst in others they are either at the stage of field study or in lab/greenhouse. The status of agricultural biotechnology in ASEAN countries are also looked at in this chapter.

Chapter three discusses the patenting of biotechnological products. One main important perimeters of patenting is the threshold of patentability; i.e. the conditions that need to be satisfied in order for a patent to be registered. The chapter continues to describe matters which are non patentable provided by section 13 of the Patents Act and under this the discussion goes on to analyse the issue of the patentability of plant and animal varieties. From here the chapter continues to delve into the issue of objections to patentability which are based on morality and public order. This part of the chapter scrutinizes the applicability of section 31(1) of the Malaysian Patents Act which is similar to Article 53(a) of the European Patent Commission (EPC). The chapter then goes on to discuss some recent developments in patenting criteria which may have an impact on biotechnological inventions. Part 3 ventures further into the drug approval process and how biotechnology related pharmaceutical products needs to undergo the drug approval process before being made available to the public. Finally, Part 4 of the Chapter provides recommendations on the 3 main issues discussed in this chapter.

Chapter four mainly looks into the ethical dimensions of research in biotechnology and any of its products, with special emphasis to the position in Malaysia. In doing so, the chapter is divided into four parts. The first part of the chapter discusses the meaning of bioethics and its relation to biotechnology. This part also briefly identifies the ethical issues raised when biotechnology is used in agricultural and health biotechnology. Meanwhile, the second part of the chapter looks at the role of bioethics committees and the importance of these committees in many parts of the developed world. Part three of the chapter continues the discussion on the position of bioethic committees in Malaysia. From here part four of the chapter looks into the influence of religion in bioethical considerations in Malaysia. Finally, the chapter seeks to provide some conclusions and recommendations that could address some of the problems that have been associated with biotechnology.

Chapter five and six of the book is devoted to the legislative framework in Malaysia as a case study. Chapter five provides a discussion of the role of several government agencies in the use and control of biotechnology in the agricultural sectors in Malaysia. The discussion is divided into three parts. Part one concentrates on the use of biotechnology in animal and animal products which is under the direct supervision on the Department of Veterinary Services (DVS). This part highlights the role of the DVS in ensuring that all animal based products are fit for human consumption and in doing so the welfare of the animals too are looked after. In this part a brief discussion is made on the application of the Animal Ordinance, 1953 and the Animal Rules of 1962. The application of certain state enactments that regulate the licensing requirements for the farming of poultry and pig-farming have been highlighted. In regards to the use of biotechnology in animal farming or production, it has been submitted that existing legislation does not directly deal with the use of biotechnology in animal farming and production of food for animal consumption. The chapter then provides some recommendations on how the DVS could improve the lacuna in the Animal Ordinance 1953 and the Food Regulations 1985.

In the second part of the Chapter, the discussion is continued on the use of biotechnology in fish and fisheries product which falls under the jurisdiction of the Department of Fisheries. Concentration is made on the standards adopted by the Department of Fisheries for aqua-farmers whereby Good Farming Practices are introduced to ensure that fish farmers are more responsible towards the consumers and the environment. Nevertheless, as in animal farming or production, the related laws do not directly deal with the use of biotechnology. Highlight is made on the results of interviews conducted which showed that the government does not allow gene manipulation for fish produce for human consumption, despite the absence of specific provisions in existing legislations and regulations.

The third part of the Chapter concentrates on the agricultural produce which is under the direct supervision of the Department of Agriculture. This area would perhaps be the largest area in which biotechnology is used. This part discusses the applicability of several legislations and how it controls the use of biotechnology in research and agricultural produces. The main concern of this part is on the use of genetically modified organisms (GMOs) its control and labeling requirements for genetically modified foods. Attention is also made to the Bio-Safety Act 2007 which is the basis for regulating bio-safety aspects of biotechnology. It sets forth a number of procedures and rules regulating the release, importation, exportation and contained use of living modified organisms and the release of such products of such organisms in order to protect humans, plants animals, the environment and to ensure biological biodiversity. Comments are also made on how current understanding and practices relating to Bio-safety, food labeling and transportation of GMOs and LMOs could be improved.

This chapter also contains a compilation of general practices on the regulation of agricultural biotechnology from Australia which the research puts forward as a good example to follow. Aside from that recommendations are also made on the need for a boost in the role of consumers in demanding for their rights to be informed on the use of biotechnology in the area of agricultural biotechnology especially when it relates to food production.

Chapter six examines the legal landscape surrounding the health biotechnology industry in Malaysia in three critical stages; research, product development and commercialization. Among issues critical at the stage of research are approval for research, lab protocol, ethical standards, bio safety, customs and access and benefit sharing. Whilst for product development, critical issues are pre clinical trial, privacy and ethics. At the stage of commercialization, the critical issues include drug approval, access and benefit sharing and labeling.

What are the lessons to be learned from the global, international and national legal standards on biotechnology? What are the lessons that could be drawn from the Malaysian experience? Should we focus on the development of the technology first? Should it be coupled with enhancement of the infrastructure and R & D facilities? When should strong legislative framework be introduced? Can Malaysia be showcased as a 'model' for other gene rich countries wanting to embark on the same journey? These are some of the conclusions that will be drawn in chapter seven of the book.

Footnotes

1. Jeremy Rifkin, The Biotech Century: Harnessing the gene and Remaking the World, (1998)
2. The scientific disciplines, biology, cell biology, molecular biology, immunology, microbiology, chemical engineering, genetics, chemistry, biochemistry, physics, computer science, forensic science, and mathematics–encompass the range of activities which comprise the underlying scientific principles of biotechnology. See Victoria Sutton, Law and Biotechnology: Cases and Materials, Carolina Academic Press 2007, p 3.
3. See Victoria Sutton, Law and Biotechnology: Cases and Materials, Carolina Academic Press 2007, p 4.
4. Intellectual Property and Biotechnology: A Training Handbook, Module 2 (A training resource for developing countries in the APEC region funded under the APEC Support Program of the Australian Agency for International Development (AusAID) December 2001).
5. Article 2, Convention on Biological Diversity.
6. *Ibid.*
7. Article 3 of the Cartagena Protocol on Bio-safety to the Convention on Biological Diversity–29 January 2000.

2

Agricultural Biotechnology

Introduction

Enough food is a prerequisite for survival of mankind on earth. With increase of the world population, food demand also increases. It is therefore necessary to keep a close proximity between population growth and agricultural output. This task can be a possibility only when agriculture becomes a matter of priority. So as to meet this challenge, in most of the developing countries, especially in India and China, policy makers in the sixties and sentries of the nineteenth century gave priority to agriculture, which is the green revolution. The noteworthy boost to the agricultural sector in these countries resulted in agriculture and agro industries being accorded numerous incentives, and several agricultural universities were established. In spite of that, many least developed countries especially in Africa, which were not so resourceful, could not meet the challenge of their food demand. These countries obtained food aid from countries that produce more food grains than they need, e.g. the United States, Canada and Australia. Some other developing countries, including Malaysia, instead gave priority to its industrial sector. It proved to be a success, but they did not have enough agricultural growth.

These countries, including Malaysia, could be able to reduce imports resulting in saving a substantial amount of money. Nevertheless, they still have to import food grains to fulfill their demands. They cannot afford to continue with this position. They will have to support their agricultural sector with suitable incentives. It is for this reason that in Malaysia, agriculture is now a priority area, and it is supported with some incentives. This has given a boost to this sector.[1] However, the country has yet to grant formal approval to any GM Crop.

In many developed countries, the population growth has been either steady or has not experienced any growth at all. The scenario in developing countries is different. It is estimated that the total population in these countries will keep on growing in at least the three coming decades, which will push food demand in these countries up; whereas the agricultural growth has its own limitations. Efforts in the traditional ways have always been made by farmers and scientists in all countries to improve existing species of food grains, especially of rice, wheat and corn. But these efforts could bring only little help. The recent scientific inventions in agricultural biotechnology have certainly brought a sigh of relief, as species developed by means of gene manipulation can give relatively more crops even in adverse weather conditions. Genetically modified corn is the best example. Biotechnology research went on to modify plant and animal species.

However, ever since their invention genetically modified seeds have always been matters of controversy. The first and foremost controversy is that genetically modified food (hereinafter GM Food) are not good for human health. It is not only limited to food grains; it goes further to genetically modified cotton (Bt Cotton), which has the quality to kill common kind of insects that cause harm to cotton crops. Seeds of Bt Cotton are used to make oil. It is argued that how can such oil be used for cooking food? The second controversy is that if genetically modified seeds (hereinafter GM-seeds) are used by farmers, the other species will vanish, with the result that there will be an irreparable loss of biodiversity further resulting in economic dependency. This has proved to be true in the case of termination seeds, which can only produce crop (hereinafter GM Crops), but cannot further be used for the next crops. Yet another controversy is that GM Crops, if grown closer to other varieties, will contaminate those other varieties. It means in due course of time, other varieties will lose their originality, and all will become like GM Crops. Some countries are totally skeptical about genetically modified organisms (GMOs) and genetically modified living organisms (LMOs), GM Food and food containing genetically modified organisms. Some other countries are supportive of all these and they have no objections concerning human consumption of these food. These are mainly producing countries. There is yet a class of countries that has taken the precautionary approach. They have allowed only some of the genetically modified cash crops for economic reasons; but others have taken a precautionary approach. The strict application of the precautionary principle is that if the effect of something is not ascertained, it is better not to introduce it. However, some countries, like India, have developed its own testing mechanism, and before their import, effects of the LMOs and GMOs and GM Food have to undergo intensive laboratory testing. Malaysia also subscribes to the precautionary approach. These countries are taking many precautions because companies engaged in developing newer genetically modified seeds and the like are not guaranteeing their safety. EU member states are very cautious about GM Crops. Given that EU countries are net importers of many agricultural commodities, EU countries have a major impact on developing and least developed countries. Many developing countries in Africa have failed to adopt GM Crops because of EU countries' advice regarding the 'Precautionary principle'.[2] It is, therefore, necessary to examine the attitude of some of the developed and developing countries' towards some important biotechnologically developed GMOs being consumed by the human mass. It is also necessary to examine regulatory and precautionary measures of these states towards GMOs.

The scenario of domesticated animals for meat and milk is different. The problem with them is limited only to GM Food. There is no danger of unwanted contamination of other species unless genetically modified LMOs are left loose to the wild. Laws that regulate use of meat and milk of genetically modified animals and GM food require proper evaluation. In many countries, there is no competent regulatory framework. It requires to be thoroughly discussed so that we can formulate a viable legal framework. Towards this end, the EU Regulations can be just a good guide.

There is lack of a competent local legal framework that protects the interest of farmers. The legal framework generally favours breeders rather than farmers. According to the Indian experience it can be said that if a breeder infringes farmers' right there is no provision to compensate them. On the contrary, if farmers infringe breeders' right, they have to recompense the breeders. This is because most of their innovations are patented. If farmers do not get good crop or suffer from a total failure while they have used certain types of genetically modified seed, law is not competent enough to protect farmers' interests. Likewise, if their crop gets contaminated because a genetically modified crop was grown close by, they can seldom be compensated. There is possibility only when farmers are able to bear the cost of justice. It is notable that the vast majority of farmers in developing and least developed countries are not able to bear this. It could be possible in a few cases. One of them is *Monsanto* v. *Schmeiser* [3] where the Canadian Supreme Court awarded compensation for such a contamination. This matter requires further investigation. We need to develop a compensation mechanism that protects the interest of all interest groups, breeders, farmers and consumers equally.

The International Convention for the Protection of New Varieties of Plants (UPOV ACT), which has been amended from time to time, provides protection to breeders. Based on it, there is union of the member states having its seat in Geneva. This convention has strengthened the TRIPS and the WTO. Malaysia is not a member of this convention. It is necessary to critically examine relevant provisions of the convention, keeping in mind the interests of developing countries and least developed countries in general and farmers in specific.

All the above raised questions are required to be answered in the context of developing countries with special reference to Malaysia, so that these countries could take appropriate steps to protect their interests. Reference to the practices and the legal framework of developed countries will be considered only as a guide. Before any practices or laws of developed countries are recommended to be followed by developing countries, including Malaysia, their suitability to these countries will have to be properly examined. And possibility to establish mutual cooperation between these countries will also be appropriate to be examined.

Status of Agricultural Biotechnology in the Contemporary World

Food safety concern has always been associated with GM Food. The public perceptions are:

Health Risks

It is said that GM Food might increase the toxin level in the human body, that they might be a reason for cancer, that they might cause allergy, and that they might develop antibiotics resistance detrimental to the human body. It was proved in the United Kingdom that the tests which are made as basis to say that GM Food might cause toxin in the human body was faulty. Some kind of hormone injected in animals for more milk was proved to be cancerous to the human body. Thus, they were banned in Canada and European Union countries. The last fear of development antibiotics resistance has not be substantiated by any scientific tests. With respect to some kind of genetically modified soybean, it was reported that they have potential to cause serious allergy. It was confirmed by safety assessments.[4]

Environmental Risks

Increased use of pesticides and herbicides will contaminate the soil. This seems to be true. There might be genetic pollution. If necessary precautions are not taken, this will prove to be true. There will be damage to beneficial insects. This is said in the context of Bt cotton. It is now said that Bt cotton can only kill one type of insect which damages the cotton crops the most. This is yet to be satisfactorily substantiated. GM soybean and canola might develop their resistance to weeds also turning them into super weeds. This fear has yet to be proven. Likewise, Bt cotton and maize might create super pests. This fear is also yet to be substantiated. Some genetically modified plant and animal species might be so strong that they might weed out other species. There is yet no scientific evidence of this fear.[5]

Socio-economic Risks

Terminator seeds might create economic dependency. This is true. Because of this reason, Monsanto has withdrawn termination seeds. The economic gap between developed and developing countries might widen. In the absence of necessary help extended by developed countries to developing and less developed countries, this might not happen. In view of this, it is said that developing countries should give high priority to the biotechnology capacity building.

Ethical Concerns

It is said that from the ethical and religious reasons, biotechnology products are not acceptable. This is not true because biotechnology researches that are for the interest of the society are means to protect human kind from hunger and poverty. No religion can disapprove anything that is in the interest of the general public. Misuse of biotechnology for developing certain harmful viruses which can be used as a biological weapon is certainly unethical and opposed to all religions.

According to Chapter 5 of the 2003-04 *State of Food of the Food and Agriculture Organization of the United Nations* (SOFA), which is based on several independent research conducted by the International Council for Science, the Nuffield Council of Bioethics, the United Kingdom GM Science Review Panel, and the Royal Society Farm-Scale Evaluation. SOFA concluded firstly that there is no exceptional food safety problems with GM Food. There are two main food safety concerns, first, introduction of allergens and toxins; and secondly, negative effects from the consumption of antibiotic-resistance marker genes, and viral promoter genes used in the transformation process. According to the report, the alleged allergenic and toxic effects have not been scientifically proven. As far as the other negative effects are concerned, their use has been discouraged and scientists have developed a clean method of genetic transformation that eliminates these substances. It is therefore warranted that this expertise have to be used in growing GM Crop.

Secondly, adverse impact on the environment is true to some extent. But if enough precautions are taken, these negative impacts can be mitigated. These negative impacts are also true with the traditional crops. But the same results are reached in different manners. For example, in Cambodia, heavy reliance of farmers on only few rice varieties resulted in vanishing other varieties. It put the scientists in such a condition that they could not conduct further research using genetic materials of local rice varieties. Fortunately those varieties were there in the gene bank of the International Rice Research Institute of Philippines. Scientists might face the same kind of problem if only genetically modified crop is adopted by farmers, or if all other species get contaminated by GM Crops. It is, therefore suggested that environmental effects–out-crossing of the genes, harm to non-targeted crops, and emergence of pest resistance, etc.-should be evaluated on a case-by-case basis depending on the crop, trait and the ecosystem where the crop is grown.[6] It is notable here that the health risk as noted above can be eliminated by using some kind of technology. It is also notable here that environmental harm cannot be ruled out. But it can be mitigated by using appropriate measures.

It is because of these reasons that both developed and developing countries are concerned about the health and environmental safety of genetically modified organisms. As developed countries are technologically advanced, they take appropriate measures based on their scientific findings on risk assessment. Developing countries are confronted with two conflicting recommendations regarding GM crops. The recommendation from most North American universities and policy research centers is that developing countries should develop food safety and environmental safety regulations so that they could do intensive risk testing to their own satisfaction. It is more important for democratic countries. It will be easier to convince their people about the use or provision on use of certain types of GM Food.

On the other hand, the recommendation from most European Union universities and policy research centers is that developing countries should take a precautionary approach. It means slower development of regulatory mechanism for the introduction of GM Crops and GM Food. It also has implications for the development of the skills associated with developing GM Crops. This is because modern plant breeding encompasses 'marker-aided selection' techniques that facilitate conventional plant breeding.[7]

The authors are of the view that the experience of Argentina, China, India, Mexico and South Africa as well as the United States reveal that Bt Cotton has been economically beneficial. It is for this reason that Bt Cotton has been approved by many countries. Governments have made regulations to protect the interests of small farmers. They have also ensured that the profit made by the private sector companies permeates down to small farmers in the form of chap seeds and general public in the form of lower price. It has also been noted that small farmers have had no difficulty in adopting new farming technology. However, these findings cannot be generalized. Countries should make their own research before introducing transgenic Bt Cotton and maize.

Based on independent risk assessments, many countries initially approved soybeans, maize, cotton and canola. This was further extended to other GM Crops and their commercial use was permitted. United States, for example, has granted such approvals to canola, chicory, cotton, flax and linseed, maize, melon, papaya, potatoes, rice, soybeans, squash, sugar beets, tobacco and tomatoes. This has been followed by many developing countries. India, Argentina, Mexico, China, South

Africa, Brazil, Uruguay, Colombia, the Philippines, Paraguay and Chile have approved GM Crops for commercial production. Some other countries like Kenya, Bangladesh, Morocco, Pakistan, Malaysia, Costa Rica, Bolivia, Zimbabwe, Thailand, Cuba, Honduras, Egypt, Tunisia and Guatemala are in the early stage of approval. A large number of developing countries are encouraging it to be studied and conducted at laboratory level. If things go favorable, they might approve GM Crops for commercial farming in times to come. For a comprehensive presentation, countries can be classified as: approval for commercial production (P), regulatory approval (A), field study (F) and lab/greenhouse study (L). The table given below depicts the stages of country-wise acceptability:[8]

Table 1
Global Biotechnology: Field Crops-2006

Field Crops Country	*Soybean*	*Cotton*	*Maize*	*Canola*	*Sugar beet*	*Rice*	*Flax*	*Wheat*
Canada	p	A	P	P	A	A	A	F
US	P	P	P	P	A	A	A	F
Australia	A	P	A	A	A			F
West Eup.	A	F	P	A	F	F		F
Argentina	P	P	P		F			F
Mexico	A	p	F	F		F	F	F
China	F	P	F	L	L	F		L
Japan	A	A	A	A	A	F		L
S. Africa	P	P	P	F				
Brazil	P	F	F			F		
East Eup.	P		A	F	L		L	F
Indonesia	F	A	F			L		
Uruguay	P		P					
Egypt		A	F	A				F
India		P		F		L		
Colombia		P						
Philippines			P			F		
Paraguay	P							
Chile	P		P					
S. Korea	A		P					
Honduras			A					
Belize		F	F	F				
Cuba			L			L		
Thailand		F				F		
Canada		F	F		F	F	F	

Contd.

Field Crops Country	*Soybean*	*Cotton*	*Maize*	*Canola*	*Sugar beet*	*Rice*	*Flax*	*Wheat*
Venezuela						L		
Zimbabwe		F						
Bolivia	F	F						
Costa Rica			L			F		
N. Zealand				F				
Malaysia						L		
Pakistan		L				L		
Morocco								L
Bangladesh						L		
Kenya			L					

Field Crop by Country	*Sugar Cane*	*Barley*	*Alfalfa*	*Cassava*	*Sunflower*	*Clover*	*Safflower*	*Sorghum*
US	F	F	F				F	
Australia	F	F				F		
W. Europe		F	F		F			
Argentina	L	L	F		F			
Mexico								
China		L						L
Japan								
S. Africa	F							
Brazil	F	L						
E. Europe		L	F		F			
Indonesia	L			L				
Uruguay								
Egypt	F	L						
India								
Colombia				L				
Philippines								
Paraguay								
Chile								
S. Korea								
Honduras								
Belize								
Cuba	F							
Thailand				L				
Venezuela	L			F				
Zimbabwe				F				
Bolivia								
Costa Rica								
N. Zealand								
Malaysia								
Pakistan								
Morocco								
Bangladesh								
Kenya								

Contd.

Note: On 7 February 2008, the Philippines became the first Asian country to approve planting of genetically modified corn. It plans to commercialize GM nutritionally enhanced rice in 2009. India's genetic Engineering Approval Committee (GEAC) has approved a new Bt cotton variety for commercial planting, making it India's first GM Crop to be developed by the public sector. The new cotton variety called Bikaneri Narma, was developed by India's Central Institute of Cotton Research (CICR) and by the University of Agricultural Sciences in Dharwar, Karnataka. The Variety contains the gene for the Bt Cry IAc protein. It will be released in North, Central and South cotton growing zones. GEAC has also approved 84 hybrid Bt cotton varieties. The original Bt cotton can be used as seeds by farmers; whereas, hybrid varieties cannot be used for re-planting. CICR is working on other GM cotton varieties. It might come in 2010. (Source: Crop Biotech update, 23 May 2008).

Table 2
Global Biotechnology–Vegetables-2006

Vegetables by Country	*Potato*	*Tomato*	*Squash*	*Pepper*	*Pea/ Bean*	*Lettuce*	*Cucumber*
W. Europe	F	F	F		F	F	
U.S.	A	A	P		F	F	F
Canada	A	A	A				
Australia	A	F					
Japan	A	A			F	L	F
China	F	P		P			
Mexico	F	A	F	F			
Brazil	F	F			F	L	
Egypt	F	F	F		L		
Thailand		F		F	L		
Argentina	F	F					
E. Europe	F	L			F		
Cuba	F	L					
Zimbabwe	F						
Bolivia	F						
Peru	F						
S.Africa	F						
Kenya	F						
Guatemala		F					
N.Zealand							
S.Korea				F			
Indonesia	L	L		L			
Malaysia				L	L		
India	L	L					
Chile	L	L					
Columbia	L	L					
Bangladesh					L		
Philippines		L					
Tunisia	L						

Contd.

Vegetable by Country	*Cabbage*	*Carrot*	*Egg Plant*	*Onion*	*Cauli-flower*	*Broccoli*	*Spinach*
W. Europe	F	F	F		F	F	F
U.S.				F			
Canada							
Australia							
Japan					F	F	
China	F	L					
Mexico							
Brazil		F					
Egypt							
Thailand							
Argentina							
E. Europe							
Cuba							
Zimbabwe							
Bolivia							
Peru							
S.Africa							
Kenya							
Guatemala							
N.Zealand				F			
S.Korea							
Indonesia							
Malaysia			L				
India	L		F				
Chile							
Columbia							
Bangladesh							
Philippines			F				
Tunisia							

Note: On 7 January 2008, Maharashtra Hybrid Seed Company of India has been allowed by the Genetic Engineering Approval Committee to conduct commercialization of Bt brinjal seeds at the company's site. The company will produce 7 Bt brinjal hybrids, which makes brinjal resistant to the Fruit and Soot Borer (FSB). The Philippines has the plan to commercialize MG insect-resistant eggplant in early 2009.

The Table 2 and 3 show the involvement levels of developed and developing countries in biotechnology crops, vegetables and fruits. Several developing countries also, including Malaysia, have shown mark advancements in agricultural biotechnology. Although it is very well understood now that Islam does not prohibit developing newer varieties of crops, vegetable, and fruits by means of gene manipulation; and they are fit for human consumption if they are *halal* (It is permitted for human consumption) and *tayeb* (It is good to be used; it

Table 3
Global Biotech – Fruits - 2006

Fruits by Country	*Papaya*	*Melon*	*Banana*	*Pine-apple*	*Apple*	*Grape*	*Plum*	*Straw-berry*	*Water-melon*	*Citrus*	*Cherry*	*Canta-loupe*	*Kiwi*	*Rasp-berry*	*Mango*	*Coconut*
U.S.	P	A	F		F		F		F							
W.Europe		F		F	F	F	F	F	F	F	F	F	F	F		
Australia	F			F	F	F										
Canada	A					F										
Mexico	F	F	F													
Cuba	F	L	L						L							
Philippines	F		F										L	L		
China	F	F														
Egypt		F	L									F				
Japan	L	F														
E.Europe								F								
Brazil	F															
Malaysia	L	L	L	L												
Chile		L			L	L	L									
Venezuela	L		L										L			
Colombia			L													
Costa Rica			L													
Bangladesh	L															
Thailand	L														S.	
Africa								F								

Note: The Philippines has a plan to commercialize virus resistant papaya in early 2009.

Table 4
Global Biotechnology – Other Crops - 2006

Other Crops by Country	*Tobacco*	*Chicory*	*Mustard*	*Peanut*	*Coffee*	*Lupins*	*Oilseed Poppy*	*Olive*	*Oil palm*	*Cocoa*	*Garlic*
U.S.	P	A		F	F						
W. Europe	A	A	F					F			
Australia			F			F	F				
China	F			F							
Brazil	F									L	
Canada			F								
E.Europe	F										
S.Korea	F										
India	F										
Mexico	F										
Indonesia	L			L	L				L	L	
Chile	L										L
Bangladesh	L			L							
Malaysia	L								L		
Venezuela					L						
Philippines	L										
Argentina	L										
Cuba					L						
Japan	L										

cannot cause any health hazards to men who consume them), many Muslim countries, especially of the Middle East, have not shown any advancement in the area of agricultural biotechnology. It does not mean that they are not making efforts. Since they have ventured into this area late, concrete results might take some time. Ernst & Young's global biotechnology report entitled "Beyond Borders: Global Biotechnology Report 2007"[9] gives us further advancement and acceptability of biotechnology innovations. The salient features of the report are as follows:

1. The global biotechnology industry has shown a robust growth in 2006. US companies' deal value was about USD 23 billion. The capital of world's biotechnology companies has raised by a massive 42%. Public companies showed robust growth (US 145, Canada 22% and Europe 14%). Product approvals also increased by 15%.
2. Biotechnology activities in the US and EU countries were faster than other countries.
3. In the Asia-Pacific, biotechnology companies are moving steadily. They are making efforts to have home grown products instead of relying on foreign companies. Governments are extending all kinds of assistance. However, according to Utkarsh Palnitker, an Indian biotechnology expert, Asian biotechnology companies are facing critical challenges in their efforts to accelerate the transitions to become enterprises driven by research and development.
4. With the biotechnology industry maturing in more regions, an increasing number of companies will have to deal with the challenges of success.

The 2006 report features results of an Ernst & Young survey of over 400 biotechnology CEOs, at small, mid size and large biotechnology companies, which found that some of the fastest growing challenges facing their companies are issues facing maturing companies: ensuring regulatory compliance for sales forces, dealing with pricing pressures, expanding globally, and managing global operations. Survey represents also were resoundingly optimistic. 94% of respondents indicated they plan to hire new talents the next two years, and 68% indicated plans to introduce new products within two years. These challenges' of success will drive even more deal activity in the years ahead according to survey respondents. (99% of American CEOs, and 875 of European CEOs plan to enter deals in the next two years with "sales and Marketing assistance" being the most popular reason for entering alliances.) Whereas, 525 of CEOs plan to establish partnerships to bring new products to the market, up from 29% of products that are currently marketed with the help of partners. Giovannetti is of the opinion that maturation brings greater responsibilities, including greater regulatory challenges and heightened investor security. Despite these challenges, the biotechnology sector still holds great promise for innovative companies and is comfortably on track to become a USD 100 billion revenue industry before the end of the decade.

The progress of the biotechnology industries around the world is quite encouraging. However, in developing countries, except China and India, the progress of biotechnology industries is not so encouraging. Some countries, including Malaysia, have been able to attract foreign investments also. It is also notable that these countries are taking all efforts to provide maximum financial support to develop their biotechnology capability.

The researchers are however of the opinion that developing countries, including Malaysia, in addition to accepting help from developed countries and their private sector industries, should concentrate on their capacity building the most. Towards this end, they should enhance south-south cooperation. This is because they cannot depend on foreign experts and multinationals as there is no guarantee that these experts and entities will stay long in their countries. Developing countries should give more emphasis on augmenting research and development, which obviously requires competent infrastructure and necessary equipments. They should maximise financial allocations to their biotechnology sector.

India, China and Singapore can be best examples for other Asian and African countries to emulate. These countries have high financial allocations to this sector and are making full efforts towards their capacity building. They are making efforts to strengthen the private sector, and with the result of that, private sector companies are thriving. M.S. Swaminathan Research Institute India has adopted a unique way to bring biotechnology expertise with the support of Asian Development Bank to villages. It is for fostering the growth of new income-raising application of agricultural biotechnology.

Position in ASEAN Countries: Special Reference to Malaysia

ASEAN[10]

Most of the ASEAN countries are developing countries. Along with other developmental activities they have to concentrate on developing agricultural biotechnology so that they are able to contribute to the economy of their countries and provide enough food to their people. C. Peter Timmer stressed on this aspect and summarized its benefits to developing countries under the following points:

1. To increase agriculture- led growth which will increase their GDP.
2. It will lower food prices.
3. It will generate employment and ensure food security.
4. Productivity gains for non-grain crops and livestock are possible from biotechnology, and these products have better developing opportunities as incomes increase and a middle class emerges. These gains will help stimulate agricultural diversification.
5. It will help solve rural poverty.
6. GM Crops offer the possibility of reduced input use, especially of pesticides, which have had very serious health consequences for farm workers in countries with inadequate safety regulations on the use of hazardous chemicals. The potential for biotechnology

to contribute to sustainable agricultural systems, through much more efficient utilization of water, nutrients and agricultural chemicals, could be achievable in the long run.

7. Bio-fortification of key food stuffs with better availability micronutrients such as iron and vitamin A is possible through biotechnology. Even this is a controversial area, as the heated debate over "golden rise" demonstrates. But even modest additions of vitamin A to the diets of poor children can have noticeable better health consequences. Provided the safety of the GM Food is ensured.[11]

Most of the ASEAN member countries have given high priority to agricultural and biotechnology innovations. The ASEAN initiative for augmenting biotechnology in member states, through the ASEAN Biotechnology Project, which is also supported by Australia. The project provided support to biotechnology projects, especially on utilisation of carbohydrates produced as agricultural by-products and identification of valuable natural products from indigenous plant species, such as search from sago palm. The scope of the project is being widened from time to time. [12]

ASEAN countries are facing the same problems that the researchers have mentioned above in the context of developing countries. ASEAN countries are also facing challenges of capacity building, developing human expertise, and developing infrastructure in biotechnology. Capacity building is not an easy task for them as it is related to augmenting research programmes, having appropriate corporate control, managing market power and distributional implications, dealing with intellectual property issues, fostering consumer acceptability, making competent regulations pertaining to protection of the environment and human health (biosafety), and making biotechnology innovations that remain sustainable.[13] Some of the ASEAN countries also faced problem pertaining to research and development. This is because they had to import relevant technology and expertise. Right now, with considerably high allocations to biotechnology, especially agricultural and medical biotechnology, some of them like Malaysia, Indonesia, Philippines, Vietnam and Thailand have been able to develop their own R&D.[14] Cambodia, Laos and Myanmar are relatively behind. It is notable that Singapore is much ahead of other ASEAN countries. The researchers have already stated above that in the area of capacity building and research and development, help of those countries, which are already advanced in agricultural and other biotechnology, to those, which have yet to achieve a certain level from where they can go ahead on their own, is crucial.[15]

In view of the above, it is necessary for the ASEAN countries to make the following efforts jointly and severally:

1. ASEAN should further widen the scope of the ASEAN Biotechnology Project and should make efforts for the mutual benefit of the member states so that they could benefit from each other's expertise and genetic resources. Singapore can play an important role in this matter.
2. The member states should increase financial allocations for biotechnology, especially agricultural biotechnology.
3. They should make efforts to enhance their capacity building and research and development. For this, they should enter into bilateral agreements with the countries that are already much ahead of them.
4. They should make efforts to attract foreign direct investment and foreign expertise in their biotechnology sector. This can be done by providing suitable incentives to investors.
5. They must have a rich gene bank having genetic materials of all indigenous food crop species and possibly of other ASEAN countries; so that if need be they are able to supply genetic materials to other countries. It is notable here that the International Rice Research Institute could supply genetic materials to Cambodia of Cambodian rice varieties when they

were not available in Cambodia and Cambodian scientists were in grave need of them.

It is notable here that no country can solely depend on foreign expertise as they might not be sustainable. For a sustained development of the biotechnology sector in any country, its own capacity and research and development is *sine qua non.* Sufian Jusoh appropriately writes:

"...*ASEAN countries may not rely on biotechnology alone as a catalyst to generate economic growth. This is because heavy reliance on foreign owned technology may mean such growth may not be sustainable. Foreign investors always look for most conducive market that offers the best incentive, cheap labour costs with the best knowledge. If they find better investment environments, ASEAN countries, being a combination of small economies will once again face problem of exodus of foreign capital, closure of factories and loss of jobs. This happened when China opened its market. One of the safeguard measures will be to develop internal human resource capacity, whilst increasing internal research and development spending. This means that member countries must start at the university level followed by having research grants for local scientists to carry out their own research and development activities.*"[16]

The Philippines

Being the third biodiversity-rich country, of the world, the Philippines gave attention to biotechnology back in 1980 with the creation of the National Institute of Molecular Biology and Biotechnology. It gave special importance to agricultural biotechnology in its biotechnology policy of 1990. In the same year it created the National Committee on the Biosafety of the Philippines, which is responsible for making guidelines for biosafety and risk assessment, for issuing regulations for contained work, large scale contained work and glasshouse trials, and to provide guidelines for field testing of agricultural biotechnology researches. The country shifted its commodity based agricultural activities to market-orients product based agriculture. The Agriculture and Fisheries Modernization Act 1997 has provided necessary facilities required to augment agricultural biotechnology in the country. In 1998, the government funded five high-level biotechnology researches in these areas: new varieties of banana resistant to banana bunchy to virus and papaya resistant to ringspot virus; delayed ripening papaya and mango; insect-resistant maize; marker assisted breeding in coconut; and coconut oil with high lauric acid content. The government of Philippines is concerned about biosafety of new products. It is for this reason that the government in 2002 issued commercialization guidelines for biotechnology products. In spite of this preventive measure, NGOs and other groups are vocal about biosafety of GMOs. This has adversely affected field testing and commercialization of transgenic crops.

Indonesia

Indonesia placed high priority to agricultural biotechnology in late 1980 when the Research Center for Biotechnology was created. In 1985, it established a National Committee on the Development of Biotechnology. In 1990, Inter University Centers for Biotechnology in Gajah Mada University, Bandung University of Technology, and Bagore Agricultural University were created. These institutions are well funded by the government. These institutions have cooperation on superior coding gene isolation, DNA recombinant development for superior variety, development of strategic commodity by tissue culture, application of simbion microbes for fertilizer, development of new food and functional food, diagnostic kit for cattle and plants, animal vaccine envelopment and the like. On 8 January 2004, a workshop under the auspices of the Ministry of Science and Technology was organized to develop a national programme on biotechnology. Along with other recommendations, the workshop stressed on strengthening development of human resources, bringing about public knowledge on biotechnology and intensifying collaborations among institutions.[17]

The first transgenic rice containing the insect resistant gene was produced by the Indonesian Institute of Sciences (LIPI) in 1997, but in the absence of appropriate regulatory framework, its field testing could not be done. So the question of commercialization did not arise. However, Bt. Rice developed by LIPI was allowed to be field tested only in off seasons.[18]

In view of the above paragraphs, the researchers could easily infer that Indonesia has the capability to develop transgenic crops indigenously, which can be field tested, undergo biosafety laboratory testing, and commercialization. But how intensely such biosafety and environmental field testing will be cannot be predicted now.

Thailand

Thailand is very much keen in developing transgenic crops. It set up the National Centre for Genetic Engineering and Agricultural Biotechnology (BIOTECH). With support of BIOTECH, biotechnology is developing fast. However, because of protests launched by some NGOs and the fear that genetically modified rice might be rejected by the EU countries and Japan, the two biggest importers of Thai rice, the country decided not to research on genetic modification of rice especially its fragrant rice. However, Thailand has achieved considerable success in developing capability for diagnosis and control of virus diseases in shrimp, which has prevented the loss of an estimated 20-50 percent of annual production, a saving of at least USD 100 million.[19]

The latest biotechnology policy in Thailand is the National Biotechnology Framework (2004-2009). The aim of the policy is to promote biotechnology to be a substantial part of the GDP of the country. It also aims to augment competitiveness, poverty alleviation, promote equitable income distribution, and improve social community development. The policy has 6 goals, namely:

1. 'Emergence and development of new bio-business'.
2. To use modern biotechnology techniques to increase production of major crops. It is put as: 'biotechnology promoted Thailand as kitchen of the world'.
3. To be a healthy society and a hub for Asian health business. It is put as: 'Thailand represents healthy community and healthcare center in Asia".

4. To use biotechnology in waste management and generating energy. It is put as: 'utilization of biotechnology to conserve the environment to produce clean energy'.
5. To use biotechnology to eradicate poverty to strengthen the economy so that poverty could be eradicated. It is put as: 'biotechnology as the key factor for self-sufficient economy'.
6. To enhance the capability in the biotechnology sector by 'development of qualified resource system.

The country is funding this sector and making efforts to enhance its capability by promoting development of human resources, and establishing collaborations. It is hoped that by the year 2011, biotechnology will be playing a vital role in the country's development. The emphasis will be placed on applying core technologies, (e.g. genomics, bioinformatics, plant and animal breading by means of molecular markers) to accelerate development in the following areas: agriculture/ food, medical care, environmental protection, new knowledge creation for the development of higher value-added products, as well as for knowledge-based policy and strategic planning. The core technologies will also help to promote biotechnology businesses, including high-end products with high value and new types of services where modern technology is required. The national goals for biotechnology development are also derived from consideration of other dimensions. These include, among others, capability in and accessibility to technology, readiness and potential of the country and implications of the economy, society and the environment.[20] The country is also making efforts to convince NGOs and the Thai people to accept genetically modified products, importantly, edibles.[21]

Singapore

Among ASEAN countries, Singapore is the most successful in developing the biotechnology industry. Since Singapore is resourceful, it can attract foreign scientists and venture into collaborative scientific research. The country aims to attract

15 top biotechnology companies by 2010. With enough funding Singapore's economic development board has been able to develop infrastructure competent enough to augment agricultural biotechnology, environmental biotechnology and medical biotechnology. Right now Singapore's emphasis is on developing medical, biomedical, bio-imaging and biomedical translational and clinical research (BM-TCR). It has established a biomedical research council to strengthen the research and come out with value added products. Singapore has planned to venture into genetic medicine and immunology-virology, stem cell technology and nanotechnology researches. The country has capability to venture into producing transgenic crops. The Singapore Biotechnology: Agricultural Biotechnology Report 2005, which is a part of Global Agricultural Information Network (GAIN) Report 2005, states that the country currently does not produce any agricultural-related GMOs in Singapore or outside Singapore. There are also no biotechnology crops under development nor does it envisage any that will be in the market in the near future. Singapore is not giving priority to this because it is a city state with limited area and relatively less population. It has a plan to develop GM Crops in future for mobilising financial resources. It has already approved the import of agricultural biotechnology products such as genetically modified corn and soybeans to be used in food and feeds. The Genetic Modification Advisory Committee, which was established in 1999, has the task to advise on research and development, production, use, handling and release of GMOs in Singapore. The committee is presently concerned about following international standards of risk assessment and acceptance of imported GMOs by its people.[22]

Malaysia

The Malaysian government realised long back that biotechnology can be an engine of fast economic growth. In view of this, the country came out with a biotechnology policy in 2005. The policy lays emphasis, along with other aspects of biotechnology, on fast developing the agricultural biotechnology sector. Some of the notable thrusts are:

1. *Agricultural Biotechnology Development*– Transform and enhance the value creation of the agricultural sector through biotechnology.
2. *R&D and Technology Acquisition*– Establish centers of excellence, in existing and new institutions, to bring together multidisciplinary research teams to co-ordinate research and communication initiatives. Accelerate technology development via strategic acquisition.
3. *Human Capital Development*– Build the nation's biotech human resource capability in line with market needs through special schemes, programmes and trainings.
4. *Financial Infrastructure Development*– Apply competitive 'lab to market' funding and incentives to promote committed participation by academia, the private sector, as well as government-linked companies. Implement sufficient exist mechanisms for investments in biotechnology.
5. *Legislative and Regulatory Framework Development*– Create an enabling environment through continuous reviews of the country's regulatory framework and procedures in line with global standards and best practices. Develop a strong intellectual property protection regime to support R&D communication efforts.
6. *Government Commitment*– Establish a dedicated and professional implementation agency overseeing the development of Malaysia's biotech industry, under the aegis of the Prime Minister and relevant government ministers. The Policy sets three implementation stages: phase I (2005-2010) capacity building; phase II (2011-2015) science to business; and phase III (2016-2020) global presence. The first phase has seven strategies: to establish an advisory and implementation council; to establish a Malaysian biotechnology corporation; to educate and provide training of knowledge to works; to develop a legal and intellectual property framework; to strive for business development

through accelerator programmes; to build Malaysian branding; and to create jobs and enhance industrial development in agricultural biotechnology, industrial biotech and bioinformatics.

Malaysia has created the Malaysian Biotechnology Corporation, which aims at being a dedicated and professional one-stop agency for developing the biotechnology sector in the country. It works under the supervision of an Implementation Council and on advice of an International Advisory Panel. These apex bodies work under the leadership of the Prime Minister of Malaysia. The Council, which comes under the Ministry of Science Technology and Innovation, will co-ordinate with relevant ministries. Some notable functions of the Council will be: catalysing commercial spin-offs to the private sector; facilitating market-driven research and development (R&D) and commerce via funding and industry development services; and advancing R&D and commerce in agricultural biotechnology, healthcare biotechnology and industrial biotechnology.

So as to enhance the biotechnology products from lab to market, networking is an essential requirement. Towards this end, BioNexus Malaysia has been created. It is a network of centers of excellence throughout the country, comprising companies, and other institutions such as educational institutions and institutes like MARDI, FRIM and PORIM. This network can provide information about infrastructure, capacity building, and research progress of one institution to other institutions. It will help in establishing cooperation among them and engage in collaborative ventures.

It has been noted that a world class center requires high class human resource and sophisticated equipments. In spite of some constraints, Malaysia is progressing satisfactorily. In the area of agricultural biotechnology, MARDI and University Putra Malaysia are the centers of excellence. But it is hoped that in the near future, the country will have additional centers of excellence in the agricultural sector. This is because the 9th Malaysia Plan gives priority to agriculture with emphasis on agricultural biotechnology. It envisages:

"In line with the National Biotechnology Policy, the application of biotechnology to agriculture will be further promoted and intensified to harness the potentials of the agriculture sector in creating new wealth. To accelerate R&D activities in biotechnology, research institutions including institutions of higher education will be equipped with the requisite facilities and equipment. In addition, public researchers will be trained in the field of advanced biotechnology including biodiversity through attachment programmes and greater collaborations with the private sector."[23]

The government is working hard in implementing the Biotechnology Policy by various strategies. The following strategies can be appreciated:

Financial Allocation

For the 9th Malaysia Plan period, a development budget amounting to RM 11.435 billion has been allocated for the development of the agricultural sector. In the 2007 budget, RM 3.7 billion has been allocated for this sector, particularly to increase productivity and efficiency in agriculture production and expand marketing capabilities. A substantial part of the allocation in given to the Ministry of Agriculture and Agro-based Industry and will be used to finance food production, to encourage farmers to venture into the non-food sector such as floriculture, livestock, and agricultural industry. In 2007, the Ministry has approved investment worth USD 613.36 million for food production sub-sector.

Attracting Foreign Investments

In view of heavy allocations in the agricultural sector and various incentives, including tax incentives (see point 4), given to the sector and foreign investors, Malaysia expects a rise in foreign investment in the agricultural and biotechnology sector. This was highlighted in the speech delivered by the then Honorable International Trade Minister Muhyiddin Yassin in his speech delivered at the opening of the agriculture office of the Netherlands in Kuala Lumpur, and in his keynote address delivered at the agriculture marketing and investment mission, in London on 3 July 2007. While speaking in London, he said:

"...we welcome entrepreneurs and investors...to consider investing in areas such as research and development in biotechnology, fruits crops production and processing, aquaculture, livestock, food production, production of seed and hatchery, and other agricultural related inputs, machineries and services, which has the potential to yield lucrative returns...There are also a number of financing facilities available, which includes credit and loan facilities from private institutions, facilitated by the government. Loan and credit can be secured from government and financial institutions, which includes the agriculture bank under my Ministry, SME bank, major commercial banks such as Maybank and CIMB bank, as well as foreign banks such as Rabobank, Citibank and HSBC. With respect of technology, product and quality development, institutions like Malaysian Agricultural Research Institute (MARDI) is available to assist investors in upgrading production and processing agro food products. In additions, there are other support services provided by government institutions and private companies relating to distribution and marketing, logistics infrastructure, distribution channels, branding and others. We recognise that to successfully penetrate into the world market, our products must meet the stringent international standard of food safety and quality of food. To this, Malaysia has introduced several acceleration schemes to ensure that Malaysia's agricultural products comply with quarantine sanitary and phytosanitary (SPS) requirements of importing countries. My Ministry has established the Malaysian Farm Accreditation Scheme (SALM) which requires our fruit farmers and producers to comply with 17 protocols and procedures specified under the scheme. Under SALM, officers under the Ministry will inspect as well as audit and thus award an acceleration on the whole range of the farming activities and practices, including production, maintenance, post-harvest handling, grading, labeling, and transporting. A few years ago, my Ministry introduced and have since developed the "Malaysia's Best" logo as a seal of guaranteed quality and safety to be used on the agricultural produce and products that meet the mark. To this end, we have also introduced the Agromas and Olemas Branding schemes."

Technical Assistance, Capacity Building and Foreign Collaborations

Although Malaysia is growing fast in its capacity building, yet it needs to enhance its technological expertise by way of transfer of technology through foreign collaborations. The Agriculture and Agro-based Industries Minister stressed on it while speaking at the opening of the agriculture office of the Netherlands in Kuala Lumpur on 14th September 2006 in these words:

"...Malaysia also requires technical assistance and capacity building in areas in which the Netherlands is strong at, such as floriculture, livestock, and R&D in biotechnology...Malaysia and the Netherlands are already working together to promote cooperation through the existing mechanisms..."[24]

Tax Incentives

Malaysia offers tax reduction incentives on investments in agricultural and agro-based industries under the Promotion of Investment Act 1986 and Income Tax 1967. Companies investing in the promoted agricultural activities are eligible to apply for Pioneer Status Incentives or investment tax allowances. Under section 7A of the Income Tax Act 1967, qualifying projects will be eligible for an allowance of 60% of qualifying capital expenditure which can be deducted against 70% of the statutory income. It is available for 15 years beginning from the assessment year in which investment allowance was first claimed. Unabsorbed allowance can be carried forward and allowed until fully absorbed. There is 100% deduction on qualifying investments in biotechnology.

Biotechnology business can also benefit from pre-packaged tax incentives currently provided by the government, including 10 year tax exemption pioneer status, exemption of import duties on approved equipments and materials, double tax deduction on qualifying expenses and R&D investment. A resident company undertaking an approved food production project or under a pre-packaged scheme for large investments in specific sectors (including biotechnology industries) is able to offset the losses of one company against the profits of another company within the same group. There is tax exemption on dividends distributed by the company. With effect from 2 September 2006, the following incentives have been granted to Bio-Nexus and biotechnology companies and investment in such companies:

- A Bio-Nexus company will be subject to a concessionary tax of 20% for another 10 years upon expiry of a 10 year exemption period;
- A company or an individual investing in a Bio-Nexus company is to be given a tax deduction equivalent to the amount of investment made in seed capital and early stage of financing;
- A Bio-Nexus company undertaking merger and acquisition with a biotechnology company within the five year period until 31 December 2011 will be given exemption from stamp duty and real property gains tax; and
- Buildings (whether purchased or constructed) used solely for the purpose of biotechnology research activities are to be given Industrial Building allowance over a period of 10 years.[25]

Research and Development

We have noted above that Malaysia is making full efforts to enhance its R&D in biotechnology. Towards this end, with government funding, MARDI, FRIM, and PORIM are actively involved. Among them, MARDI is concentrating on agricultural biotechnology. Along with them, institutions of higher learning are also engaged. For infrastructure development, these institutions get grafts from the government. They have been able to develop expertise in various areas of biotechnology. Experts working with these institutions may get grants from their respective universities and various ministries. Notable grants are: Science Fund; Techno Fund; and Fundamental Research Grant (FRGS). Although proper scrutiny of applications are done at various levels, if proposed projects are viable and falls within the scope of the 9th Malaysia Plan, one can easily get the grant. However, these universities have not been able to attract experts from developed countries because of low emoluments to be paid to them. In spite of all efforts in the UNDP Project Document (Government of Malaysia) (Mal/03/G31-OIMS 2182), 2006, it has been stated that there are insufficient capacities in risk assessment and risk management.[26]

Although Malaysia has not been able to produce any transgenic commercial crop, it has been able to successfully genetically modified, at laboratory level, several crops containing traits of value at the experimental stage. At MARDI, rice has been successfully modified to resist the tungro virus, and papayas manipulated to resist ring-spot virus infection and to have a prolonged shelf life. These papaya varieties have been allowed for field testing. The government will implement the strategic thrust of the National Biotechnology Policy under the 9th Malaysia Plan. Malaysia is also developing genetically engineered oil palm, with a focus on increasing value-added products from the palms such as high oleate and high stearate oil, nutraceuticals (vitamin A and E), biodiesel and bioplastics.[27] The country has developed certain types of genetically modified pepper, beans, and eggplant. But they are also at the lab scale. This level of success is not a significant breakthrough.

The aspirations of the country will be fulfilled when the country becomes a exporting country of transgenic food grains. Then only agricultural biotechnology can be valued as a money generating sector. For achieving that ambition, the country will have to make the following efforts, firstly to review its strategy to attract foreign investment and establishing foreign collaborations. Secondly, the country will have to work more in enhancing the capacity with better technology and foreign experts. The country has the financial capability to acquire sophisticated technology; but for attracting foreign experts, it will have to consider the emoluments to be offered to them. It is notable here that Singapore has been able to attract foreign experts because the pay structure there is lucrative. The capacity building has to be at a faster rate, because no country can rely on foreign investments and foreign experts. Foreign experts should be appointed for a relatively longer period so that local scientists could get enough time to learn from them. We have the example of China and India. These countries are opening up their markets with better incentives to foreign investors and foreign collaborators. With the result of that in these countries the growth of biotechnology is at a faster rate (6-7 % per annum). In Malaysia the agricultural growth is 5%; whereas the growth of biotechnology is not recorded. In the year 2000, there were 50 biotechnology companies in the country. Malaysia aims to increase it to 100 companies by the end of the year 2008 with 280,000 job opportunities.[28] Researchers are of the opinion that to achieve this goal and to go further, research and development expenditure should be increased. Malaysia has already increased it from .5% of the GDP to 1.5% of the GGDP, but it has to be further increased. Perhaps, because of this reason, Malaysia does not have enough R&D multinational companies in the country.

Thirdly, Malaysia should establish world class laboratories under the auspices of the Ministry of Science and Technology (MOSTI), Ministry of Health and Ministry of Natural Resources and the Environment, and Ministry of Agriculture and Agro-based Industries. Before any transgenic crop developed in the lab is to go through intensive risk assessment and risk management strategies, field testing and its ultimate internal and external marketing should not be allowed. This is necessary for confidence building in transgenic crops. It is also necessary that custom officers, who are responsible to monitor export and imports of LMOs and GMOs and food containing GMOs, must be sufficiently trained. This capacity building is also necessary for confidence building among the local people and foreign buyers.

Other ASEAN countries are also interested in agricultural biotechnology, but due to limited financial resources and lack of sufficient infrastructure and human resources, they are yet to achieve any success in developing any transgenic crop. Among them, Myanmar is keen to develop its capability in agricultural biotechnology in order to overcome the limitations of conventional plant breeding methods so that the country becomes able to produce more rice, maize, beans and pulses and export them.[29] Myanmar is already doing micropagation in banana and pineapple. Research is being made to produce virus free potato, banana and strawberry using *in vitro* techniques. It is also making efforts to produce certain rice varieties that will have shorter breeding periods. It has established at the National Institute of Technology and Evaluation of Pathein University, a Biotechnology Development Centre in May 2004. This Centre is getting technical support from Japan. The Centre has several on-going projects with some Japanese institutions. One project team has discovered 1,835 micro-organisms, including 26 items of micro-organisms that can be used to produce glucose from rice, potato, maize and tapioca; five items of micro-organisms that can fight against insects, and various kinds of micro-organisms to be used in manufacturing medicines.[30]

There are five big players around the world in transgenic crops. They are: United States, Canada, Argentina, Brazil and South Africa. Uruguay and Chile are fast coming up. Other developing countries are struggling to produce and market their biotechnology products. In order to market a product, it is necessary to have an innovative transgenic crop, get it patented, and to conduct intensive risk assessment to the satisfaction of the buyers. At present, other developing countries have to import it from time to time.

We have noted above that Malaysia is keen to be the hub in South-East Asia. This has been said by the Chief Executive Officer of the Malaysian Biotechnology Corporation.[31] Towards this end, the country is making considerable efforts in expanding infrastructure, enhancing workforce, wooing foreign investments, and establishing foreign collaborations with large foreign private biotech companies. With the result of that Malaysia's capability to conduct biotech research, especially in the area of agricultural biotechnology, is showing remarkable results. The number of agricultural researchers, due to rise in public expenditure, is steadily growing. MARDI has been successful in establishing collaborations with many foreign biotechnology companies. However, the private sector participation in agricultural biotechnology has been sluggish.[32] The authors are of the view that along with other efforts, public spending and foreign collaborations should be maximized. Wooing foreign investments is also a key factor in developing the biotechnology sector of the country. The Malaysian government is trying hard to attract foreign investments. Recently, the Malaysian Biotechnology Corporation has sealed five collaboration agreements with large biotechnology companies of the world, which will reap about RM 1 billion as foreign investment between 2008 and 2011. Malaysia aims to get more then RM 9 billion from 25 strong biotechnology companies with a total revenue of RM 80 billion, as the country wants to be one of the exporters of biotechnology products, especially agricultural products.[33] Malaysia wants to be a big player in D-8 countries and other Muslim countries as stressed in the recent meeting of representatives of D-8 countries (It is a group of 8 Muslim developing countries including Malaysia, Indonesia, Iran, Egypt, Nigeria, Bangladesh, Turkey) in Kuala Lumpur.[34] The authors are of the view that to achieve the target, Malaysia should develop its own capability by increasing public spending on the biotechnology sector. It has the potential to be one of the important players in food biotechnology.

It will be better if ASEAN takes up the issue of capacity building among ASEAN countries. Since capacity building includes scientific and technical training, in the area of risk assessment and risk management, and improvement of technological and institutional biotechnology skills, including biosafety skills, ASEAN will have to develop a mechanism suitable for the member states with help of biotechnology experts and financial resources from some international institutions, including Asian Development Bank, which is keen in extending financial support in this area. We have the example of Latin American countries, especially Chile, Peru and Colombia where the Organization of American States, with the help of government agencies and independent NGOs, and with the fund provided by some international financial agencies, especially International Development Research Centre and

Canadian International Development Agency came in to extend assistance. The *modus operendi* was to develop the competence of these countries through transfer of technology for risk assessment and risk management, by bringing about consciousness among the people about the probable impact of LMOs and GMOs on the human health and the environment, and by establishing cooperation mechanisms among these countries and other countries.[35] Cooperation is also warranted in the area of developing a viable bio-safety legal and institutional framework.

Law on Biosafety (Risk Assessment) of GM Crops and Export and Import Control

A bio-safety mechanism requires sustainable use of biological products, including GMOs. There can be sustainable use only when an LMO or food containing genetically modified elements is safe to human, animal, and plant use and which is environmentally friendly. FAO defines it as: "...the safe and environmentally sustainable use of all biological products and applications for human health, biodiversity and environmental sustainability, in support of improved food security.[36] For ensuring an LMO to be within this precinct, there has to be a competent risk assessment and risk management within a competent bio-safety legal and institutional framework. Risk assessment and risk management is necessarily warranted for determining safe use of any GMO and its public acceptability.

The problem is that the public perception about GMOs has not been favourable. This public perception is the negative attitude of many NGOs and skeptical approach of the EU countries. Public acceptability can be improved only when it is proved on the basis of reliable risk assessment done by the producing-consuming countries (If it had been imported, by the importing country or any independent reliable agency) that certain GMOs are safe for human consumption, for using them in animal feed, and/or they are safe for the existing biodiversity in specific and the environment in general. Right now, the five big producing countries in producing and commercializing GMOs, stress on safety of the GMOs. However, in most of the cases, risk assessment is done by the producing private sector, which as a matter of principle cannot be fully relied upon even though they may be of high standard; and producing countries plead for their safety. It is a matter to worry that no state or producing company gives guarantee for the safety of GMOs being produced by them. In view of this, it is necessary either to have an intensive risk assessment mechanism in importing countries, and import and marketing licenses should be issued only when they are found safe, or to rely on an internationally accredited risk assessment mechanism run by any independent body. If safety of certain GMOs cannot be determined on the basis of risk assessment done on acceptable scientific procedures, the precautionary principle should be applicable, which would require that those GMOs should not be introduced. The authors are of the opinion that in view of this, ASEAN countries should have their own capability to determine safety of GMOs based on an acceptable scientific procedure. For this, member states should have a competent legal and institutional framework.

There are two international legal instruments in this area, Agreement on the Application of Sanitary and Phytosanitary Measures (hereinafter SPS Agreement) under the WTO, and the Cartagena Protocol on Bio-safety under the Convention of Biological Diversity (hereinafter Cartagena Protocol). These two legal instruments are not coextensive and coexistent. This is because the primary objects of both are different. One has been made to protect unnecessary obstruction of international trade of GMOs and their products if they are safe to human, plant and animal health. Whereas, the Cartagena Protocol has the object to protect the environment and human health. However, both require risk assessments. Many ASEAN countries are members of the SPS Agreement and the Cartagena Protocol. It is necessary to have a critical appraisal of these legal instruments and discuss the area of conflict among them and to offer suggestions to make them compatible with each other.

The Cartagena Protocol

In the late nineties, OECD countries and some other countries expressed concern about the probable negative impact of GMOs on human health and environment. It resulted in a strong opinion in favour of applicability of the Precautionary Principle to GMOs. This was supplemented with the right to information, which requires labeling of GMOs and substances containing them. This approach of OECD countries and some other countries formed a negative perception about genetically manipulated living and non-living organisms, especially about their human consumption. This negative perception about GMO became a matter of great concern to GMO producing countries because their exports suffered tremendously. If we look at this from the point of view of the object of the WTO and agreements made under it, we find that there was a need to have an international agreement that would provide a common framework for market access and environmental protection. The Cartagena Protocol of 2000, which came into force on 11th September 2003, and which was a result of a long negotiation among different interest groups,[37] attempts to solve the pertinent problems pertaining to trans-boundary movement of LMOs. The Bio-safety Protocol supports international trade in biotechnology products while at the same time seeks to ensure that the human health and the environment are not adversely affected. Protection of the environment has to be determined based on scientific process along with application of the precautionary principle.[38]

The Cartagena Protocol allows trans-boundary movement of GMOs only on Advanced Informed Agreement (AIA) basis so that the importing country gets enough information from the exporting country and also, if it likes, can perform scientific tests, and imports only if it wishes to import. It means every country has a sovereign right either to import or not to import certain GMOs. This is justified by Article 10.6 of the protocol, which reads, 'lack of scientific uncertainty, due to insufficient relevant scientific information and knowledge regarding the extent of the potential adverse effects of a living modified organism on the conservation and sustainable use of biological diversity in the Party of import, taking also into account risks to human health, shall not prevent the Party from taking a decision, as appropriate, with regard to the of the LMOs, in order to avoid or minimise such potential adverse effect.'

So as to ensure human health and protection of the environment, the Protocol has heavy dependence on the Precautionary Principle.[39] Precautionary Principle (PP) generally requires something not to be introduced into the environment or allowed for human consumption if its adverse impacts are not known or cannot be ascertained. PP is the recognition that lack of certainty regarding the threat of environment harm or human health should not be used as an excuse for not taking action to avert the threat. It recognises that delaying action until there is compelling evidence of harm will often mean that it is then too costly or impossible to avert the threat. Use of the PP promotes action to avert risks of serious or irreversible harm to the environment in such cases. In fact, PP is based on the recognition that a false prediction that a human activity will not result in significant harm will typically be more harmful to the society than a false prediction that it will result in significant harm. In short, the Principle provides a fundamental policy basis to anticipate, avoid and mitigate threats to human health and the environment.[40] The Principle is applicable where the following elements are present, first, where there is uncertainty. It means if the threat is relatively certain, only some preventive measures will need to be taken; Secondly, where there is a threat to the environment or human health. It means if there is no indication of harm, the principle will not apply; and thirdly, where the threatened harm is of serious or of irreversible nature. It means, where threatened damage is trivial or easily reversible, the principle will not be relevant. For enforcing PP, states are free to follow certain regulatory measures (certain conditions) based on scientific procedures. It means risk and its extent has to be based on risk assessment conducted according to scientific requirements. Applicability of PP by a state will not prove the existence of the risk. For example, ban on import of certain varieties of GM rice will itself not be sufficient proof that they are not fit for human consumption. Once existence of risk is proven, the precautionary principle can be invoked to either avoid or minimize the risk. Minimisation of risk can be done by application of an appropriate risk management procedure. Minimisation of the risk can be done by contained use of GMOs or any GM Food. So as to protect human health, certain GMOs can be used only for research purposes or for animal or plant use. They can be used only when it is proven that they are safe for human consumption. Likewise, contained cultivation of GM crops in order to protect other varieties from contamination can also be practiced.

Under the Cartagena Protocol, it is incumbent upon each Party to take the necessary and perform appropriate scientific procedure for measuring the risk assessment, if any; and to take measures that prevent or mitigate the risk. They are also required to have appropriate legal, administrative and other measures to implement the AIA obligation. (Articles 7-12) In order to fulfill these requirements, importing Parties must have enacted appropriate bio-safety legislation for development, handling, transport, use, transfer and release of any GMO. A large number of states have already enacted laws and approval mechanisms for commercial use of GMOs.[41] It is the duty of the exporting country to get informed consent for export. The exporter must provide detailed information in advance of first shipment. It is the duty of the exporting country to provide documentation accompanying LMOs in addition to handling, transport, packaging and identification. (Article18). The Conference of Parties in 2006 ascertained the detailed requirements about the documentation accompanying shipments.[42]

One of the key-components of AIA is an appropriate risk assessment as per Annex III of the Protocol, the cost of which will be borne by the exporting country. In view of this, it has been provided that the importing country can extend the time of import up to one year. It can seek more information, or it can cancel import notification, or can import with conditions, or can impose prohibition on import. It is to be noted here that any measure adopted by the importing country should be only to the extent necessary to meet the identified risk. (Article 16) This is of trade law origin, and includes a requirement well defined under trade law for the measure to be as least trade restrictive as possible to meet the identified risk. This is a stringent trade law test that requires several alternative mechanisms to be considered before a significant impact on trade is found acceptable under the test. For capacity building and bringing about awareness among the people, 'Bio-Safety Cleaning House' mechanism has been suggested. It requires sharing of information and assisting each other in implementing the Protocol. As an additional part of the decision-making process, the parties can consider the socio-economic issues, which might arise from impact of LMOs on biological diversity, related to the import. (Article 26) This may expand the issue that can be considered through a risk assessment, and provide additional latitude for conditions or prohibitions on certain imports.[43]

Approval for commercial use has been one of the most controversial aspects of the GMO trade. In some countries, including India, experts are of the opinion that the approval body should not rely on the scientific data released by GM Crop producing companies. They suggest that it is the duty of the producing state and importing state to perform certain appropriate scientific tests. It is necessary because a small quantity of GMO might have the potential to cause a big harm, sometimes irreparable damage. The author is of the opinion that their demand is genuine and must be given heed by the member states.

By virtue of Article 18.2(a) all shipments of LMOs-FFPs (example, corn and soybean), which are intended to be used as food, feed or processing, must be accompanied with a document stating that the shipments 'may contain' LMOs' and are 'not intended for international introduction into the environment'.[44] This is to ensure the protection of the environment. Further, there must also be sufficient information about the identity, traits and characteristics of LMOs, including their safe handling, storage, transport and use, and information about the imports and exports without having intention to alter the rights and obligations under the WTO or other existing international agreement.

The Cartagena Protocol has excluded five types of LMOs from the AIA procedure. They are: pharmaceuticals for humans; LMOs in transit to a third Party; LMOs destined for contained use; LMO-FFPs (subject to simplified, less restrictive procedure in Article 11); and LMOs that have been declared safe by a meeting of the parties. These exclusions (in particular, the exclusion of LMO-FFPs) means that the AIA covers only a small percentage of traded LMOs, only those destined for direct introduction to the environment for the importer, such as seeds and micro-organisms.[45] Under the AIA scheme, the exporting Party is duty bound to make necessary declaration about the LMO-FFPs. In view of this, the importing Party has to develop and notify a regulatory procedure. It is, thus, the responsibility of the importing country to develop a necessary regulatory mechanism. The exporting country does not have to wait to receive the notification from the importing country. Also, the exporting Party does not have burden of proof established for exporters of other LMOs, who may have to conduct and finance risk assessment in support of their notification[46]. It is notable that this provision encourages international trade of LMOs-FFPs.

It is because of the Cartagena Protocol that the trans-boundary movement of LMOs is being properly regulated. It has provided an important stimulus for developing safety laws in LMOs importing countries. However, it is conspicuous that the operationalisation of fully functional biosafety mechanisms varies from country to country because of availability of scientific skills, institutional infrastructure and financial resources. It is notable that the Protocol does not address the issue of food safety. It means the exporting country is not duty bound to give a safety guarantee. It also does not require segregation of bulk shipments of commodities that may contain LMOs. This is because the exporting countries have simply to make a declaration that the LMOs are being shipped. It is now the duty of the transporter to ensure their safe carriage. After the import, it is the duty of the importing country to deal with the LMOs-FFPs according to the regulations made by it. The mandate of the Protocol is to address potential risks to biodiversity that may be caused by LMOs. Human, animal and plant health is incidental to it.

Bio-safety Protocol and International Trade

GM crops, although having suffered from negative perceptions about their probable impacts on human health and environment, failure of compliance containing GMOs, to market requirements prescribed by various countries, e.g. labeling on food stuffs, has created new opportunities for international trade. However, beneficiaries of GM crops were major producers of the world. The Bio-safety Protocol is not intended to directly facilitate the grain trade. We have noted above that the Protocol does not put safety obligations on exporting countries, they have to provide all information, under the AIA procedure, necessary to make informed consent; importing countries have to ensure its safety on the basis of risk assessments funded by exporting countries. It is notable here that major GM crop exporters, including USA, Canada, Australia, and Argentina are not members to the Protocol. In that situation, international trade between an importing member state and a non-member exporting will take place on the basis of the bilateral agreement entered into between them and this will govern the sale. The position will be the same if both a seller country and a buyer country are non-members.

The international trade in GM crops is directly affected by the consumers' sentiments of segregating them from non-GM crops. Applicability of the 'segregation requirement' will not affect international trade of GM crops. It will instead boost their sale.[47] Segregation becomes more important in case of hybrid species. Thus, the concept of 'identity preservation', i.e. maintaining separate identities of GM and non-GM crops becomes a necessary requirement of their trade. This requires labeling and traceability for minimizing 'adventitious presence'[48] of GM crops. However, labeling law of one country is different than the labeling law of another country. Some examples are: EU regulations require food products containing more than 0.9 percent of genetically engineered material (GE material) to be labeled as such; Japan has a threshold of 5 percent of GE material; and Australia, New Zealand, and Brazil have a threshold of 1 percent. It is notable that these labeling requirements do not have the basis of any risk assessment. They are just a precautionary measure. The author is of the opinion that it is not logical to require to have labeling at certain threshold levels. Labeling mechanism is a segregation device. For this reason, all products having any amount of GE material should be labeled if labeling at all is required by any country pertaining to any international trade. It cannot have any political basis, or a trade restrictive measure.

It is also to be noted that if labeling is required, it should not have any discriminatory application. On the contrary, labeling requirement will be considered as a violation of the international trade law. For a smooth international trade in GM crops, regulatory procedures in producing countries, which grant commercialisation of crops, is curtailed. It is equally important in importing countries. Regulations of both countries have to have the basis of some scientific procedure to be followed for risk assessment. It is necessary for confidence building. If risk assessment is not trust worth, international trade of MG crops will certainly be affected. In that situation, the attitude of the people will be skeptical, they will demand for labeling, they will ask for application of the precautionary principle, and will prefer only to consume non-GM crops. People of the EU countries are the best example. It is because of non-satisfactory risk assessment that in EU Countries GM crops are least demanded. Since risk assessment requires scientific and technical capabilities, developing and least developed countries are in dire need of assistance from outside. It is notable that some developed countries, FAO and the Asian Development Bank and the African Development Bank are extending help to needy countries. Majority of FAO activities are undertaken either through the relevant technical units through the International Working Groups on Biotechnology that provides a forum for biotechnology related activities of multidisciplinary flavor in a complementary manner. Bio-safety in food is generally managed within a bio-security framework coordinated by the international Working Group on Biotechnology to promote a strategic and integrated approach to analyze and contain risks in the sectors of food safety, animal life and health, as well as plant life and health.[49] Through the production and dissemination of technical publications, FAO has also taken the lead in expanding knowledge base in biotechnology and bio-safety. The assistance extended by these institutions will certainly help in capacity building and reflecting the public perception based on scientific testing rather than on conjecture. The authors are of the opinion that risk assessment conducted by the GM crop producing companies should not be the sole criterion for allowing them to be commercialized. Producing companies' risk assessments should be considered only as *sine qua non* for conducting such assessments by exporting and importing countries. Commercialization of a GM crop found safe by producing companies must be substantiated on the basis of independent risk assessment carried out by these states. If this is done, the confidence about GM crops that are being traded internationally will get a boost.

WTO Sanitary and Phyto-Sanitary Agreement (SPS Agreement)

The SPS Agreement provides basic rules pertaining to food safety and animal and plant health standards to be adhered to by Members of the Agreement. Members are under an obligation to develop their own rules based on science setting standards to be applied for the protection of human, animal and plant life or health. Under the Agreement, international standards are to be used whenever possible. Where specific quality-oriented standards are not available, international procedural standards for reaching national decisions on appropriate standards becomes the next available type of international standard. Several WTO cases that have considered the SPS Agreement have made reference to such standards.[50] These rules have to be applied uniformly. No state has the right to discriminate. For example, no state can discriminate between domestic products and foreign products. Likewise, no state can discriminate one state against another state.

The SPS Agreement has been made to facilitate international trade and to restrict or prohibit any unreasonable sanitary and phyto-sanitary measures that restrict international trade.[51]It is because out of over precaution, some countries may take very stringent measures to be applied about imports. Under the SPS Agreement they might be considered as trade restrictive, as they might hamper international trade. So as to avoid such situations, the Agreement prescribes certain basic rules. First, as far as possible a restrictive rule must have the basis of a scientific finding. Next, among the alternative measures, the state will opt for the measure which is not more trade restrictive than is required to meet the health objective. Third, if the measure is accentuated by other state(s), it will strengthen the measure. Fourth, the measure should have the basis of an appropriate assessment of the actual risk involved, and if requested, it should be made known. Fifth, any change in the measure should be notified. Sixth, in case where the relevant scientific evidence is insufficient, a member may provisionally adopt sanitary or phyto-sanitary measures on the basis of available pertinent information including that from relevant organizations. In that situation, if the state needs more information for taking its decision, such information will be provided to it within a reasonable period. Seventh, a member state is required to observe the provisions of Annex C in the operation of control, inspection and approval procedures, including national systems for approving the use of additives or for establishing tolerances for contaminants in food, beverages or feedstuffs, and to ensure that their procedures are not inconsistent with the provisions of the SPS Agreement. Under paragraph one of Annex C of the agreement, the state has to ensure, with respect to any procedure to check and ensure the fulfillment of sanitary or phyto-sanitary measures, that such procedures are undertaken and completed without undue delay and in no less favourable manner for imported products than for like domestic products.[52] Eighth, under the 'transparency obligation' member states are under obligation to notify 'measures' and 'obligations' taken by them, any change made in them, including answering reasonable questions and publishing regulations. To facilitate them to fulfill this obligation, certain procedures have been developed without altering provisions of the SPS Agreement. It is a significant part of the 'transparency obligations' that member states have to designate a National Notification Authority (in a federal form of government, or a central government authority) and a National Enquiry Point. It is the general practice of the member states that an authority serves both the purposes. Member states are obliged to inform about these and any changes there to, to the WTO Secretariat, which through certain websites, notifies all member states.

Members of the WTO deliberated on the revised recommendations and agreed on certain improvement with regard to information they share with each other on food safety and animal and plant health. They were approved by the SPS Committee on 2-3 April 2008. These have been confirmed because no objections were raised within the 30th May 2008 deadline. The revised recommendations deal with how governments provide information on new or proposed measures they adopt on sanitary and phyto-sanitary measures. New recommendations are the third revision of the set, and include new forms and procedures for countries to submit information, together with details of new on-line databases where notifications and other relevant information are complied.[53] They also encourage WTO members to notify when they adopt international standards – this would be voluntary because members are only required to notify when their measures do not follow international standards. These recommendations have made the transparency obligation contained in article 7 of the SPS Agreement as the accepted standard.[54] A brief account of important aspects of the recommended notification procedures is as follows:

1. For application of Annex B, paragraph 5, states are required to notify any regulations which are distinct from internationally accepted standards (obligation). Nevertheless, they can notify regulations that have international standards (optional).

2. To assess any significant effect on trade relevant available information will be taken into consideration.
3. New regulations or any amendments in the existing ones will be notified at an early stage and in such a manner to enable interested member states to know about it. The procedure requires that notification should be made before 60 calendar days of their finalisation. The author is of the opinion that it is a general practice that regulations are gazetted. If so, it should be informed within reasonable time to the WTO Secretariat. Member states notification obligation should be considered to have been complied with. The state will still be under obligation to answer any enquiry after that. In the author's opinion, it is not appropriate to comply with the notification obligation when regulations are in draft stage. Instead of giving 60 days time for affected states to make any comments, affected states have the right to forward any questions or clarifications, and the state concerned is under obligation to respond to them.
4. The state should provide the document of regulations, if required by any member state.
5. Notification should provide about, the address of the body who can be contacted. If the enquiry has been responded to or the document has been received, it should be acknowledged. If translations of the document exist or its summery exists, it should be notified.
6. An authority must be fixed to receive any comments on the notification of the draft document. Any such comments should be acknowledged by that authority. This has no relevance in view of the author's above comment.
7. The 60 days time may be extended on request where there have been delays in receiving and translating the document. In view of the author's above comment, this point is not relevant.

8. There can be addenda, revisions, and corrigenda in the regulations.
9. A member which has made a determination to recognise the equivalence of sanitary or phyto-sanitary measures of another Member or Members will notify other Members.[55]

The author has expressed the view that when a Member state has made notification and forwarded a copy to the WTO Secretariat, its only duty that remains is to answer any comments or questions put forth by other Members. There is no point notifying the draft regulation in advance. In a way, it seems to be good and helpful in improving the draft, but it will be a delaying tactic. The best course is to make comments on new regulations or amendments to existing ones. This will be a faster way to promote international trade. However, the notifying Member state should be at liberty to accept any suggestion, comment and answer or not to answer any questions. This is because no state can be compelled to accept any of the suggestions made by other Member states to improve the notified regulations. So as to bring about uniformity and certainty, Members should be encouraged to accept international standards unless its interests are gravely affected. It will be better if members situated in a region have one set of regulations to be followed by the members of the region, and cooperate with each other to improve on it from time to time.

To further the implementation of Article 6 of the SPS Agreement, in the 2-3 April 2008 SPS Committee meeting, WTO members recognized that there can be SPS regionalisation within a country or spanning borders, provided no country objects by 15 May 2008. The regionalisation guidelines include various recommended steps to be taken by an importing and an exporting country discussing the recognition of a region's status. For regionalisation, the key concept is recognition that an exporting region (all or part of the country or a border-trading zone) is disease free or pest free (or has a lower incidence). When importing countries recognise different situations in different regions, their restrictions on product from areas with disease do not apply to whole countries. It is often raised as a specific trade concern as well as being discussed as a subject in its own right.[56]

At the outset, we should be clear: that these guidelines are facilitative in nature, that they do not affect the existing rights and obligations of members under the SPS Agreement; and that they are subject to review from time to time by the Committee in light of experience gained through the implementation of the Agreement and the use of the guidelines. A brief account of the non-binding guidelines can be put under the following points:

1. Importing Members are required to publish the basis for such recognition.
2. Members should proceed with a recognition process without undue delay.
3. The process should be applied without discrimination.
4. There should be transparency.
5. The veterinary or phyto-sanitary authorities of exporting members should be competent and should work independently.
6. The importing member should take into account any relevant knowledge of and prior experience with the authorities of the exporting member.
7. All information previously provided should be taken into account by the importing country.
8. In an exporting member puts more than one request, it should fix its priority.
9. An importing Member should provide information sought by exporting Members. All disputes should be resolved on the basis of mutual discussions between the importing Member and the exporting member.
10. The guidelines prescribe administrative steps to be followed. Members should give heed to them.
11. An importing member should resort to an expedited process.

12. The Committee will monitor the implementation of Article 6. In this regard, members are encouraged to inform the Committee about a request for recognition of pest free or disease free area or area of low pest or disease prevalence is made, and/or a determination on whether to recognise such areas. Members are encouraged to share their experiences.[57]

As noted above, Article 6 are non-binding guidelines, but they are of great persuasive value. It gives importance to regional conditions, and ensures an effective and transparent mechanism for enforcing Article 6 of the SPS Agreement. The Member states should adhere to them.

Analytical Account of the cases under the SPS Agreement: Various provisions of the SPS Agreement that resulted in disputes between exporting and importing countries were attempted to be resolved by the WTO's Panel Reports and Appellate Body Reports in *European Communities – Measures Concerning Meat and Meat Products,* Panel Report, WT/DS26/A/R (hereinafter *EC-Hormones*); *European Communities – Measures Affecting Approval and Marketing of Biotech Products,* WTO Panel Report, WT/DS291/R, WT/DS292/R, and WT/DS293/R (hereinafter *EC-Biotech*); *Australia – Measures Affecting Salmon (i),* Appellate Body Report, November 1998, WT/DS18/AB/R (hereinafter *Australia Solomon*); *Australia – Measures Affecting the Importation of Salmon* , Recourse to Article 21.5 by Canada, Panel Report, WT/DS/18/RW (hereinafter Australia Solomon 21.5); *Japan – Measures Affecting Agricultural Products,* WT/DS76/AB/R (hereinafter *Japan-Agriculture*); *Japan – Measures Affecting the Importation of Apples,* WT/DS245/AB/R (hereinafter *Japan–Apple*).

EC-Biotech[58]*:* In 2003, Argentina, Canada and the United States, who are among the biggest producers and exporters of GMO and products containing them, brought a complaint under the WTO Dispute Settlement Understanding against various parts of the regulatory regime of EC and certain of its member states for the approval and marketing of biotech products.[59] The following were the key measures in the issue:

- An alleged *de facto* moratorium imposed by the European Communities (hereinafter EC) on the approval of new biotechnology products;
- The alleged failure by the EC to approve specific biotechnology products for which application for approval had been made; and
- 'Safeguard' measures taken by six EC members to prohibit certain biotechnology products that had been approved by the EC level.

The Panel found the following violations of the SPS Agreement:

1. The de facto moratorium on approvals of biotechnology products led to 'undue delay' in the completion of the approval process, in violation of SPS Agreement Annex C(1)(a), first clause;
2. Delays in approval process for a number of products violated the same provision; and
3. The member state's 'safeguard' measures were not 'based on' a 'risk assessment' in violation of SPS Agreement Article 5.1, and these measures could not be justified under SPS Agreement Article 5.7.

It is notable here that Annex A provides that: "Sanitary and Phytosanitary measures include all relevant laws, decrees, regulations, requirements and procedures including end product criteria; process and production methods; testing, inspection, certification and approval procedures; quarantine treatment including relevant requirements associated with the transport of animals or plants, or with the materials necessary for their survival during transport; provisions on relevant statically methods, sampling procedures and method of risk assessment; and packaging and labeling requirement directly related to food safety.

The Panel ruled that for determination any of the measures, its objective, form and nature are to be ensured. It further ruled that the *nature* requirement was not fulfilled, *as there was unnecessary delay*, and as the application to export was neither approved nor rejected.[60] This amounts to violation of Annex C(1)(a), first clause.[61] This is because the EU did not undertake and complete the approval procedure without undue delay; it thus amounted to *de facto* moratorium, which violated the provisions of Annex C(1)(a), first clause.[62]

The Panel considered Argentina's claim that biotechnology products had been treated less favourably than novel non-biotechnology products, and prior to 1998, the EC granted approvals for the marketing of biotechnology products, whereas it had not done so since 1998. The Panel rejected the claim on a technical ground. The Panel ruled that Argentina had focused on specific sub-categories of the product, and had not shown that *imported* products as a group were treated less favourably than the comparable group of *domestic* products.

The Complainants made a series of claims concerning 'safeguard' measures adopted by certain EC member states. It is notable that an EC member state can invoke in certain situations the following: 'as a result of new or additional information made available since the date of the consent and affecting the environment risk assessment or reassessment of existing information on the basis of new or additional scientific knowledge', and 'there are detailed grounds for considering that a GMO as or in a product... constitutes a risk to human health or environment'. They claimed that in absence of any of these reasons there was violation of Article 5.1 of the SPS Agreement,[63] which requires that SPS measure be "based on' a 'risk assessment', and could not be justified under Article 5.7 of the Agreement,[64] which allows a 'provisional measure' when 'relevant scientific evidence is insufficient'. Before giving its verdict on this compliant, the Panel compared Article 5.1 and 5.7.

According to the Panel, Article 5.7 should be characterized as a right in relation to Article 5.1, rather than as an exception to the 'general obligation' under Article 5.1. In view of this, the Panel ruled: "...in cases where a complaining party alleges that an SPS measure is inconsistent with Article 5.1, it is incumbent on the complaining party, and not the responding party, to demonstrate that the alleged measure is inconsistent with at least one of the four requirements set forth in Article 5.7"[65] The Panel found that; (a) for each safeguard, the measure was not 'based on' a 'risk assessment' under Article 5.1.[66] (b) because the first requirement of Article 5.7, which states that members may provisionally adopt an SPS measure if the measure is imposed in respect of a situation where 'relevant scientific evidence is insufficient', was not met, the safeguard measures were, thus inconsistent with Article 5.7...[67]

The findings of the Panel demonstrate that a moratorium or undue delay in the approval process will be considered as a violation of Article 5.7 of the SPS Agreement. This is acceptable as there can be no other opinion. Perhaps it is for this reason that appeal was not made by any of the parties. In view of this, it is suggested that all states, especially developing countries should follow an internationally accepted speedy approval process. It will be appropriate for them if they do not have a competent person or body of person to correct and take a speedy decision, the help of foreign expert(s) should be taken. Only then the imperative set out in Annex A(1) can be complied with.

Australia–Salmon: In this case, Australia prohibited the import of Salmon (fresh, chilled or frozen ocean-caught Canadian Salmon and certain other Canadian Salmon) from Canada. Canada challenged the Australian ban and pleaded that the ban had violated Article 5.1, Article 5.5 and Article 5.6 of the SPS Agreement. Under Article 5.6 Member states are authorized to take an 'appropriate level of protection', which is defined in paragraph 5 of the Annex A as 'the level of protection deemed appropriate by the Member establishing a sanitary measure.' The Appellate Body observed that it was a prerogative of the member state concerned and not of a panel or of the Appellate Body.

The Appellate Body clarified that the 'appropriate level of protection' established by a member and the SPS measure had to be clearly distinguished. They were not one and the same thing. The first was an objective, the second was an instrument chosen to attain or implement the objective.[68] The Appellate Body ruled: "We thus believe that the SPS Agreement contains an implicit obligation to determine the appropriate level of protection. We do not believe that there is an obligation to determine the appropriate level of protection in quantitative terms. This does not mean, however, that an importing Member is free to determine its level of protection with such vagueness or equivocation that the application of the relevant provisions of the SPS Agreement, such as Article 5.6 becomes impossible…We believe that in cases where a member does not determine its appropriate level of protection or does so with insufficient precision, the appropriate level of protection may be established by panels on the basis of the level of protection reflected in the SPS measure actually applied. Otherwise, a member's failure to comply with the implicit obligation to determine its appropriate level of protection – with sufficient reason–would allow it to escape from its obligations under this Agreement and , in particular, its obligation under Article 5.5 and 5.6."[69]

It may be observed that the Appellate Body reversed the Panel's finding that the heat-treatment violated Article 5.6 was 'more trade restrictive than necessary', because heat treatment was the wrong measure. In view of this is submitted that Members while determining 'appropriate level of protection', must ensure that they are not more trade restrictive than necessary. It is submitted that the ruling of the Appellate Body does not resolve the problem once and for all. The word 'necessary' might give rise to disputes in future.

The 'sufficient scientific evidence' in Article 2.2 and 'risk assessment' in Article 5.1 of the SPS Agreement are related because they are essential for the maintenance of the delicate and careful negotiated balance in the Agreement between the shared and, but sometimes competing, interest of promoting international trade and protection of life and health of human beings. In this context the Panel in *EC – Hormones* (see infra) ruled that Article 5.1 may be viewed as a specific application of the basic obligation contained in Article 2.2 of the SPS Agreement. And the Appellate Body ruled that both should consistently be read together.[70]

In this case, the Appellate Body shed light on a very intricate problem of the type of risk assessment and degree of risk assessment under Article 5.1 of the SPS Agreement. The Appellate Body gave the following three imperatives to be complied with: 1. *Identify* the diseases whose entry, establishment or spread a member wants to prevent within its territory, as well as the potential biological and economic consequences associated with the entry, establishment or spread of these diseases; 2. *Evaluate* the likelihood of entry, establishment or spread of these diseases, as well as the associate potential biological and economic consequences; and 3. *Evaluate* the likelihood of entry, establishment or spread of these diseases *according to the SPS measures which might be applied.*[71] In short, it is indentifying and evaluates the likelihood of risk. About the *degree of risk* the Appellate Body determined: "We note that the first type of risk assessment in paragraph 4 of Annex A is substantially different from the second type risk assessment contained in the same paragraph. While the second require only the evaluation of the potential for adverse effect on human or animal health, the first type of risk assessment demands an evaluation of the likelihood of entry, establishment or spread of disease, and of the associated potential biological and economic consequences. In view of the very different language used in paragraph 4 of Annex A for the 2 types of risk assessment, we do not believe that it is correct to diminish the substantial differences between these 2 types of risk assessments..."[72]

From this it can be noted that for a risk assessment to fall within the meaning of Article 5.1 and the first definition in paragraph 4 of Annex A, it is not sufficient that a risk assessment concludes that there is a *possibility* of entry, establishment or spread of diseases and associated biological and economic consequences. A proper risk assessment of this type must evaluate the 'likelihood', i.e. the 'possibility' of entry, establishment or spread of diseases and associated biological and economic consequences as well as the 'likelihood', i.e. 'probability' of entry, establishment or spread of diseases according to the SPS measure which might be applied. The

Appellate Body ruled: "...We do not agree with the Panel that a risk assessment of this type needs only some evaluation of the likelihood or probability. The definition of this type of risk in paragraph 4 of Annex A refers to 'the evaluation of the likelihood' and not to some evaluation of the likelihood. We agree, however, ... that the SPS Agreement does not require that the evaluation of the likelihood needs to be done quantitatively. The likelihood may be expressed either quantitatively or qualitatively...there is no requirement for a risk assessment to establish a certain magnitude or threshold level of degree of risk."[73]The author appreciates this interpretation because this brings about a meaningful balance between protection of human, animal and plant life and international trade. This interpretation has further been clarified in *Japan – Apple*. (See infra)

Article 2.3 of the SPS Agreement enjoins not to take any measure arbitrarily or unjustifiably discriminate between Members where identical or similar conditions prevail. This non-discrimination obligation has to be read in light of Article 5.5 of the Agreement. This has been clarified by the Appellate Body in these words: "...a finding of violation of Article 5.5 will necessarily imply a violation of Article 2.3, first sentence, or ...second sentence. Discrimination 'between Members, including their own territory and that of other members' within the meaning of Article 2.3 first sentence can be established by following the complex and direct route and is not the only route leading to a finding that an SPS measure constitutes arbitrary or unjustifiable discrimination according to Article 2.3 first sentence can be found to exists without any examination under Article 5.5." [74]

Article 5.5 of the SPS agreement prohibits any disguised restriction. In this case the Appellate Body decided that the Australian measure was not an SPS measure based on an assessment of the risk to human, animal or plant life or health–either because there was no risk assessment at all or because there was insufficient risk assessment–was a strong indication that the measure was not really concerned with the protection of human, animal, plant life or health but was instead a trade measure taken in disguise of an SPS measure, i.e. a 'disguised restriction on international trade'.[75] (For a detailed jurisprudential delineation, see *EC – Hormones*, infra).

Article 5.6 of the SPS Agreement entails that any SPS measure should not be 'more trade restrictive than required to achieve the appropriate level of protection'. The Appellate Body agreed with the three-pronged test for this Article of the Agreement. These three elements are: 1. It should be reasonably available taking into account technical and economic feasibility; 2. It achieves the Member's appropriate level of sanitary or phytosanitary protection; and 3. It should be significantly less trade restrictive than the SPS measure contested.[76] These three are cumulative in nature. This has been affirmed by the Appellate Body in *Japan - Agriculture* (see infra).[77]

Japan–Apple: In this case, on request of the United States, the Panel was established to consider a complaint by the United States concerning certain restrictions and prohibitions imposed by Japan with respect to the importation of Apple fruits from the United States. The Panel Report was given on 15 May 1984, which was considered by the Appellate Body and its report came on 26 November 2003, which was adopted on 10 December 2003. The issues were on Article 2.2, 5.1 and 5.7 of the SPS Agreement.

The Panel ruled that:

- That the phytosanitary measure was 'without sufficient scientific evidence'. Thus, there was violation of Article 2.2;
- That it was not based on 'risk assessment' within the meaning of Article 5.1 of the SPS Agreement; and
- That the restriction did not qualify for provisional measure under Article 5.7 as it was not imposed in respect of a situation 'where scientific evidence was insufficient'.

The Appellate Body broadly accepted the findings of the Panel that can be put under these points:

1. That Japan's phytosanitary measure was 'without sufficient scientific evidence' within the meaning of Article 2.2 of the SPS Agreement.
2. That Japan's measure at issue was not imposed in respect of a situation 'where relevant scientific evidence is sufficient', and, therefore, that it was not a provisional measure justified under Article 5.7 of the SPS Agreement; and
3. That Japan's risk analysis did not satisfy the definition of risk assessment set out in paragraph 4 of the Annex A of the SPS Agreement because (i) it failed to 'evaluate the likelihood of entry, establishment or spread of' the plant disease at issue, and (ii) failed to conduct such an evaluation 'according to the SPS measure which might be applied'. Consequently, the Appellate Body upheld the Panel's findings, that Japan's measure was not 'based on' risk assessment, as required by Article 5.1 of the SPS Agreement.

Detailed accounts at certain points of the Articles referred above are appropriate to be given. On Article 2.2, the Panel says that the measure was clearly disproportionate to the risk identified on the basis of the scientific evidence available. Such a 'clear disproportion' implies that the 'rational objective relationship' does not exist between the measure and the relevant scientific evidence, and, therefore, the measure is 'without sufficient scientific evidence'. It can be noted here that the Panel found no 'rational or objective relationship between an SPS Measure and the scientific evidence'.

On this, the Appellate Body ruled: "We emphasize...that whether a given approach or methodology is appropriate in order to assess whether a measure is maintained 'without sufficient scientific evidence'...depends on 'the particular circumstances of the case' and must be 'determined on a case-by-case basis'. Thus, the approach followed by the Panel in this case – disassembling the sequence of events to identify the risk and comparing it with the measure – does not exhaust the range of methodologies available to determine whether a measure is maintained 'without scientific evidence'. Approaches different from that followed by the Panel in this case could also prove to evaluate whether a measure is maintained without sufficient scientific evidence. Whether or not a particular approach is appropriate will depend on the 'particular circumstances of the case'."[78]

On 'risk assessment', the Appellate Body ruled that "the evaluation of the entry, establishment and spread of a disease" be conducted 'according to the SPS measures which might be applied'. We agree with the Panel that this phrase 'refers to the measures 'which are being applied' is used in the conditional sense. In this sense, 'might' means: 'were or would be or have been able to, were or would be to have been allowed to were or would perhaps.' We understand this phrase to imply that the risk assessment should not be limited to an examination of the measure already in place or favoured by an importing Member."[79]

In other words, the Appellate Body delineates that the evaluation contemplated in paragraph 4 of Annex A to the SPS Agreement should not be distorted by preconceived views on the nature and the content of the measure to be taken; nor should it develop into an exercise tailored to and carried out for the purpose of justifying decisions *ex post fact.*

On Article 5.7 of the SPS Agreement, the Appellate Body ruled: "...the first requirement of Article 5.7 is that there must be insufficient scientific evidence.

When a panel reviews a measure claimed by a Member to be provisional, that panel must assess whether 'relevant scientific evidence is insufficient'. This evaluation must be carried out, not in the abstract, but in the light of particular enquiry. The notions of 'relevance' and 'insufficiency' in the introductory phrase of Article 5.7 imply a relationship between the scientific evidence and something else. Reading this introductory phrase in the broader context of Article 5 of the SPS Agreement, which is entitled 'Assessment of Risk and Determination of the Appropriate level of Sanitary and Phyto-sanitary Protection', is instructive in ascertaining the nature of the relationship to be established. Article 5.1 sets out a key discipline under Article 5, namely that 'Members shall ensure that their sanitary or phyto-sanitary measures are based on an assessment...of the risk to human, animal or plant life or health'. This informs the other provisions of Article 5, including Article 5.7.

We note, as well, that the second sentence of Article 5.7 refers to a 'more objective assessment of risks'. These contextual elements militate in favour of a link or relationship between the first requirement of Article 5.7 and the obligation to perform a risk assessment under Article 5.1: relevant scientific evidence will be insufficient within the meaning of Article 5.7 if the body of available scientific evidence does not allow, in qualitative or qualitative terms, the performance of an adequate risk assessment as required under Article 5.1 and as defined in Annex A to the SPS Agreement.

Thus, the question is not whether there is sufficient evidence of a general nature or whether there is sufficient evidence related to a specific aspect of a phyto-sanitary problem, or a specific risk. The question is whether the relevant evidence, be it 'general' or 'specific', in the Panel's parlance, is sufficient to permit the evaluation of the likelihood of entry, establishment or spread of, in this case, fire blight in Japan."[80] The Appellate Body further clarified that the application of Article 5.7 could be triggered *not by the existence of scientific uncertainty, but rather by the insufficient scientific evidence*. The text of Article 5.7 was clear. It referred to 'cases where relevant scientific evidence was insufficient', and 'not to scientific uncertainty'. The two concepts were not interchangeable. In view of this the Appellate Body rejected Japan's claim that Article 5.7 should be interpreted through the prism of 'scientific uncertainty.[81]

On the basis the Appellate Body report we can discern the following three cardinal principles to be relevant for Article 5.7:

1. The application of Article 5.7 is triggered not by the existence of scientific uncertainty, but rather by insufficient scientific evidence;

2. This has to be ascertained by the panel; and
3. 'Relevant scientific evidence' will be 'insufficient' if the body of available scientific evidence does not allow, in qualitative or quantitative terms, the performance of an adequate assessment of risk as required under Article 5.1 and as defined in Annex A of the SPS Agreement. The author are of the opinion that as stated above, the provisional measure taken by a Member is not of permanent nature. It will be operative within a reasonable period of time. When the relevant scientific evidence becomes 'sufficient', the measure will have to be lifted. There are, in fact, four requirements of Article 5.7. This has been spelled out in *Japan–Agriculture.* (See infra).

Japan–Agriculture Products: Japan prohibited the importation of eight agricultural products originating from the United States on the ground that they were potential hosts of codling moth, a pest of quarantine significance of Japan. The import prohibition could, however, be lifted if the United States could propose an alternative quarantine treatment which achieves a level of protection equivalent to the import prohibition. The dispute was on the Japan's requirement of varietal testing and confirmation of the efficacy of the quarantine treatment for each variety of certain agricultural products. The Panel found that Japan had acted inconsistently with Article 2.2, 5.6 and 7 of the SPS Agreement. The Appellate Body upholding the findings of the Panel, decided that there was: violation of Article 2.2, as there was not sufficient scientific evidence within the meaning of this Article; there was violation of Article 5.1, as the variety testing was not based on a risk assessment; and there was violation of Article 5.7 of the SPS Agreement, as Japan did not fulfill the requirements contained in the second sentence of the Article. A detailed account of the essential aspects of the Report is as follows:

On the word 'sufficient' used in the phrase 'sufficient scientific evidence' in Article 2.2 of the SPS Agreement it was ruled that it was a rational concept. 'Sufficiency' requires the existence of a sufficient or adequate relationship between two elements, *in casu*, between the SPS measure and the scientific evidence. The context of the word 'sufficient' or more generally the phrase 'maintained without sufficient scientific evidence' in Article 2.2 includes Article 5.1...and Article 5.7.[82]

The Appellate Body agreed with the Panel that the obligation in Article 2.2 that an SPS measure cannot be maintained without sufficient scientific evidence required that there be a rational and objective relationship between the SPS measure and the scientific evidence. It is required to be made on a case-by-case basis and would depend on particular circumstances of the case, including the characteristics of the measure at issue and the quality and quantity of the scientific evidence.[83] It should be determined on a case-by-case basis.[84]

We have noted above that the provisional measures can be adopted if the scientific evidence is not sufficient. The Appellate Body, thus, ruled that Article 5.7 operated as a qualified exemption from the obligation under Article 2.2 not to maintain SPS measures without sufficient scientific evidence. An overly broad and flexible interpretation of the obligation would render Article 5.7 meaningless.[85]The Appellate Body ruled that, "Article 5.7 of the SPS Agreement sets out four requirements which must be met in order to adopt and maintain a provisional SPS measure. Pursuant to the first sentence of Article 5.7, a member may provisionally adopt an SPS measure if this measure is imposed in respect of a situation where 'relevant scientific information' is insufficient; and adopted on the basis of available pertinent information.

Pursuant to the second sentence of Article 5.7, such a provisional measure may not be maintained unless the Member which adopted the measure:

- Seeks to obtain the additional information necessary for a more objective assessment of risk; and
- Reviews the measure accordingly within a reasonable period of time.

These four requirements are cumulative in nature and are of equal importance for the purpose of determining consistency with this provision. Whenever one of these requirements is not met, the measure at issue will be inconsistent with Article

5.7 of the Agreement.[86] The Appellate Body concluded in these words, "We, therefore, conclude that the Panel did not err in its application of Article 5.7 by first examining whether the varietal testing requirement meets the requirements of the second sentence of Article 5.7" There was no need for the Panel to examine the requirement of the first sentence."[87] Reasonable period of time to review the measure has to be determined on case-by-case basis.[88]

We have noted above that by virtue of Article 5.6 of the SPS Agreement, any measure should 'not be more trade restrictive than required' to achieve the appropriate level of protection. Interpreting this Article, the Appellate Body in *Australia - Salomon* gave three elements of this test: it should be reasonable; it should achieve the Member's appropriate level of sanitary and phyto-sanitary protection; and it should significantly be less trade restrictive than the SPS measure. These three points were reiterated in this case.[89]

EC–Hormones: In *EC–Hormones*, adopted on 13 February 1998, EC had banned import of meat and meat products from animals treaded with certain hormones. The United States opposed this measure. The Appellate Body ruled that since the measure was not based on a risk assessment within the meaning of Article 5.1 of the SPS Agreement, it was inconsistent with the Agreement. It was the first case when the Appellate Body had the opportunity to consider the SPS Agreement. It is notable that the SPS Agreement marks a departure from the GATT discrimination-based regime. The Agreement does not allow those measures which are arbitrary in the sense that they do not really serve to advance their purported purpose of protecting life and health. Any measure, thus, will be invalidated if it is not based on any objective 'risk assessment'. Important among the points discussed are: 'discrimination or a disguised restriction on international trade', meaning of the phrase 'based on' and meaning and scope of precautionary principle in the context of the SPS Agreement. Since we have already taken the view point of the Appellate Body in the cases discussed above, we will highlight only those aspects on which sufficient light was not shed in previous cases.

The Appellate Body determined that Article 2.2 informs Article 5.1 as without risk assessment, we cannot determine 'sufficient scientific evidence', and thus we cannot establish a meaningful balance between international trade and protection of life and health.[90]

Generally speaking, the objective and purpose of Article 3 of the SPS Agreement is to promote the harmonisation of the SPS measures of Members on as wide a basis as possible, while recognising and safeguarding, at the same time, the right and duty of Members to protect the life and health of their people. The ultimate goal of harmonisation is to prevent the use of such measures for arbitrary or unjustifiable discrimination between Members or as a disguised restriction on international trade, without preventing members from adopting or enforcing measures which are both 'necessary to protect' human life and health and 'based on scientific principles', and without requiring them to change their appropriate level of protection.

With regard to 'measure based on...international standards', the Appellate Body ruled that the measure of consistency with relevant provisions of the SPS Agreement that arose under Article 3.2 in respect of measures that conform to international standards might well be an *incentive* for Members so as to conform their SPS measures with such standards. It was clear, however, that a decision of a Member not to conform a particular measure to an international standard did not authorise imposition of a special or generalised burden of proof upon that Member, which may, more often than not, amount to a *penalty*.[91] The Appellate Body further ruled, "We cannot lightly assume that sovereign states intended to impose upon themselves the more onerous, rather than the less burdensome, obligation by mandating conformity or compliance with such standards, guidelines and recommendations. To sustain such an assumption and to warrant such a far-reaching interpretation, treaty language far more specific and compelling than that found in Article 3 of the SPS Agreement would be necessary."[92]

Under Article 3.1 of the SPS Agreement, a Member may choose to establish an SPS measure that is based on the existing relevant international standard, guideline or recommendation.

Explaining this, the Appellate Body said, "Such a measure may adopt some, not necessarily all, of the elements of international standard. The Member imposing this measure does not benefit from the presumption of consistency set out in Article 3.2; but...the member is not penalized by exemption of a complaining Member from the normal burden showing a prima facie case of inconsistency with Article 3.1 or any other portions SPS Agreement or of the GATT 1994"[93]. It is notable that Article 3.2 of the SPS Agreement is about presumption of consistency with relevant provisions of the SPS Agreement with respect to measures that conform to international standards and may be an incentive for a Member so to conform their SPS measure to such standards. It is clear, however, that a decision of a Member not to conform to a particular measure to an international standard does not authorise imposition of special or generalized burden of proof upon that Member, which may, more often than not, amount to a penalty. Thus, the Appellate Body ruled, "Under Article 3.2 of the SPS Agreement, a Member may decide to promulgate an SPS measure that conforms to an international standard. Such a measure would embody the international standard completely and, for practical purposes, converts it into a municipal standard. Such a measure enjoys the benefit of a presumption (albeit a rebuttable one) that is consistent with the relevant provisions of the SPS Agreement and of the GATT 1994."[94]

Under Article 3.3 of the SPS Agreement, a Member state may decide to set for itself a level of protection different from that implicit in the international standard, and to implement or embody that level of protection in a measure not 'based on' the international standard. The Member's appropriate level of protection may be higher than that implied in the international standard. The right of a Member to determine its own appropriate level of sanitary protection is an important right.

On this the Appellate Body has given the following clarifications, First, it is not an absolute or unqualified right. Second, this is an autonomous right and not an exception from a general obligation under Article 3.1. Third, that Member will have to comply with requirements in promulgation of the SPS measure to achieve that level. These are:

- scientific 'justification for the measure'; or
- as a consequence of the level of protection a Member determines to be appropriate in accordance with the relevant provisions of paragraph 1 through 8 of Article 5.[95]

The Appellate Body further ruled, *"It is true that situation (a) does not speak of Article 5.1 through 5.8. Nevertheless, two points need to be noted. First, the last sentence of Article 3.3 requires that 'all measures which result in a [higher] level of protection', that is to say, measures falling within situation (a) as well as those falling within situation (b), be 'not consistent with any other provision of this Agreement' textually included in Article 5. Secondly, the footnote to Article 3.3, attached to the end of the first sentence, defines scientific justification as 'an examination and evaluation of available scientific in conformity with relevant provisions of this Agreement...' This examination and evaluation would appear to partake of the nature of the risk assessment required in Article 5.1 and defined in paragraph 4 of Annex A of the SPS Agreement."*[96] It means Article 3.3 requires complying with the requirements of Article 5.1 of the Agreement.

We have noted in the above cases that for maintaining a balance between international trade and protection of human, animal and plant life and health, it is necessary to have SPS measures based on risk assessment within the meaning of Article 5.1 and 'sufficient scientific evidence' under Article 2.2. This was actually first said by the Appellate Body in *EC – Hormones*.[97] The Appellate Body clarified that Article 5.1 may be viewed as a specific application of the basic obligation under Article 2.2 of the Agreement. So, both should be read together.[98]

As reiterated in the above cases, according to the Appellate Body the definition of 'risk assessment' is a two-step process: (1) to identify the adverse effects on human health (if any)..., and (2) if any such adverse effects exist, evaluation of the potential or probable occurrence of such effect.[99] It is not necessary for the state that takes sanitary or phyto-sanitary measure to conduct its own risk assessment, but the measure must be based on an assessment carried by another Member state.[100] The Appellate Body has rightly ruled that since science cannot provide absolute certainty, theoretical uncertainty did not constitute the kind of risk which, under Article 5.1, is to be assessed.[101] According to the Appellate Body, "...It is essential to bear in mind that the risk that is to be evaluated in a risk assessment under Article 5.1 is not only risk ascertainable in a science laboratory operating under strict controlled conditions, but also risk in human societies as they actually exist, in other words, the actual potential for adverse effects on human health in the real world where people live, work and die."[102] However, there has to be a rational relationship between the measure and the risk assessment. This has been stressed by the Appellate Body in *EC – Hormones*[103] and *Japan – Agriculture.*[104]

Article 5.5 stipulates that ***consistency*** be maintained in the application of the appropriate level of protection. In this connection the Appellate Body ruled that there can be inconsistency among measures as each state takes measure according to its own judgment. Therefore it will only be arbitrary or unjustifiable inconsistencies that are to be avoided.[105] It further ruled that the compliant of violation of Article 5.5 must show the presence of three distinct elements: 1. The Member imposing the measure complained of has adopted his own appropriate levels of sanitary protection against risks to human life and health in several different situations. 2. Those levels of protection exhibit ***arbitrary or unjustifiable*** differences ('distinctions' in the language of Article 5.5) in their treatment of different situations. 3. The arbitrary or unjustifiable differences result in *discrimination or a disguised restriction* of international trade. These three elements are cumulative.[106] The Appellate Body requires that Article 5.5 must be interpreted in the context of Article 2.3. When we read them together, Article 5.5 may be seen to be marking out and elaborating a particular route leading to the same destination set out in Article 2.3.[107]

We have noted above that Article 5.7 of the SPS Agreement allows a Member to resort to provisional measures where 'relevant scientific evidence is insufficient'. In *Japan – Agriculture,* the Appellate Body gave these four requirements for the application of a provisional SPS measure: 'relevant scientific information is insufficient', it is based 'on the basis of available pertinent information', it 'seeks to obtain additional information necessary for a more objective assessment of risk', and it has to be 'subject to review'.[108] In *Japan – Apple,* the Appellate Body ruled that the relevant scientific evidence would be insufficient if the body of available scientific evidence did not allow... the performance of an adequate assessment of risks as required under Article 5.1 and as defined in Annex A to the SPS Agreement. Thus, the application of Article 5.7 is triggered not by the existence of scientific uncertainty, but rather by the insufficiency of scientific evidence.[109] This is, in fact, reflection of the precautionary principle. With respect to the precautionary principle, the Appellate Body stated that the status of the principle was still debated in international law. It is not clear whether the principle has crystallized into a general principle of customary international law.[110]

However, the Appellate Body clearly stated that "*It appears to us important, nevertheless, to note some aspects of the relationship of the precautionary principle to the SPS Agreement. First, the principle has not been written into the SPS Agreement as a ground for justifying SPS measures that are otherwise inconsistent with the obligation of Members set out in particular provisions of the agreement. Secondly, the precautionary principle indeed finds reflection in Article 5.7 of the SPS Agreement. We agree at the same time, with the European Communities, that there is no need to assume that Article 5.7 exhausts the relevance of the precautionary principle. It is reflected also in the sixth paragraph of the preamble and Article 3.3. These explicitly recognise the right of Members to establish their own appropriate level of sanitary protection, which level may be higher (i.e. more cautious) than that implied in existing international standards, guidelines and recommendations. Thirdly, a Panel charged with determining, for instance whether 'sufficient scientific evidence' exists to warrant the maintenance by a Member of a particular SPS measure may, of course, and should, bear in mind that responsible, representative governments commonly act from perspectives of produce and precaution where risks of irreversible, e.g., life-terminating, damage to human health are concerned. Lastly, however, the precautionary principle does not, by itself, and without a clear textual directive to that effect, relieve a panel from the duty of applying the normal (i.e. customary international law) principles of treaty interpretation in reading the provisions of the SPS Agreement".*

GMOs and WTO Rules (SPS Agreement): International trade in GMOs touches the SPS Agreement under the following circumstances:

To Protect	*From*
Human	Risk arising from additives, contaminations, toxins
Animal Life	Disease-causing organisms in their food, beverages, food stuffs
Human Life	Plant or animal carried diseases (zoonoses)
Animal or Plant Life	Pests, diseases, or disease-causing organisms
A Country	Damage caused by the entry, establishment, or spread of pests

In the context of international trade in GMOs, the first and the last point of the above table seem relevant, i.e. protection from food safety risks and invasive species risks from genetically modified plants. In the case of food safety, however, the SPS agreement applies to risks from additives, contaminants, toxins or disease-causing organisms, and it is not clear if potential risk from GMO foods fit into one of those categories. If the SPS Agreement did apply, regulations on GMOs would have to conform to the provisions of the Agreement, such as scientifically based risk assessment, least trade restrictive measure, and prohibition of disguised measure that results in trade restriction. If a scientific risk assessment proves that certain GMOs might be harmful to human, animal or plant life and health or to any or two of them, an SPS measure can be taken and import of such GMOs can be banned. In case there is lack of 'sufficient scientific evidence', provisional SPS measures can be taken. Such restrictions must maintain a balance between the appropriate level of protection and the SPS measure so that international trade and protection of life and health go hand-in-hand. The measure must not be excessive or taken in disguise. Is so, international trade will impede, and if challenged, it might be determined to be violative to the SPS Agreement. In the cases discussed above, we have taken a detailed and critical account of various aspects of Article 2.2, 5.1, 5.5, 3.1-3 and 5.7 of the SPS Agreement which demanded interpretations. The interpretations given by the Panel and Appellate Body are clear.

Among all cases, with respect to trade in GMOs, the *EC – Biotech* is important. The Panel's conclusion focused on three issues: 'Undue delay' in approving biotechnology products for commercial use (Article 8 and Annex C, paragraph Ia); the requirement of a scientifically based risk assessment for an SPS measure (regulation, law, recommendation, judicial ruling) (Article 5.1 and paragraph 4 of Annex A); and application of an SPS measure when there is insufficient scientific information about a product (Article 5.7; application of precautionary principle). The Panel ruled that the EC violated by taking three kinds of SPS measures; a general moratorium, product specific SPS measure and member states safeguard measures against biotechnology products. This is because SPS measures lacked scientific risk assessments. Further, in no case did the Member state demonstrate that 'the relevant scientific evidence was insufficient to perform a risk assessment, such that the Member state might have had recourse to provisional measures under Article 5.7 of the SPS Agreement (i.e., precautionary principle will not be applicable).

It is notable here that unlike international environmental law, application of the precautionary principle in WTO rules is too controversial and unsettled. On the basis of the above cases, we can say that even if a Member takes the plea of precautionary principle for justifying its SPS measure, it has to be based on sufficiently warranted or reasonably supported by a risk assessment;[111]and that any risk assessment done under the Cartagena Protocol for any GMO approval does not have value in the SPS Agreement. In effect, the Panel in *EC – Biotech,* made domestic measures based on the Protocol, including the Protocol's Articles on risk assessment…indefensible if they are if they were challenged by a non-party…under the definition of risk assessment in the SPS Agreement. Not becoming a party to the Protocol, while intervening to prevent its implementation...was apparently a bullet proof litigation strategy against any attempt by WTO Members who were also protocol parties to defend their environmental regulation of GMO with reference to fulfilling their protocol commitments.

Thus, non-membership in protocol also allows non-parties to avoid having to inform Protocol parties of the lamentable state of environmental regulations of GMOs. A NGO amicus brief sought to bring the impoverished scientific basis of GMO approvals to the attention of the Panel in *EC – Biotech,* but the Panel chose not to take amicus briefs into account. By disregarding evidence of the weak regulation of GMOs, the Panel's jurisdiction based ruling on the Protocol defense of environmental regulation of GMOs would annul any benefits of Protocol implementation in the event that Protocol implementation in the event that Protocol consistent modes of compliance conflict with WTO Agreements, particularly the SPS Agreement.[112]

It is generally accepted that many provisions of a number of Multilateral Environmental Agreements (MEAs) are in conflict with the WTO rules.[113]It is because these two sets of legal regimes have developed in different paradigms. After the two world wars that had crippled the world's economy and had taken millions of lives, the world community emphasised on economic development as fast as possible. It is better known as 19th century *laissez-faire*. Protection of the environment came in the limelight only in 1972 at the United Conference on Human Environment (UNCHE). Only after this conference, sovereign states started making specific legislations and a large number of treaties, known as multilateral environmental agreements (MEAs), came into existence. Some of these MEAs became so popular that they have more members than the WTO. Some of these MEAs are in conflict with WTO rules.[114] Although under the Cartagena Protocol 'trade and environment agreements should be mutually supportive with a view to achieving sustainable development, there are possibilities of collision between it and the SPS Agreement, and the *EC – Biotech* is the proof of this situation.[115]

As protection of the environment is no less important than ensuring international free trade, even a person like Jagdish Bhagwati, who is a staunch supporter of free trade, pleads for an amicable co-existence of both the regimes.[116]

There is a large group of experts who are of the opinion that the two regimes can be made mutually supportive: either by considering MEAs as an exception to WTO rules, which has been done in the NAFTA, or by making suitable amendments in the GATT as Article xx of the GATT has filed to have an amicable co-existence of both the regimes. But for one or the other reason, these two suggestions are found not viable solutions because NAFTA is a small treaty between three countries and because unfortunately WTO has been a centre of a lot of groupings and politicking,[117] which is proven by the July 2008 meeting on the Doha Round.[118] It is unfortunate that all cases, except the *EC – Asbestos,* decided under Article XX of the GATT and GATT-94 have gone in favour of free trade. It is because the provisions of Article xx were given strict interpretation and narrow application. Perhaps it could go like that because members at the GATT and WTO Panels and Appellate Body had only experts of trade laws and did not have enough insight in environmental laws. It has been unfortunate that even in the *EC – Biotech* the trade law contained in the SPS Agreement was given preference over the Cartagena Protocol.

The Panel made domestic measures based on the Protocol, including the protocols. Articles on risk assessment and risk management, indefensible if they were challenged by a non-party or freer rider to the Protocol under the definition of risk assessment in the SPS Agreement. Although the EC, in this case, evoked the Protocol in the defence of environmental protection regulations, the panel did not need to confine its ruling to jurisdictional issues. Instead, it could have declined to rule given the lack of consensus about risk assessment and risk management options in multilateral agreements.[119] It is also notable that in *EC – Hormones,* the Appellate Body simply said that unlike international environmental law, the precautionary principle was not so developed in international trade law. The Appellate Body could have deliberated on it in detail and could have determined its nature and scope in line with the nature and scope in MEAs, especially in the Cartagena Protocol. It is necessary to mention that in totality, the Cartagena Protocol gives an articulate and expansive version of the precautionary principle than the SPS Agreement.

In spite of these odds, some are optimistic and think that both the regimes can be made supportive to each other.[120] It is for this reason that Paragraph 31 of the Doha Declaration strives for having such a situation. Paragraph 32 of the Declaration provides for constituting a Special Session of the Committee on Trade and Environment (CTE). It is unfortunate that in spite of repeated request by the Director General Lamy, there is no significant breakthrough. The Committee is still working but its success is loomed by the clouds of uncertainty. The latest failure of the July 2008 meeting has further blurred the possibility of an amicable co-existence of both the regimes.

So far as co-existence of the Cartagena protocol and the SPS Agreement is concerned, some solutions can be suggested. The popular solution is that for providing a greater degree of freedom of risk assessment the states should suitably amend Articles 5.5 and 5.7 to bring them in line with CODEX assessment guidelines and the Cartagena Protocol. But will it be advisable, as the two legal instruments have two different objectives? The predominant purpose of the Cartagena Protocol is to regulate transboundary movement of LMOs from one country to another country and to protect the environment; whereas, the emphasis of the SPS Agreement is to protect human, animal and plant life and health. It is for this reason that the requirement of risk assessment in the SPS Agreement has to be based on more objective scientific procedure not only done in the lab, but also outside in the society, so that only in genuine cases SPS measures are taken and they are neither trade restrictive nor arbitrary. The whole scheme, in effect, favours international trade. Even where the state has taken precautionary measure under Article 5.7, it will have to review its measure from time to time. Sovereignty of the state has got to play an important role in the SPS Agreement. On the contrary, in the Cartagena Protocol also risk assessment has to be done before enforcing import embargo; but in this, states have greater degree of freedom. It is because Article 2.2 of the Protocol reads: "Nothing in this Protocol shall be interpreted as restricting the right of a party to take action that is more protective of the conservation and sustainable use of biological diversity than that called for in this Protocol, provided that such action...is in accordance with the Party's other obligations under international law." Article 10.6 and 12 espouse that, "Lack of scientific certainty due to insufficient relevant scientific information and knowledge regarding the extent of the potential adverse effects of a living modified organism...shall not prevent that Party from taking a decision, as appropriate with regard to the import of the living modified organism in question" (CBD 2000, Article 10.6)

"A party of import may at any time in light of new scientific information on potential adverse effects... review and change a decision regarding an international transboundary movement" (CBD, Article 12.1)

"A Party of export or a notifier may request the Party of import to review a decision it has made...where the Party of Export or the notifier considers that (a) a change in circumstances has occurred that may influence the outcome of the risk assessment upon which the decision was based; or (b) additional relevant scientific or technical information has become available." (CBD 2000, Article 12.2).

It is notable that in case of SPS Agreement review has to be made within a 'reasonable period of time'; whereas, in the Protocol, a review is sought only when new scientific information or circumstances is considered relevant. In this case the period of review may be longer. It is supported by the new CODEX procedure, which says that 'precaution is an inherent element of risk analysis'. It might be true in case of the Protocol. But if it is applied in the SPS Agreement, international trade might suffer. It is also obvious that even in the SPS Agreement, review of the measure will be done within a reasonable period of time, but the continuity of the measure will depend on the scientific-based risk assessment.

To conclude, the Cartagena Protocol, which has its prime object to conserve the environment, provides a viable mechanism for transboundary movement of GMOs. In view of the five exclusions, its scope is limited to seeds and LMOs. Movement of LMOs depends on the AIA mechanisms, which has the basis of risk assessment. Risk assessment is generally done by the producing country before it allows commercialisation of any LMO. It is also done by the importing country if it intends to impose import ban of any LMO. It has been observed that in some cases, risk assessment done by the company with respect to an LMO produced by it, and on that basis, the state, where the company is situated, has allowed commercialisation of that LMO. This is a wrong practice.

Once a state has imposed import ban with respect to any LMO, it has to review it in view of any new scientific information or circumstances. It is different than the precautionary measure taken under the SPS Agreement. The Agreement requires review of the provisional SPS measure taken by a Member state within a reasonable period of time. The authors are of the opinion that under the Protocol, the period of review may be longer, which might prove to be more restrictive to international trade. But for the sake of a greater degree of protection of the biodiversity, which includes all living entities, the application of the precautionary principle in the Protocol is better than the provisional measure taken under Article 5.7 of the SPS Agreement.[121] However, it is suggested that in both the legal regimes, application of measure, which requires scientific experimentation, must not only depend on laboratory findings. Actual effect on the ground must also be performed.

The authors are of the opinion that there is conflict between the Cartagena Protocol and the SPS Agreement. There exist inconsistencies between the two, but these inconsistencies can be resolved amicably by making suitable amendments in the SPS Agreement. This is warranted because conservation of the biodiversity in effect contributes to the protection of human, animal and plant lives and health in manifest ways. Some are suggesting that Article 5.5 and 5.7 of the SPS Agreement should be amended in order to bring them in line with the Cartagena Protocol and the CODEX procedure. It is suggested that before we opt for such an amendment, a proper study should be done by the Special Session of the CTE, so that an amicable balance between international trade in and conservation of the biodiversity may be created. It was expected that decisions of the Panels and the Appellate Body in the cases discussed above, will make efforts to harmonise the two inconsistent legal regimes, but they contributed little.

Conclusion and Suggestions for Reform

Food biotechnology has a notable breakthrough in many countries, including some developing countries. Biotechnology companies of these countries are producing and exporting LMOs, generally in the form of LMOs, seeds and edibles containing GM content. The ASEAN countries, are striving hard to get into the arena of production, consumption and export of LMOs and GM food. For example, Malaysia's Agricultural Policy and efforts to enhance the agricultural sector in the country all kinds of support, but the result in terms of new GM food varieties are yet to be seen. The pace of their progress in almost all ASEAN countries, in this area, is not so encouraging. It is because of lack of enough expertise and infrastructure, including sophisticated technology. The authors are of the view that their collaborative research with developed countries and South-South cooperation can provide an impetus to the biotechnology sector in general and agricultural biotechnology in specific. Collaborative research with the able guidance of Singapore and Philippines can help other ASEAN countries. Although Singapore is ahead of many countries in medical biotechnology, it has the capability to help other countries in the area of agricultural biotechnology also. India, China and Brazil can also be of great help. If ASEAN countries keep on augmenting such efforts, with rather greater degree of emphasis, they will be able to develop GM varieties which might have international market.

In Malaysia, biotechnology is a priority area. The Malaysian government is extending all sorts of incentives to this sector. In spite of these incentives, the sector is growing steadily. So as to have a faster growth, the country should increase financial allocations, should review incentives, should emphasize on collaborative work, and should bring certain incentive-based schemes to attract foreign experts. Foreign experts can help augmenting the biotechnology research and enhancing indigenous human resource.

All countries should develop their own capabilities for bio-safety tests, both lab testing and field lab testing. The capability should be world class so that their products become acceptable around the globe. This is because biotechnology companies do not give safety guarantee of their LMOs and edibles containing genetically modified stuff. However, they provide bio-safety data based on their bio-safety testing. For economic reasons, states heavily rely on them. This practice of exporting and importing states has been resented by biotechnologists, environmentalists and NGOs, who are concerned about human and animal consumption of GMOs. This was clearly observable in the recent Indian Bt. Brinjal squabble between the biotechnology company and the central government on one side and scientists, environmentalists and NGOs on the other side.

Actually, researchers are of the opinion that data provided by biotechnology companies can only be used as only a basic material for further testing of bio-safety of GMOs. It is for this reason it is suggested that states should have their own experimentations for determining effects of GMOs on the environment and human, animal and plant life and health. If experimentations fall in the garb of uncertainty, the precautionary principle should be applied i.e. LMOs should not be allowed for field testing; if they are safe for field testing with a meaningful buffer, they should not be allowed for marketing within the country and for export. It is a fallible argument that because use of pesticides are more harmful than certain LMOs, LMOs (for example Bt varieties) should be allowed for human and animal consumption. For example, the EU allowed import of GM soy because an independent bio-safety test revealed that it is safe for human consumption. For bio-safety testing, there should be competent human resource and a sophisticated lab working under a competent body created by law. India has such a law. This law has undergone amendments in order to make testing mechanism more realistic. Based on a decision of the Indian Supreme Court, two renowned experts will be present when the designate body meets to consider approval applications of genetically modifies organisms. The authors are of the opinion that ASEAN countries should have similar mechanism so that nothing spurious hastily comes into the market and cause irreparable loss to the environment, or endangers human and animal life and health. Under the Malaysian Bio-safety Act of 2007, such an arrangement can easily be made.

The researchers hold the view that there is conflict between the Cartagena Protocol and the SPS Agreement. There exist inconsistencies between the two, but these inconsistencies can be resolved amicably by making suitable amendments in the SPS Agreement. This is warranted because conservation of the biodiversity in effect contributes to the protection of human, animal and plant lives and health in manifest ways. Some are suggesting that Article 5.5 and 5.7 of the SPS Agreement should be amended in order to bring them in line with the Cartagena Protocol and the CODEX procedure. It is suggested that before we opt for such an amendment, a proper study should be done by the Special Session of the CTE, so that an amicable balance between international trade in and conservation of the biodiversity may be created. It was expected that decisions of the Panels and the Appellate Body in the cases discussed above, will make efforts to harmonize the two inconsistent legal regimes, but they contributed little.

Based on discussions in this chapter, the authors offer following suggestions:

1. All developing countries, including Malaysia, should augment their biotechnology efforts by making it a priority area of research and development and supporting it by all means.
2. All governments are keen to expand their biotechnology sectors and develop new GM crops; and

for achieving their ambitions, they are providing all sorts of supports, financial and others, to them. But desired results can only be seen when, along with facilities, indigenous expertise is also enriched. In order to achieve this, collaborative researches in biotechnology companies, government-funded independent laboratories, and educational institutions are not given priority. Towards this end, South-South cooperation can be a fruitful choice.

3. GM crops should be allowed for human or animal consumption only when their safety tests are positive beyond any doubt. For this purpose, all states, developed and developing, should have competent labs equipped with sophisticated equipments and experts.
4. In no case, safety tests conducted by the biotechnology company, which has developed the GM crop, should be considered as a conclusive proof for its safe human or animal consumption.
5. All foods containing GM stuff must be subject to labeling. If we do so, in fact, it will be nothing but honouring the right to information of consumers.
6. Safety tests and labeling should be governed by appropriate laws. These laws should be properly enforced.

Footnotes

1. See Bruce Chassy, "The Role of Agricultural Biotechnology in World Food Aid", at: http://usinfo.stste.gov/journals/ites/0903/ijee/chassy.htm. 20 July 2008, 3.00 p.m.
2. See Robert E. Evension, "Status of Agricultural Biotechnology: An International Perspective" in Richard E. Just *et.al*, (eds.), Status of Agricultural Biotechnology: An International Experience, Vol. 30 "Regulating Agricultural Biotechnology: Economics and Policy (U.S.: Springer, 2006).
3. [2004] 1 SCR 902; 2004 SCC 34.
4. See Asian Development Bank, Agricultural Biotechnology, Poverty Reduction, and Food Security", Working Paper (Manila: ADB, 2001), p. 35.

5. See *ibid*, p. 37.
6. See Chapter 5 of the FAO of the UN, Rome–The State of Food and Agriculture 2003-04 (Agricultural Biotechnology, Meeting the Needs of Poor) At: http://www.org/docrep2006/y5160E/Y5160E00.HTM
7. See Robert E. Evension, footnote 2, pp. 105-106.
8. This is heavily based on the studies conducted by Robert E. Evension, footnote 2, pp. 107-112; C.F. Runge and B. Ryan (2004) "The Global Diffusion of Plant Biotechnology: International Adoption and research in 2004", Report Prepared for Council of Biotechnology Information, Washington DC, which is available at: http:www.scidev.net/en/news/gm-boom-could-spell-economic-growth-for-poor-nati.htm; and A, Sobolevsky, G. Moschini and H. Lapan, "Genetically Modified Crops and product differentiation: Trade and welfare Effects with Soybean Complex", American Journal of Agricultural Economics, 2007, Vol. 87, pp. 621-644; Ernst Young, "Beyond Borders: Global Biotechnology Report 2007", see the repot at: www.ey.com/perspectives.
9. See footnote 8.
10. This part is mainly based on Sufian Jusoh, footnote 14; 2001 ADB Report and annual reports of the member states.
11. C. Peter Timmer, "Biotechnology and Food Systems in Developing Countries", The American Society for Nutritional Sciences, 133: 3319-3322, November 2003.
12. FAO, "Implications and development of Biotechnology", 25th FAO Regional Conference for Asia and the Pacific, Yokohama, Japan, 28 August, 1 September 2006, p. 6.
13. See Joel Kohen, John Komen and Jose Falck Zepeda, "National Agricultural Biotechnology Research Capacity Building', Working Paper 4-14 (FAO-ESA). Available at: http://ideas.repec.org/p/fao/0414.html
14. See the ASEAN Biotech Annual Report 2002-2003.
15. See W. Janssen, C. Falconi and J. Comen, "The Role of National agricultural Research Systems in providing Biotechnology Access to the Poor", in M. Qaim, A.F. Frattinger and J. Von Brown, Agricultural Biotechnology in Developing Countries: Towards Optimizing the Benefits for the Poor (London: Kluwer Academic Publishers, 2000), Ch. 21.
16. Sufian Jusoh, Biotechnology Law and Regulations: The ASEAN Perspective (London: Cameron, 2007), Ch. 2, p. 4.
17. See Leonarddus B.S Kardono, "Indonesia Country Report: programs and Activities on Biotechnology in Indonesia (2005)", at http://www.binasia.net/binesiaownload/downloadFile. asp?file= EGM_CP_Indonesia.doc.
18. See Sufian Jusoh, footnote15, Ch. 2.
19. See the Report of the Asian Development Bank, footnote 4 , p: 21.
20. See The Thailand's National Biotechnology Policy Framework 2004-2009, at: www.biotech.or.th.
21. See Sufian Jusoh, footnote 15, Ch. 2.
22. See the GAIN Report, 2005, dated 13 July 2005.

23. See MOSTI, Biotechnology for Wealth Creation and Social Well-being; The way forward, 28 April 2005.
24. See the Speeches at: http://mao.gov.my/moa/index2.php? option= com_content&task=view&id...
25. See Jayapalan Kasipillai, A Comprehensive Guide to Malaysian Taxation (Shah Alam: Mc Graw Hill, 2007), pp. 778 and 807.
26. See the Report, at p. 4.
27. See Muslamah Johan, The Star, 1 August 2006.
28. See Treasury of Malaysia, Malaysian Economic Report 2002/2003, and 2005/2006.
29. See Pierre van der Eng, "Productivity and Comparative Advantage in Rice Agriculture in South-East Asia Since 1870", 18 Asian Economic Journal, 2004, pp. 345-370.
30. See http://www.Bio.nite.go.jp/ndbc/c/atom-agron-e-htm.
31. See Raziah Hamzah, "Malaysia To Evolve as a Regional Biotechnology Hub" Bernama, 3 July 2008.
32. See various country-reports of the Agricultural Science and Technology Indicators (ASTI) at its website.
33. See Leslean Arshad, "Malaysia Concludes Five Biotechnology Pact at Bio San Diego, 2008", Bernama, 20 June 2008.
34. See Raziah Hamzah, footnote 31.
35. See Javier Verastegui, Victor Martinez, Willey Roca, Myriam de Pena and Leonel Gil, "The Multinational Bio-safety Project of the Organization of American States", Electronic Journal of Biotechnology, Vol. 7, N0. 1. April 15, 2004.
36. FAO, Implementation and development of Biotechnology: Twenty-Fifth FAO Regional Conference for Asia and the Pacific (Project Paper), Yokohama, Japan, 28th August .to 1st September, 2000, p. 9.
37. The following were the groups: 1. The Miami Group (Canada, United States, Argentina, Uruguay, Chile and Australia). This group wanted free trade of GMOs without burdensome bureaucratic approval procedures and without allowing for protectionist trade barriers masquerading as environmental protection. 2. The Like-Minded Group (G-77/China). This group supported a strong protocol. 3. The EU. It also argued for a strong protocol including coverage of risk to human health because they were under pressure of their people. 4. The Compromise Group (Japan, New Zealand, Norway, Singapore, South Korea and Switzerland). They supported for a compromise protocol that ensures international trade alongwith protection of human health and the biodiversity.
38. The Protocol can be discussed under ten heads: Scope of coverage, applicability of precautionary principle, requirement for advanced informed agreements, requirement of assessment and content of assessment, responsibility for conducting an assessment, decision-making parameters: least trade restrictive provisions, ongoing assessment options and responsibilities, labeling, capacity building, and liability. For an overview on these, see Howard Mann, "The Cartagena

Protocol on Bio-safety: An Analysis", paper presented at the ASEAN Workshop on International Trade in ASEAN Agreement and Forest Products and Measures to Align Trade and Environment, 1 June 2000, Bangkok, Thailand.

39. See Preamble, article 1, Article 10(6), Article 11(8) and Annex III, Article 4, on the conduct of risk assessment of the Protocol.
40. See Abdul Haseeb Ansari, Parveen Jamal and Maizatun Mustapha, "Meaning Scope and Implementation of the Precautionary Principle: A Critical Appraisal" in Hunud Abia Kadouf and Sharifah Zubaidah Aljunid, Land Use Planning and Environmental Sustainability in Malaysia: Policies and Trends (K.L.: IIUM, 2006), p. 64-93; IUCN, Guidelines for Applying the Precautionary Principle to Biodiversity Conservation and natural resource management, approved by the 67th meeting of the IUCN Council 14016 May 2007.
41. Nearly 82 countries have enacted bio-safety laws. See at: http://www.unep.ch/biosafety/news.htm#nbf; FAO-Committee on Commodity Problems, Joint Meeting of the Intergovernmental Group on Grains (31st Session) and the International Group on Rice (42nd Session), Istanbul, 14-17 May 2007, CCP:GR-RI 07/3.
42. See COP-MOP 3, 3-17 March 2006(BS-III/8/9/11) at: http://www.biodiv.org/decisions/default.aspx?m=MOPo3&id=11064&lg0
43. Howard Mann, footnote 38 , p. 8.
44. It is to be noted here that this labeling has no relevance for consumers.
45. Aaron Cosby and Stas Burgeil, The Cartagena Protocol on Bio-safety: An Analysis of Results, IISD Briefing Note, IISD, Canada. See at: http://www.iisd.org/pdf/biosafety.pdf
46. *Ibid.*
47. FAO carried a study to quantify the investments and costs involved in segregating the chains of production, transportation and embarking for GM and non GM soya bean and maize in Argentina in conformity with the Cartagena Protocol. Since the cost was not significant, it was considered to be practicable. See TCP/ARG/2903 (A).
48. It refers to the unintentional and incidental co-mingling of trace amounts of one type of seed, grain or food product with another. It is also warranted for biological reasons.
49. See CT/BRM/Rep. Technical Consultation on Biological Risk Assessment in food and Agriculture, Bangkok, 13-17 January 2003.
50. See infra.
51. See The World Trade Organization, WTO Agreement Series, Sanitary and Phyto-sanitary Measures, Geneva: WTO (2002), 6.
52. See Sufian Jusoh, footnote 5, Chapter 4. For the ASEAN perspective, see Sakaridr Bhumiratana, Report on Bio-safety Policy Options and Capacity Building Related to Genetically Modified Organisms in the Food Processing Industry of ASEAN, June 2002. This report was prepared for UNIDO and is available at: http://www.fao.org/biotech/news-list.asp?thexpad=1&cat=131. It is notable that except Laos and Vietnam, all other ASEAN members have ratified the SPS Agreement.

53. The document will be known as: G/SPS/7/Rev.3, the draft of which can be seen at the web as: G/SPS/W/215/Rev.2.
54. Under the SPS Agreement, notifications are used to inform other members about new or changed regulations that may significantly affect their trading partners. It also includes answering reasonable questions, and publishing regulations. It is notable that the Agreement uses the term 'measures' and 'regulations' somewhat interchangeably when referring to any sanitary or phyto-sanitary measure such as laws, decrees, or ordinances applied to protect human, animal or plant life or health as defined under paragraph 1 of Annex A to the SPS Agreement.
55. See WTO, Recommended Procedures for Implementing the Transparency Obligation of the SPS Agreement (Article 7), G/SPS/W/ 215?Rev.2, 22 April 2008.
56. The text that Members conditionally accepted comes from the work of a small group of countries, coordinated by New Zealand and is a compromise after about one year of work within the group and five years of discussion in the SPS Committee.
57. See WTO, Guidelines to Further the Practical Implication of Article 6 of the Agreement on the Application of Sanitary and Phyto-sanitary Measures, G/SPS/48, 16 My 2008.
58. Dated 29 September 2006, and adopted on 21 November 2006.
59. These member states were: Austria, Luxemburg, France, Italy, Greece and Germany.
60. Paras. 7.1327-1465
61. It states: "1. Members shall ensure, with respect to any procedure to check and ensure the fulfillment of sanitary and phyto-sanitary measure, that: (a) such measures are undertaken and completed without undue delay [...].
62. See paras. 7.1326-1465; 7.1466-1570; 7.1628-1633; 7.1680-1778; 7. 1779-2391.
63. Article 5.1 provides: "members shall ensure that their sanitary measures are based on an assessment, as appropriate to the circumstances, of the risk to the human, animal or plant life or health, taking into account risk assessment techniques developed by the international organizations."
64. Article 5.7 provides: "In cases where relevant scientific evidence is insufficient, a member may provisionally adopt sanitary or phyto-sanitary measures on the basis of available pertinent information, including that from the relevant international organizations as well as from sanitary or phyto-sanitary measures applied by other Members. In such circumstances, Members shall seek to obtain the additional information necessary for a more objective assessment of risk and review the sanitary or phyto-sanitary measure accordingly within a reasonable period of time." It is notable that this Article can be invoked if any of the requirements set out by it is present.
65. See paras. 7.2562-2922; 7.3000-3001.

66. Paras 7.3036-3213.
67. Paras. 7.3215-3371.
68. See para 199.
69. Paras 206 and 207.
70. See para. 180 of WT/DS48/AB/R. It was held by the Appellate Body in Australia–Solomon that by maintaining an import prohibition...in violation of Article 5.1, Australia had, by implication, also acted inconsistently with Article 2.2 of the SPS Agreement.
71. Para 121.
72. Footnote 69 to para 123.
73. Para 124.
74. Para 252.
75. Para 166.
76. Para 194.
77. Para 95.
78. Para. 164.
79. Para 208.
80. Para. 179.
81. See para. 184.
82. Para. 73-74.
83. It is to be noted here that the Appellate Body in EC–Hormones (infra) has clearly indicated that Article 2.2 and Article 5.1 of the SPS Agreement should be read together as the 'sufficient scientific evidence' and risk assessment are closely related as the Article 5.1 is the basic application of Article 2.2. Only then can there be a meaningful balance between international trade and protection of the human, animal and plant life and health.
84. Para. 84. It is notable that in Japan – Apple the Appellate Body held the same. (supra)
85. Para. 80.
86. See para 89.
87. Para. 91-92.
88. See para. 93.
89. Para. 95.
90. See para. 250, 177 and 180. It is notable that this was maintained in subsequent cases.
91. See para. 102.
92. Para 165. It is notable that the Panel interpreted that 'based on' means the same thing as 'conform to'. The author agrees with the interpretation given by the Appellate Body as it is closure to the object that Article 3 aims to achieve.
93. Para. 171.
94. Para. 170.
95. See paras 104, 172, 173, and 175.
96. Para. 175.
97. See para. 177.
98. See para. 180.

99. We have noted above in Australia–Salomon that a proper risk assessment must evaluate the 'likelihood', i.e., the 'probability', of entry, establishment or spread of diseases and associated biological and economic consequences as well as the 'likelihood', i.e., of 'probability' of entry, establishment or spread of diseases according to the SPS measures which might be applied.
100. See paras. 183-184, 190.
101. See para. 186.
102. Para. 187.
103. See para. 193
104. Para. 84.
105. See para. 213.
106. See para. 214-215.
107. See para. 212. Article 2.3 of the SPS Agreements reads: "Members shall ensure that their sanitary and phyto-sanitary measures do not arbitrarily or unjustifiably discriminate between Members where identical or similar conditions prevail, including between their own territory and that of other members. Sanitary and Phyto-sanitary measures shall not be applied in a manner which would constitute a disguised restriction on international trade.
108. See para. 89
109. See paras. 179 and 184.
110. See para. 123.
111. See Steven Suppan, "EC Biotech Products" Ruling at the WTO and the Cartagena Protocol on Biosafety", at: http://www.save ourseeds.org/downloads/wto_ruling_cartagena.pdf
112. ibid. Also see, Mark Philbrick, "Disputed Hormones:: Risk Assessment, the Cartagena Protocol, and the Legitimacy of WTO", at: http://are.berkley.edu/courses/EEP131/old_files/notablestudent04/carta gena%20harmones%philbrick.pdf.
113. Abdul Haseeb Ansari, "Future Directions in Conservation of Biological Diversity: An Interdisciplinary Approach" in Micheal I. Jeffery, Jeremy Firestone and Karen Bubna-Litic (eds.) Biodiversity Conservation, Law and Livelihood (New York: Cambridge University Press, 2008); Jgdish Bhagwati, "After Seattle: Free Trade and the WTO", International Affairs, 2001, 77(1), pp. 15-29; Ken Conca, The WTO and Undermining of Global Environmental Governance", Review of International Political Economy, 2000, 7(3), pp. 484-494; Daniel C. Esty, "Environment and the Trading System: Picking up the Post Seattle Pieces", in J.J. Scott (ed.) The WTO After Seattle (Washington: Institute for International Economics, 2000), pp. 243-252; Mitsuo Matsushita, "Governance of International Trade under World Trade Organization Agreements– Relationship Between WTO Agreements and other Trade Agreements", Journal of World Trade, 2004, 38(2), pp. 185-474; and Bondi Ogolla A. Markus and Xueman Wang, International Biodiversity and the World Trade Organization: Relationship and Potential for Mutual Supportiveness", Environmental Policy and Law, 2003, 33(3-4), pp. 117-132.

114. See Abdul Haseeb Ansari, footnote 113.
115. See Sabrina Safrin, "Treaties in Collision? The Bio-safety Protocol and the World Trade Organization Agreements", The American Journal of International Law, 2002, 96(3), pp. 1109-1134; Gilbert R. Winham, "International regime Conflict in Trade and Environment: The Bio-safety Protocol and the WTO", World Trade Review, 2003, 2(2), pp. 131-155.
116. See footnote 113.
117. See Abdul Haseeb Ansari, footnote 113.
118. See Bridges, dated 30 Sept. 2008.
119. See Steven Suppan, footnote 111.
120. Abdul Haseeb Ansari, footnote 113; Mitsuo Matsushita, footnote 113, Ogola et.al, note 113; Tarish Kelly, "The WTO the Environment and Health and Safety Standards", The World Economy, 2003, 26 (1), pp. 131-151; and Gary p. Sampson, "Effective Multilateral Environment Agreements and Why the WTO Needs Them", The World Economy, 2001, 24(9), pp. 1109-1134.
121. For a greater degree of discussion on application of the precautionary principle in two legal instruments, see J. Peel, 'The Precautionary Principle in Practice–Environmental Decision-Making and Scientific Uncertainty", 2005; Gateway to Precautionary Priciple in WTO Law", Journal of Environmental Law, 2007:19, 155-156; J. Peel, "Precautionary Only in Name: Tensions Between Precautions and Risk Assessment in the Australian GMO Regulation Framework", in E. Fisher, J. Jones and R.V. Schomberg (eds.), Implementing the Precautionary Principle (2006), pp. 202-204; R.F. Quijano, "Elements of the Precautionary Principle", Precaution, Environmental Science and Preventive Public Policy, 2003, 21;, pp. 23-26. Some are of the opinion that application of the precautionary principle should not solely depend on scientific findings. It should also take into consideration the public perception, especially of those who are going to consume or use LMOs and GMOs or food containing GMOs. The author is of the opinion that this suggestion will certainly democratise the applicability of the precautionary principle, but it will certainly frustrate the purpose for which the principle has been developed. So far international trade is concerned no prediction can be made at this stage. See D. Winicoff. S. Jasanoff. L. Busch, R.G. White, B. Wynne, "Adjudicating the GM Food Wars: Science, Risk and Democracy in the World Trade Law", Yale Journal of International Law, 2005:30, pp. 18-118.

3

Biotechnology and Patents

Introduction

The Malaysian National Biotechnology Policy (2005), together with the Malaysian Biotechnology Master Plan (2006 to 2020), have as their main objective, the use of biotechnology as a new economic driver for growth. Policies and incentives have been devised by the Government to encourage research and development in biotechnology and commercialisation of the results of these researches. However, for these incentives to have the desired effects, the fruits of the labour of these researchers need to be effectively protected. There is a need to ensure that whatever inventions relating to products and processes that are devised by the researchers are safeguarded, at least for a specified duration, to give them a head start over their competitors. Of the various branches of the intellectual property system, the patent system is deemed the most viable system for the protection of the results of these researches.

The chapter examines the various issues relating to the patenting of such inventions. The scope of unpatentable subject matters is first discussed, with the aim of providing a clearer picture of what cannot be patented under Malaysian law in relation to the products of biotechnology-related inventions. Other issues relating to the requirements of novelty, inventive step and industrial application are then examined. As there is a dearth of judicial pronouncement in Malaysia on these issues, the decisions of the courts in other jurisdictions are relied upon to provide some guidelines on how the Malaysian courts would decide on these matters were they to be raised before them. Where relevant, suggestions are made to address some of the problems in relation to the patenting of biotechnology-related inventions.

Protection of Biotechnology-Related Inventions Under the Patent System

Since research and development relating to biotechnology involve vast amount of expenditure and human and technical resources, it is understandable that the parties involved would want to protect the fruits of their research. "The development of this powerful process established the conditions for the final enclosure of the planet. The vast interior commons that makes up the insides of nature, the cells, is now being enclosed and converted to commercial property that can be manipulated and exchanged in the world market."[1] For this purpose, the patent system would be the most viable for obtaining a monopoly control over these results for a specific term. In principle, the various techniques, processes and products resulting from the use of biotechnology could be patented provided certain conditions are satisfied. In addition to these positive requirements, the invention must not fall within the class of inventions that are statutorily deemed un-patentable.

Conditions to be Satisfied

Section 11 of the Patents Act 1983 (the Act) states that an invention is patentable if it is - new, involves an inventive step and is industrially applicable .

Section 12 of the Act states that an invention may be or may relate to a product or process. A "product" is defined in section 3 of the Act as referring to "apparatus, article, device, equipment, implement, machine, substance, composition", while "process" includes art, new use or method".

Therefore, in principle, all the above products and processes could be patented provided, first, the essential conditions mentioned in section 11 are satisfied, and secondly, the invention does not fall within the prohibition of section 13, which lists the subject matters that could not be patented.

Non-patentable Subject Matters

Section 13 of the Act specially provides that the following shall not be patentable subject matters:

Notwithstanding the fact that they may be inventions within the meaning of section 12, the following shall not be patentable:

(a) discoveries, scientific theories and mathematical methods;

(b) plant or animal varieties or essentially biological processes for the production of plants or animals, other than man-made living micro-organisms, micro-biological processes and the products of such micro-organism processes;

(c) schemes, rules or methods for doing business, performing purely mental acts or playing games;

(d) methods for the treatment of human or animal body by surgery or therapy, and diagnostic methods practiced on the human or animal body;

Provided that this paragraph shall not apply to products used in any such methods.

For the purposes of this chapter, the restriction on patenting which are most relevant are those found in section 13(1)(b).

Plant or Animal Varieties

Section 13(1)(b) of the Act provides that plant or animal varieties or essentially biological processes for the production of plants or animals could not be patented. However, man-made living micro-organisms, micro-biological processes and the products of such micro-organism processes could be patented.

The question to be considered, therefore, is the meaning to be attributed to the term "variety". The scope of this term has been considered by various decision-making bodies of the European Patent Office (EPO) in relation to Article 53(b) of the European Patent Convention (EPC), which is *in pari materia* with section 13(1)(b).[2] In *Ciba-Geigy/propagating material*, various claims were made to propagating materials for cultivated plants possessing certain characteristics. Two of the claims are as follows:

Claim 13: Propagating material for cultivated plants, treated with an oxime derivative according to formula 1 in claim 1.

Claim 14: Propagating material according to claim 13, characterised in that it consists of seed.

The application was rejected by the Examination Division of the European Patent Office on the ground that such subject-matters are debarred by Article 53(b) EPC from patentability. The Examination Division went on to hold that "if this were the case for new varieties, it applied all the more so to the known plant varieties according to claims 13 and 14, even if these had been advantageously treated with oxime derivatives." On appeal, the Technical Board of Appeal reversed,[3] holding that Article 53(b) of the EPC merely provided that patents shall not be granted in respect of plant varieties. The term "varieties" is to be understood to mean "a multiplicity of plants which are largely the same in their characteristics and remain the same within specific tolerances after every propagation or every propagation cycle".

This definition reflected the definition of a plant variety in the International Convention for the Protection of New Varieties of Plants (UPOV Convention). Plant varieties in this sense are all cultivated varieties, clones, lines, strains and hybrids which can be grown in such a way that they are clearly distinguishable from other varieties, sufficiently homogeneous, and stable in their essential characteristics. The legislator did not wish to afford patent protection under the European Patent Convention to plant varieties of this kind, whether in the form of propagating material or of the plant itself. Since no specific varieties had been claimed, a claim directed to a propagating material, treated with chemical agents, for certain genera of plants (in this case cultivated plants) without specific varieties being claimed individually, did not contravene the prohibition on the patenting of plant varieties in Article 53(b) EPC. Therefore both claims were allowed.

In *Plant Genetic Systems/Glutamine Synthetase Inhibitors*, the invention related to techniques used to integrate into the genome of certain plants or seeds heterologous DNA encoding a protein capable of inactivating or neutralising certain herbicides.

Claim 7 was directed to producing a plant or reproduction material of such plant, including the stably integrated heterologous DNA.

Claims 14, 21 were respectively directed to corresponding plant cells and eventual plants.

The Opposition Division held,[4] relying on the *Ciba-Geigy* case, that plants in general were not excluded from patentability. Article 53(b) only prohibits the patenting of plant varieties. Since the present claims were directed to plants, plant cells and seeds which possess a foreign gene encoding resistance to glutamine synthetase inhibitors, these claims were clearly not restricted to a specifically defined narrow group of plants such as a variety, but relate to a much broader group of plants. It is true, as argued by the opponent, that all the examples were carried out on plants belonging to plant varieties and that the claims furthermore embrace plant varieties in their scope. However, it is the long-standing practice of the EPO to allow claims directed to groups of plants larger than plant varieties if the invention is applicable to such larger plant groups. Any other interpretation would disregard the purpose of Art. 53(b), which is to draw an appropriate dividing line between plant variety and patent law.

On appeal,[5] the Technical Board of Appeal held that the term "plant varieties" in Article 53(b) refers to any plant grouping within a single botanical taxon of the lowest-known rank which, irrespective of whether it would be eligible for protection under the UPOV Convention, is characterised by at least one single transmissible characteristic distinguishing it from other plant grouping and which is sufficiently homogeneous and stable in its relevant characteristics. Interestingly, it held that a product claim which embraces within its subject matter "plant varieties" as just defined, is not patentable under Article 53(b) EPC.

In view of the conflicting approaches within the Technical Boards of Appeal, a reference was made to the Enlarged Board of Appeal in Novartis AG.[6] The question reads:

> Does a claim which relates to plants but wherein specific plant varieties are not individually claimed *ipso facto* avoid the prohibition on patenting in Article 53(b) EPC even though it embraces plant varieties?

The Enlarged Board held that a claim wherein specific plant varieties are not individually claimed is not excluded from patentability under Article 53(b) EPC, even though it may embrace plant varieties.

The scope of the exclusion to the patenting of "animal varieties" can be exemplified by the *Onco-Mouse* saga. At the examination Division, it was held that the exclusion of "animal varieties" in Article 53(b) means that animals in general are to be excluded from patentability. The provision refers not only to those cases where a specifically designated variety is claimed but also to cases where varieties are covered by a claim. Since Claims 17 and 18 refer to 'A ... mammalian animal' and to 'rodent', respectively, thus any individual animal/rodent having the oncogene in question is covered by these claims.[7]

On appeal against this decision, the Technical Board of Appeal held that the exception to patentability should be strictly construed. Article 53(b) did not exclude the patenting of animals as such. The true issue was whether or not the subject-matter of the application was an animal variety within the meaning of Article 53(b).[8] This issue was remitted to the Examining Division. The economic consideration in adopting the narrow approach could be seen in the statement of the Technical Board of Appeal: .

"It is now the task of the European Patent Office to find a solution to the problem of the interpretation of Article 53(b) EPC with regard to the concept of "animal varieties", providing a proper balance between the interest of inventors in this field in obtaining reasonable protection for their efforts and society's interest in excluding certain

categories of animals from patent protection. In this context it should, inter alia, be borne in mind that for animals - unlike plant varieties - no other industrial property right is available for the time being."

On remittal, the Examination Division held that although the term 'animal variety' is not entirely clear, in particular in view of the differing wording in the three equally binding languages of the EPC, it nevertheless can be stated with certainty that rodents or even mammals constitute a taxonomic classification unit much higher than species (*Tierart*). An "animal variety" or "*race animale*" is a sub-unit of a species and therefore of even lower ranking than a species. Accordingly, the subject matter of the claims to animals per se is considered not to be covered by the above three terms of Article 53(b) EPC.[9]

The latest statement in relation to this question is that of the decision of the Technical Board of Appeal in *Harvard/ Transgenic animal* (T315/03).[10] It was there held that the principle adopted in G1/98 in respect of plants and "plant varieties" should be followed in respect of animals and a patent should not be granted for a single animal variety (or species or race, depending on which official language was used) but could be granted even if varieties fell within the scope of its claims. In the absence of the identification of a specific plant variety in a product claim, the subject-matter of the claimed invention is not directed to a plant variety or varieties within the meaning of Article 53(b) EPC.

The question that has to be resolved by the Malaysian Courts when this issue arises is which approach should be adopted. According to the substantive approach, it is necessary to decide, irrespective of the precise wording used, whether any claim is in whole or in part directed to a subject-matter for which a patent shall not be granted. The literal approach, however, is that as long as the word "variety" is not used in the claim, the claim is acceptable. It is submitted that the literal approach adopts an artificial and questionable reasoning to justify the patenting of plant and animal. In the absence of any strong policy ground for excluding plant and animal varieties from being patented, it is recommended that the restriction against the patenting of plant and animal varieties be removed. This will allow for legal certainty. The fact that there may, in certain situations, be overlapping protection for certain varieties of plant under the Protection of New Plant Varieties Act 2000 and the Patent Act 1983 should not be an obstacle to removing this restriction. Such overlapping protection is found in the United States system under the Patents Act, 35 USC, Chapter 15 Plant Patents and the Plant Variety Protection Act of 1970.

To ensure humans are not patented, regulations can usefully be drafted along the lines of the European Biotechnology Directive or the USPTO Notification in April 1987, after a series of cases which held that there was nothing objectionable about patenting life forms. Hence plants and animals are statutory subject matters.

The US Patent Office declared that it considered "non-naturally occurring non-human multicellular living organisms, including animals, to be patentable subject matter". However, a claim directed to or including within its scope a human being will not be considered to be a patentable subject matter under 35 USC 101. The grant of a limited, but exclusive property right in a human being is prohibited by the Constitution. Accordingly, it is suggested that any claim directed to a non-plant multicellular organism which would include a human being within its scope include the limitation "non-human" to avoid this ground of rejection."

Morality and Public Order Objections to Patentability

A morality objection to patentability could be made out based on the prohibition under section 31(1) of the Act. This section provides that "The grant of a patent shall not be refused and a patent shall not be invalidated on the ground that the performance of any act in respect of the claimed invention is prohibited by any law or regulation, except where the performance of that act would be contrary to public order or morality." A similar provision is found in Article 53(a) of the EPC which provides that: European patents shall not be granted in respect of (a) inventions the publication or exploitation of which would be contrary to *"ordre public"* or morality, provided that the exploitation shall not be deemed to be so contrary merely because it is prohibited by law or regulation in some or all of the Contracting States.

Morality Objection

In the *Onco-Mouse* case mentioned earlier, at first instance, the Examining Division considered the various objections:

- the desirability of applying non-animal models in the sort of cancer tests concerned,
- that the present invention is not aimed at improving any specific feature, but at producing tumours in the test animal,
- the fact that animals are regarded as an object,
- the danger that descendants of the transgenic animals might escape into nature and spread through mating the foreign malignant genes, and
- the problem of drastically disrupting evolution.

The Examining Division concluded, however, that the patent law is not the right legislative tool for regulating problems which may arise in view of the dangers mentioned above.

However, on appeal, the Technical Board of Appeal set aside the decision of the Examination Division and remitted the application for further prosecution. The Examination Division was directed to consider whether or not the exploitation of the invention was contrary to *'ordre public'* or morality within the meaning of Article 53(a), weighing the possible suffering to animals and risks to the environment on the one hand against the invention's usefulness to mankind on the other hand.[11] On remittal, it was concluded that the benefits outweighed the disadvantages, and thus the morality objection was rejected.[12]

When similar objection was made in the *Plant Genetic System* case,[13] the Board of Appeal adopted the "Acceptability Test". The Board held:

"The concept of morality [is] one which is related to the belief that some behaviour is right whereas other behaviour is wrong, this belief being founded on the totality of the accepted norms which are deeply rooted in a particular culture which, in the case of the EPC, is the culture inherent in European society and civilisation."

The Board went on to hold that seeds and plants per se do not constitute an exception to patentability under Article 53(a) merely because they represent living matter. Further, plant biotechnology per se cannot be regarded as being more contrary to morality than traditional selective breeding, since both involve the introduction of novel genetic material in order to change plant properties. Since the subject matter of the patent did not concern activities which were wrong as such in light of conventionally accepted standards of conduct of European culture, the morality objection was again rejected.

To add to the "balancing" test and the "acceptability" tests, the Opposition Division of the European Patent Office introduced yet another test, the "abhorrence" test. It held in *Greenpeace UK v. Plant Genetic Systems N.V.* that "The exclusion of patentability in Article 53(a) EPC for inventions which are contrary to public order and morality concerns extreme cases which are universally regarded as outrageous."[14]

The Problem of Deciding on the Morality Issue: The determination of whether a patent should be rejected on morality ground is based on an assessment of whether the exploitation of the patent would be contrary to *"ordre public"* or morality. The problem is that examination at the patenting stage requires that morality be determined before exploitation has become assured. The examiner, or the decision maker, would need to foresee future industrial application of the patent if granted. Since new applications may subsequently be discovered post-patenting, moral consideration of these cannot be regulated by the patent system.

Further, morality is a nebulous concept and the public's view about where it lies in a particular case is difficult to access. This would result in different forums applying different tests. A related difficulty is that morality changes temporally. A good example is the case of *Riddlesbarger's Application* (1935),[15] where the Royal prerogative was exercised so as to refuse the grant of a patent for a contraceptive. It is also worth noting that the temporal change in morality is not always more permissively. Therefore, there is a possibility of a decision of immorality being outmoded by the date of exploitation. The task for the decision maker is to search for a common morality code, not invent or impose one. It may be that the decision on whether the morality objection should be allowed or rejected may be too heavy a task to be carried out by patent examiners. It would be useful if the Registrar sets up a committee consisting of people experienced in the various disciplines of human endeavour to formulate a guideline on morality which could be relied upon both by the examiners and the Court.

Public Order Objection

Unlike the situation regarding morality, the case law relating to the public order objection is scant.[16] The only reported case is the case of *Plant Genetic Systems/Glutamine Synthetase Inhibitors*.[17] The Technical Board of Appeal held that:

1. The concept of "*ordre public*" encompasses also the protection of the environment.
2. Revocation under Article 53(a) on the basis of serious prejudice to the environment requires that the threat to the environment be sufficiently substantiated at the time of the EPO decision.
3. The evidence submitted in the case (for example, as to transformation of crops into weeds, spreading the herbicide-resisting gene to other plants, damage to ecosystem) did not justify such a conclusion. There was evidence only of possible hazard.
4. Inadequacies in the existing regulatory framework did not vest the EPO with authority to carry out tasks which should properly be the duty of regulatory bodies.

Methods of Medical Treatment Objection

As mentioned earlier, section 13(1)(d) of the Act provides that "Methods for the treatment of human or animal body by surgery or therapy, and diagnostic methods practised on the human or animal body are not patentable.[18]

Surgery: In *Occidental Petroleum's Application*, the Court concluded that, while therapy in section 4(2) of the Patents Act 1977, United Kingdom [Malaysia, section 13(1)(d)] covers curative and prophylactic (prevention) non-medical treatment, the term "surgery" is not limited to therapeutic surgery but includes any method of surgical treatment and such treatment need not necessarily involve making an incision into the body tissue. On this basis, claims to embryonic transplantation were rejected.[19]

In *See-Shell/Bloodflow*, the application related to a method of measuring bloodflow to a specific tissue in an animal, the method involving use of labelled microspheres of a size adapted to flow through the circulatory system of the animal but to become trapped in the capillaries of the tissue. Subsequent to introduction of the microspheres, the animal was sacrificed and the trapped microspheres counted. The Examining Division had, inter alia, rejected the application as directed to a method of surgery. On appeal, the Technical Board of Appeal held that "there is general agreement that treatments may only be excluded from patentability if they are carried out on a living human or animal body.[20] Further, the term *'surgery'* even comprises 'closed surgery' which, according to said dictionary, means the 'manipulation of a part, organ, or tissue without making a skin incision'. In other words, 'surgery' as the branch of medicine concerned with the healing of disease, accidental injury or bodily defects by operating on the living body - including both conservative (non-invasive) procedures such as repositioning, and the far more numerous operative (invasive) procedures using instruments.[21]

In relation to the present appeal, the Board held that "although the term 'surgical treatment' is not restricted to a treatment serving a curative purpose, the distinction between surgical and non-surgical procedures cannot be so broadly drawn that 'surgical treatment' includes any kind of manual or instrumental intervention by one human being on another, or on an animal. Clearly, the guillotining of people, or the slaughter of animals, is not a form of surgical treatment (indeed, methods for the slaughter of animals have traditionally been considered patentable). In the Board's view, methods consciously ending in the laboratory animal's death (cf. feature (c) of Claim 1) are not in their nature methods of surgical treatment, even if some of the steps they involve may have a surgical character." Hence, a method which includes a surgical step practised on a living laboratory animal and, in addition, a step of sacrificing said animal, which step is also necessary to carry out the method, cannot be regarded in its entirety as a method for treatment of the animal by surgery in the sense of Article 52(4) EPC.[22]

Therapy: In *Unilever Ltd (Davis's) Application*, the court held that the word "therapy" in section 4(2) is to be construed in its wide meaning as including preventive, that is to say, prophylactic, treatment as well as curative treatment of disease of the human body and the animal body."[23] Furthermore, it would appear from the case that "irrespective of the origin of pain, discomfort or incapacity, its relief, by the administration of an appropriate agent, is to be construed as "therapy" or "therapeutic use" in the sense of article 52(4) EPC".[24] On that basis, a claim "for a method of relieving the discomfort of a human female attendant to menstruation, which method comprises administering thereto an effective amount of an amidino-urea of a certain general formula" was upheld by the EPO because it related to a method of medical treatment by therapy.

Diagnostic Methods Practised on the Human or Animal Body: Prior to the Enlarged Board of Appeal decision in *Diagnostic Methods*,[25] there were two contrasting approaches to the interpretation of the term "diagnostic methods". *BRUKER/Non-invasive measurement* represents the narrow interpretation of the exception - the "all steps" test.[26] In that case, the Technical Board of Appeal held that the only methods to be excluded from patent protection as diagnostic methods were those whose result immediately made it possible to decide on a particular course of medical treatment. That, in turn, was only the case if the claimed method contained all steps involved in reaching a medical diagnosis, viz. examination, recording any significant deviation from the normal value, and attributing that deviation to a particular clinical picture. That meant that methods providing only interim results were not diagnostic methods, even if the results could be utilised in making a diagnosis. The consequence of such a narrow interpretation was that methods not containing all the steps involved in making a medical diagnosis were not excluded from patentability under Art. 52(4) EPC, i.e., methods providing only interim results are thus not diagnostic methods within the meaning of Art. 52(4). Therefore, all intermediate steps are perfectly patentable. A narrow interpretation of the scope of the exclusion presupposes that Art. 52(4) EPC excludes diagnostic methods practised on the human or animal body only if all of the preceding steps which are constitutive for making a diagnosis as an intellectual exercise are performed on a living human or animal body. Further, *Re Bruker* called for a further test to establish whether there was at least one step that had to be performed by the physician himself or herself.

On the other hand, *CYGNUS/Diagnostic method* represents the broad interpretation of the exception – the one step test.[27] In this case, another Technical Board of Appeal held that "the expression "diagnostic methods practised on the human or animal body" should not be considered to relate only to methods containing all the steps involved in reaching a medical diagnosis. Article 52(4) EPC was meant to exclude from patent protection all methods practised on the human or animal body which related to diagnosis or were of value for the purpose of diagnosis. Consequently, all that was needed to justify exclusion under Art. 52(4) EPC was that the claimed method comprised one step which served diagnostic purposes or related to diagnosis and was to be regarded as an essential activity pertaining to diagnosis and practised on the living human or animal body. A broad interpretation of the scope of the exception implies that this provision excludes all methods practised on the human or animal body which relate to diagnosis or which are of value for the purpose of diagnosis. Further, *Cygnus* made the character of the activity the deciding factor, and the personal presence of the physician, when the method was carried out, appeared not to be an essential precondition. *Cygnus* could, therefore, be construed to mean that a "diagnostic method" within the meaning of Art. 52(4) EPC might be present even if a physician did not necessarily have to bear responsibility for any of the steps.

In the light of the conflicting decisions by the Boards of Appeal, the President of the EPO referred to the Enlarged Board of Appeal the following questions:

1. (a) Are "diagnostic methods practised on the human or animal body" within the meaning of Art. 52(4) EPC only those methods containing all the procedural steps to be carried out when making a medical diagnosis, i.e. the examination phase involving the collection of relevant data, the comparison of the examination data thus obtained with the standard values, the finding of any significant deviation (a symptom) during the comparison and, finally, the attribution of the deviation to a particular clinical picture (the deductive medical decision phase), or

   (b) Is a claimed method a "diagnostic method" even if it only contains one procedural step that can be used for diagnostic purposes or relates to the diagnosis?

2. If the answer to 1(b) is in the affirmative: Does the claimed method have to be usable exclusively for diagnostic purposes or relate exclusively to the diagnosis? According to which criteria is this to be assessed?

3. (a) Is a claimed method a "diagnostic method" if:

   (i) it contains at least one procedural step considered as essential for a "diagnostic method" and requiring the presence of a physician (Alternative 1), or

(ii) it does not require the presence of a physician, but presupposes that a physician bears the responsibility (Alternative 2), or

(iii) all procedural steps can also or only be practices by medical or technical support staff, the patient himself or an automated system (Alternative 3)?

(b) If the participation of a physician (by being present or by bearing the responsibility) is decisive, does the physician have to participate in the procedural step practised on the body, or does he only have to participate in the procedural step considered as essential for a diagnostic method?

4. Does the requirement "practised on the human or animal body" mean that the procedural step takes place in direct contact with the body and that only such steps practised directly on the body can provide a method with the character of a diagnostic method, or is it sufficient if at least one of the procedural steps is practised directly on the body?

The Enlarged Board of Appeal held that the correct responses to the questions were as follows:[28]

1. In order that the subject-matter of a claim relating to a diagnostic method practised on the human or animal body falls under the prohibition of Art. 52(4) EPC, the claim is to include the features relating to:

   (i) the diagnosis for curative purposes *stricto sensu* representing the deductive medical or veterinary decision phase as a purely intellectual exercise,

   (ii) the preceding steps which are constitutive for making that diagnosis, and

   (iii) the specific interactions with the human or animal body which occur when carrying those out among these preceding steps which are of a technical nature.

2. Whether or not a method is a diagnostic method within the meaning of Art. 52(4) EPC may neither depend on the participation of a medical or veterinary practitioner, by being present or by bearing responsibility, nor on the fact that all method steps can also, or only, be practised by medical or technical support staff, the patient himself or herself or an automated system. Moreover, no distinction is to be made in this context between essential method steps having a diagnostic character and non-essential method steps lacking it.
3. In a diagnostic method under Art.52(4) EPC, the method steps of a technical nature belonging to the preceding steps which are constitutive for making the diagnosis for curative purposes *stricto sensu* must satisfy the criterion "practised on the human or animal body".
4. Art. 52(4) EPC does not require a specific type and intensity of interaction with the human or animal body; a preceding step of a technical nature thus satisfies the criterion "practised on the human or animal body" if its performance implies any interaction with the human or animal body, necessitating the presence of the latter.

The Special Exception to the Novelty Requirement: Section 14(4) of the Patents Act, 1983 provides that "the provisions of subsection (2) shall not exclude the patentability of any substance or composition, comprised in the prior art, for use in a method referred to in paragraph (d) of subsection (1) of section 13, if its use in any such method is not comprised in the prior art."[29] The equivalent of this provision in the United Kingdom was construed in *Schering's and Wyeth's Applications*.[30] The invention of the Wyeth application was based on the discovery that certain guanidines compounds disclosed in an earlier Wyeth patent No. 1530675 and known from that disclosure as drugs effective in lowering blood pressure, as hyperglycaemic agents and for anti-ulcer activity, unexpectedly have the property of treating or preventing diarrhoea in mammals and poultry. It was accepted that the therapeutic activity of these compounds so discovered had not previously been recognised and was not suggested by the disclosures of the earlier patent and that there appeared to be no question of obviousness.

Three distinct types of claims were made:

Type 1 Claims

Claim 10: "A guanidine of formula 1 or a pharmaceutically acceptable acid addition salt thereof for use as an antidiarrhoeal agent".

Claim 11: "Compound X or a pharmaceutically acceptable acid addition salt for use as an antidiarrhoeal agent".[31]

Type 2 Claims

Claim 1: "The use of a guanidine of formula 1 or a pharmaceutically acceptable acid addition salt thereof in treating or preventing diarrhoea in mammals or poultry"

Claim 2: "The use of compound X or a pharmaceutically acceptable acid addition salt in treating or preventing diarrhoea in mammals or poultry".[32]

Type 3 Claims

Claim 3: 'The use of a guanidine of formula 1 or a pharmaceutically acceptable acid addition salt thereof in 'the preparation of an anti-diarrhoeal agent in ready-to-use drug form for treating or preventing diarrhoea in mammals or poultry."

Claim 4: "The use of compound X or a pharmaceutically acceptable acid addition salt in the preparation of an antidiarrhoeal agent in ready-to-use drug form for treating or preventing diarrhoea in mammals or poultry."[33]

In other words, the Court basically held that the provision of the equivalent of the Malaysian section 14(4) should be read thus: "The provision of subsection (2) shall not exclude the patentability of any substance ... comprised in the prior art, for use in [a medical method], if its use in any methods for the treatment of human or animal body by surgery or therapy, and diagnostic methods practised on the human or animal body is not comprised in the state of the art."

Based on this approach, the Court disallowed both the type 1 and 2 claims, and only allowed the claims in the form of the Swiss claims.

Recent Developments in Patenting Criteria which may Impact on Biotechnological Inventions

Novelty

A patent will not be granted to an invention which has been anticipated by the prior art for the reason that "it would be wrong to enable the patentee to prevent a man from doing what he has lawfully done before the patent was granted".[34] The Act provides that an invention is new if it is not anticipated by the prior art. Further, the prior art is constituted by "everything disclosed to the public, anywhere in the world, by written publication, by oral disclosure, by use or in any other way, prior to the priority date of the patent application claiming the invention.[35]

Besides the widely accepted principles relating to the question of when a piece of prior art is deemed to be made available to the public,[36] and when a prior art anticipates an invention,[37] a recent decision addressed the question of whether a product-by-process claim would satisfy the requirement for novelty. In *Kirin-Amgen Inc v Hoechst Marion Roussel Ltd*,[38] the appellant, Kirin-Amgen Inc (Amgen), was the proprietor of European Patent EP 0148605B2 relating to the production of erythropoietin (EPO) by recombinant DNA technology, As a defence to Amgen's claim that the respondents' GA-EPO infringed the claims of the patent, Hoechst/TKT sought a declaration of non-infringement and revocation of the patent, in particular, claim 26.[39] The main ground relied upon was that claim 26 was invalid on the ground of anticipation, and the question was whether it is new or the same as the EPO which was already part of the state of the art, namely the uEPO which a prior inventor, Miyake and others had purified from urine. It was found as a fact that there was no difference between uEPO and EPO made according to claim 26. The practice in the United Kingdom under the Patents Act 1949 and earlier was to treat the fact that a product was made by a new process as sufficient to distinguish it from an identical product which was already part of the state of the art.[40] This, Lord Hoffmann, observed, "was not particularly logical, because the history of how a product was made is not an attribute which it carries around and makes it something new. It was still the same product, even if made in a different way."[41] Moreover, he further noted that the only case in which the European Patent Office will accept a claim to a product defined in terms of its process of manufacture is when the product is new in the sense of being different from any existing product in the state of the art but the difference cannot be described in chemical or physical terms.[42] His Lordship, therefore, went on to hold that "a difference in the method of manufacturing an identical product does not make it new. It is only if the product is different but the difference cannot in practice be satisfactorily defined by reference to its composition, etc. that a definition by process of manufacture is allowed." Claim 26 was, therefore, held to be invalid on the ground of anticipation.[43]

Hence, while it is still permissible to have a claim to a product defined in terms of a process of manufacture, such claims should only be granted in cases when the product cannot be satisfactorily defined by reference to its composition, structure or other testable parameter. If the product has already become part of the prior art before the priority date, it can never be regarded as satisfying the novelty requirement just because it was made by a different process. It is worth being reminded that "Patents exist today to reward and thereby encourage inventors; they are not intended to make it possible to take out of public use processes or products already made available to the public."[44] The expression 'matter... made available to the public' in s 2(2) is to be construed in a way which will promote the purpose of the statutory provisions, not defeat them."

Inventive Step

In addition to satisfying the requirement of novelty, the inventing must also be regarded to be inventive. An invention shall be considered as involving an inventive step if, having regard to any matter which forms part of the state of the prior art under paragraph (a) of subsection (2) of section 14, such inventive step would not have been obvious to a person having ordinary skill in the art.[45] The rationale for requiring an inventive step is explained by Justice Oliver in the *Windsurfing* case, i.e., "that it would be wrong to prevent a man from doing something which is merely an obvious extension of what he has been doing or of what was known in the art before the priority date of the patent granted".[46] Various approaches have been used by the courts in the assessment of the presence of an inventive step, from the *Windsurfing* 4-Step test in the United Kingdom,[47] the European Patent Office "Problem-Solution" approach,[48] to the *Graham* test in the United States.[49] All these approaches sought to provide techniques based on an objective basis in the inventive step analysis and there is nothing much to choose between these approaches. The question ultimately hinges on how the decider of fact views the attributes and ability of the person skilled in the art in deciding the question whether he would find it obvious. The ultimate purpose is to achieve a proper balance to ensure that worthy inventions are rewarded by a grant of a patent and that non deserving inventions are rejected, by not pitching the standard of inventiveness too high or too low. In the words of Lord Moulton, "It must be remembered that the relevance of Butler's Specification is as a publication, i.e., a communication to the public which renders that which it contains public knowledge. In ascertaining its effect, the Court must consider what it would convey to the public to who it was addressed, i.e. to mechanicians. I recognise that it would be most unfair to subsequent patentees if we tested this by what it would convey or suggest to a mechanical genius; but, on the other hand, it would be equally unjust to the public to take it as though it were read only by mechanical idiots."[50]

Whether an invention satisfies the requirement for an inventive step is judged on the standard of "a person having ordinary skill in the art, commonly referred to as the "skilled person". Where highly developed technology is involved, the skilled person may not be a single person but a multidisciplinary team.[51] Previous authorities show that the person skilled in the art, although "supposed to have an unlimited capacity to assimilate the contents of, it may be, scores of specifications" but was "incapable of a scintilla of invention".[52] Similarly, in *Genentech Inc.'s (Human Growth Hormone) Patent,*[53] Falconer, J. agreed that "the addressee is to be assumed to be "reasonably well-versed in the art..." and of "standard competence without being of an inventive or imaginative turn of mind".

In view of the kind of technology involved in biotechnology, the attributes of such a skilled person may have to be reassessed. The notion of a skilled person being incapable of possessing any imaginative capacity at all was alluded to by the Court of Appeal in *Genentech Inc's Patent.*[54] Lord Justice Mustill distinguished the prior authorities on the ground that they were mainly dealing with cases of insufficiency and "could not be transferred uncritically to a research team operating in a field where some substantial measure of ingenuity is an essential qualification for being involved in the enterprise at all". There is a need to distinguish between situations where "they are addressees who start with the patent and try to make it work, or persons who start with the prior art and try to get to the patent."[55] To work the patent, "the addressees follow the instructions, filling in gaps and clarifying obscurities by common sense and trial and error. This may require skill and experience, but not inventive facility. But the discovery team has no instruction to follow. Unlike the addressees it does not know the answers in advance, and in practice the people who constitute it will be required to exercise different talents from those who take information disclosed in the patent and put it into practice."[56] Hence, where "one is looking at the research team, one cannot treat them as dull plodders, for such people would not be members of the team at all, except as laboratory assistants. We have to envisage people who are skilled, and skilled in the art. Here we have a difficult art, in which the skill consists in a substantial degree of an ability to solve problems. It must, I consider, follow from this that the hypothetical skilled man must be credited with that particular ability in the appropriate degree" and hence, "where the art by its nature involves intellectual gifts and ingenuity of approach, it would ... be wrong to assume that the hypothetical worker is devoid of these gifts."

A similar trend could also be observed in the United States jurisprudence. The leading case on the analysis of inventive step, or "non obviousness" in the United States is the case of *Graham v John Deere Co of Kansas City.*[57] The Supreme Court in that case held that obviousness should be determined firstly by looking at the scope and content of the prior art; the level of ordinary skill in the art; and the differences between the claimed invention and the prior art. Secondly, factors like the commercial success of such invention, the long-felt need of such invention in the industry and the failure of others in finding a solution to the problem at hand, must also be considered. Such secondary considerations could be utilised to give light to the circumstances surrounding the origin of the subject matter which is sought to be patented.[58]

As to the attributes of the "person of ordinary skill in the art", that person was "someone of intelligence and imagination who kept himself or herself informed of developments in the arts pertinent to his or her work". The *Graham* court also said that "technology, however, has advanced-and with remarkable rapidity in the last 50 years. Moreover, the ambit of applicable art in given fields of science has widened by disciplines unheard of a half century ago. It is but an evenhanded application to require that those persons granted the benefit of a patent monopoly be charged with an awareness of these changed conditions. The same is true of the less technical, but still useful arts. He who seeks to build a better mousetrap today has a long path to tread before reaching the Patent Office."[59]

As had been applied by the Court of Appeals for the Federal Circuit, "A person of ordinary skill in the art is ... one who thinks along the line of conventional wisdom in the art and is not one who undertakes to innovate, whether by patient, and often expensive, systematic research or by extraordinary insights, it makes no difference which."[60] The attributes of such a person, as identified by the Federal Circuit, was usefully summarised by Quillen, "He (or she) is a literalist, without imagination or creativity, uninterested in developments pertinent to his or her work; one who is incapable of considering collectively the combined teaching of relevant prior art references unless motivated to do so by explicit directions in the references themselves."[61]

Furthermore, in an effort to reduce the possibility of hindsight-based obviousness analysis and to resolve the obviousness question with more uniformity and consistency, the Federal Circuit has employed a "teaching, suggestion, or motivation" (TSM) test which requires the patent examiner to show that some suggestion or motivation exist to combine known elements to form a claimed invention.[62] Under the TSM test, a patent claim is only proved obvious if the prior art, the problem's nature, or the knowledge of a person having ordinary skill in the art reveals some motivation or suggestion to combine the prior art teachings.[63]

However, too rigid and formalistic an application of the TSM test had lead to a situation where patents were granted even for inventions that clearly appeared to be obvious, even to a layman. The Federal Circuit at times seemed to have treated the "person having ordinary skill in the art" as incapable of seeing anything other than what had been specifically pointed out to him. The matter came to a head in the case of *KSR International Co v Teleflex Inc*,[64] where the Federal Circuit reversed the decision of a District Court which held that a patent for an accelerator pedal assembly was invalid for obviousness based on a combination of the prior art references. The Federal Circuit held that the District Court's recourse to the nature of the problem to be solved was insufficient because, unless the prior art reference addressed the precise problem that the patentee was trying to solve, the problem would not motivate an inventor to look at those references.

On appeal, the Supreme Court took the opportunity to reaffirm the Graham test. After stating the Graham analysis, the Court held: "While the sequence of these questions might be reordered in any particular case, the factors continue to define the inquiry that controls. If a court, or patent examiner, conducts this analysis and concludes the claimed subject matter was obvious, the claim is invalid under s. 103."[65]

Further, the test of "teaching-suggestion-motivation" was deemed by the Supreme Court as a "helpful insight" and that there is no necessary inconsistency between the idea underlying the TSM test and the *Graham* analysis. However, the Court went on to say that "helpful insights, however, need not become rigid and mandatory formulas; and when it is so applied, the TSM test is incompatible with our precedents," and that "the obviousness analysis cannot be confined by a formalistic conception of the words teaching, suggestion, and motivation, or by overemphasis on the importance of published articles and the explicit content of issued patents."[66] The Court further cautioned that "rigid preventative rules that deny fact finders recourse to common sense, however, are neither necessary under our case law nor consistent with it."[67]

The Supreme Court specifically addressed the issue of the Federal Circuit insisting on a specific reference for an obviousness rejection by stressing on the need for a common sense approach. The Court held: "The second error of the Court of Appeals lay in its assumption that a person of ordinary skill attempting to solve a problem will be led only to those elements of prior art designed to solve the same problem. The primary purpose of Asano was solving the constant ratio problem; so, the court concluded, an inventor considering how to put a sensor on an adjustable pedal would have no reason to consider putting it on the Asano pedal. ... Common sense teaches, however, that familiar items may have obvious uses beyond their primary purposes, and in many cases a person of ordinary skill will be able to fit the teachings of multiple patents together like pieces of a puzzle. Regardless of Asano's primary purpose, the design provided an obvious example of an adjustable pedal with a fixed pivot point; and the prior art was replete with patents indicating that a fixed pivot point was an ideal mount for a sensor. The idea that a designer hoping to make an adjustable electronic pedal would ignore Asano because Asano was designed to solve the constant ratio problem makes little sense. A person of ordinary skill is also a person of ordinary creativity, not an automaton."[68]

The Supreme Court also resurrected the "obvious to try" standard, which the Court of Appeals has consistently rejected.[69] The Court held that "the same constricted analysis led the Court of Appeals to conclude, in error, that a patent claim cannot be proved obvious merely by showing that the combination of elements was "obvious to try." When there is a design need or market pressure to solve a problem and there are a finite number of identified, predictable solutions, a person of ordinary skill has good reason to pursue the known options within his or her technical grasp. If this leads to the anticipated success, it is likely the product is not of innovation but of ordinary skill and common sense. In that instance the fact that a combination was obvious to try might show that it was obvious under s. 103."[70]

More importantly for present purpose is the statement of the Court that the non obviousness analysis "need not seek out precise teachings directed to the specific subject matter of the challenged claim, for a court can take account of the inferences and creative steps that a person of ordinary skill in the art would employ."[71] The Court stressed that "a person of ordinary skill is also a person of ordinary creativity, not an automaton".[72]

The Supreme Court in the *KSR* case has made a significant decision in clarifying the standard of obviousness under section 103. A common sense approach in the analysis is encouraged. The days of the artisans, who is merely capable of carrying out instruction and incapable of being inventive are long gone. In the words of Lord Justice Purchas, "In the modern world of science such as the sphere in which teams of highly qualified molecular biochemists, protein sequencers, protein chemists and others work, the artisan has receded into the role of laboratory assistant and the others have become segregated into groups of highly qualified specialists in their own spheres of all whom must possess a high degree of inventiveness. If this were not so the specialists would not have been there at all."[73]

The Previous US Approach to Patenting Biotechnology Process Inventions: In the United States, there was formerly a problem associated with inventive step in relation to biotechnology process inventions. *In Re Durden,* the appellants filed a parent application on June 21, 1976, claiming novel oxime compounds, novel insecticidal carbamate compounds and a novel process for producing the carbamate compounds, employing the novel oxime compounds as the starting materials. A patent issued in 1980 for the carbamate compound *products* and the oxime compound *starting materials.* However, the claim for the *process* of making the novel carbamate products from the novel oxime starting materials was rejected as directed to obvious subject matter in view of the single reference patent to Punja, assigned to Imperial Chemical Industries. On appeal to the CAFC, the Appellants' "Summary of the Argument" states: A chemical process which

- employs a novel and unobvious starting material *or*
- is for the production of a novel and unobvious product compound *or*
- which employs a novel and unobvious starting material *and also* is for the production of a novel and unobvious product compound, is patentable, regardless of the extent of other similarities to prior art processes.

The issue to be decided is whether a chemical process, otherwise obvious, is patentable *because* either or both the specific starting material employed and the product obtained, are novel and unobvious.

Justice Rich held that: "The same arguments appellants are making here were made in *Albertson* 332 F.2d 379, 141 U.S.P.Q. (BNA) 730. The starting materials used in and the product produced by the claimed process were the subjects of allowed claims; the process claims were rejected as obvious in view of references showing the same chemical reduction process applied to other materials. The board affirmed the rejection and the CCPA affirmed the board. *Larsen* was relied on by the *Albertson* board and the appellant attempted to distinguish it, together with two similar CCPA decisions, on the ground that "the specific reactants in a process 'are a vital, significant part of any process,' and therefore the 'use of an unobvious starting material renders a process unobvious'."[74]

The court stressed that "We do not agree with appellant's proposition that the "use of an unobvious starting material renders a process unobvious." Were this true, every step, for example, dissolving or heating, when performed on a new compound would result in a patentable process. We reiterate that all of the evidence must be considered on the "subject matter as a whole," from the viewpoint of one skilled in the art, in the determination of obviousness, and not simply the patentability of one of the starting reactants in a process. "[75]

The court went on to say that "We find it unnecessary to discuss the other cases cited by the dissenters on the board. We suspect the possibility, in connection with these highly debatable matters, that there has been a failure to distinguish between novelty and unobviousness. Of course, an otherwise old process becomes a *new* process when a previously unknown starting material, for example, is used in it which is then subjected to a conventional manipulation or reaction to produce a product which may also be *new*, albeit the *expected* result of what is done. But it does not necessarily mean that the whole process has become *unobvious* in the sense of s 103. In short, a *new* process may still be obvious, even when considered "as a whole," notwithstanding the specific starting material or resulting product, or both, is not to be found in the prior art. To conclude, and possibly to put an end for now to this potentially endless debate on what the "law" is, which is not unlike sitting under a tree discussing good and evil with Socrates, we revert to appellants' statement of the issue, supra, and the use of the word "because" therein."[76]

Justice Rich continued, "... The argument is that an otherwise old process with a predictable outcome is *unobvious because* it is applied to a new material, notwithstanding the new material is similar or analogous to materials identically manipulated or treated before. To anyone other than a patent lawyer and therefore unfamiliar with the mysteries of patent claims, this would make little sense, we believe. ... We hold the process claim before us to be directed to obvious subject matter in view of Punja. For the foregoing reasons, the decision of the board is affirmed."[77]

The Biotechnology Process Patent Act 1995: As a result of the above decisions, the Biotechnology Process Patent Act 1995 was enacted, amending section 103 of the US Patent Act. The new section 103 provides that:

S 103. – (a) A patent may not be obtained though the invention is not identically disclosed or described as set forth in section 102 of this title, if the differences between the subject matter sought to be patented and the prior art are such that the subject matter as a whole would have been obvious at the time the invention was made to a person having ordinary skill in the art to which said subject matter pertains. Patentability shall not be negatived by the manner in which the invention was made.

Biotechnology Process Patent Act 1995

S 103. – (b) (1) Notwithstanding subsection *(a)*, and upon timely election by the applicant for patent to proceed under this subsection, a biotechnological process using or resulting in a composition of matter that is novel under section 102 and nonobvious under subsection *(a)* of this section shall be considered nonobvious if

(A) claims to the process and the composition of matter are contained in either the same application for patent or in separate applications having the same effective filing date; and

(B) the composition of matter, and the process at the time it was invented, were owned by the same person or subject to an obligation of assignment to the same person.

(2) A patent issued on a process under paragraph (1)

(A) shall also contain the claims to the composition of matter used in or made by that process, or

(B) shall, if such composition of matter is claimed in another patent, be set to expire on the same date as such other patent, ...

Biotechnology Process Patent Act 1995

(3) For purposes of paragraph (1), the term "biotechnological process" means

(A) a process of genetically altering or otherwise inducing a single-or multi-celled organism to

(i) express an exogenous nucleotide sequence,

(ii) inhibit, eliminate, augment, or alter expression of an endogenous nucleotide sequence, or

(iii) express a specific physiological characteristic not naturally associated with said organism;

(B) cell fusion procedures yielding a cell line that expresses a specific protein, such as a monoclonal antibody; and

(C) a method of using a product produced by a process defined by subparagraph *(A)* or *(B)*, or a combination of subparagraphs *(A)* and *(B)*.

(c) Subject matter developed by another person, which qualifies as prior art only under one or more of subsections *(e)*, *(f)*, and *(g)* of section 102 of this title, shall not preclude patentability under this section where the subject matter and the claimed invention were, at the time the invention was made, owned by the same person or subject to an obligation of assignment to the same person.

The Effects of the Biotechnology Process Patent Act 1995: The following are the effects of the above amendment:

(a) To benefit from the Act, a novel and non-obvious composition of matter and the process linked to it must be either in the same application or, if they are in separate applications, have the same filing date.

(b) The purpose of this provision is to ensure that the patent rights derived from a composition of matter and a process patented under the Act terminates on the same date.

(c) Since in most cases once the products are known, the process claims would become obvious, expiration of the two different rights at different dates would result in unjustifiable extension of patent terms.

(d) Therefore, if the disclosure of a patentable biotechnological product does not make the process of using or making the product obvious, the inventor is better off to take the traditional approach and not use the Act. This is because the "same application" or "same effective filing date" requirement need not be met under the traditional conditions of patentability.

(e) If the benefits of the Act are desired, an applicant must make a timely election in order to proceed under the provisions of the Act.

(f) Further, under the Act the patentable subject matter linked to an analogous process is limited to a composition of matter. Thus, a patentable machine or apparatus would not make an otherwise obvious biotechnological process per se nonobvious. Such exclusion of machines from the Act is essential in limiting the Act to biotechnology.

(g) It should be noted that the real purpose of the Biotechnology Process Patent Act of 1995 is only to ensure that those patentable biotechnological processes using or resulting in a patentable composition of matter are in fact patented.

(h) It does not intend to make otherwise obvious biotechnological processes non-obvious and patentable, even though its practical consequence may seem to be so.

(i) Novelty and utility are still required under the Act. Furthermore, the limitations included in the Act narrow its scope, and thus reduce the negative effects discussed above that are inherent in any per se rule of non-obviousness.

Industrial Application and Utility[78]

Besides having to show that the invention is new and inventive, the applicant has also to satisfy the third basic requirement for patentability, i.e., industrial applicability. Section 16 of the Act states that, "an invention shall be considered industrially applicable if it can be made or used in any kind of industry." This mirrors section 4(1) of the Patents Act 1977 United Kingdom and Article 57 EPC which states that an invention shall be considered as "susceptible of industrial application" if it "can be made or used in any kind of industry, including agriculture". An applicant has also to demonstrate the "utility" of his invention under section 101 of Title 35 of the U.S. Code.

The case law, until recently, adopts a *de minis* approach to industrial applicability and that as long as the invention can be shown to be capable of being made or used in industry, this requirement is satisfied. Cases in the United Kingdom and the European Patent Office are usually confined to the application of section 4(2) of the Patents Act 1977 United Kingdom and Article 52(4) of the European Patent Convention which essentially provide that methods of medical treatment are incapable of industrial application. This situation should be contrasted with a more rigorous test applied in the United States even before the advent of biotechnology. In *Brenner, Commissioner of Patents v. Manson,* the United States Supreme Court, concerned with creating an unwarranted monopoly to the detriment of the public, stated: "Whatever weight is attached to the value of encouraging disclosure and of inhibiting secrecy, we believe a more compelling consideration is that a process patent in the chemical field, which has not been developed and pointed to the degree of specific utility, creates a monopoly of knowledge which should be granted only if clearly commanded by the statute. Until the process claim has been reduced to production of a product shown to be useful, the metes and bounds of that monopoly are not capable of precise delineation. It may engross a vast, unknown, and perhaps unknowable area. Such a patent may confer power to block off whole areas of scientific development, without compensating benefit to the public. ... This is not to say that we mean to disparage the importance of contributions to the fund of scientific information short of the invention of something "useful," or that we are blind to the prospect that what now seems without "use" may tomorrow command the grateful attention of the public. But a patent is not a hunting license. It is not a reward for the search, but compensation for its successful conclusion."[79]

The case of *Re Dane K. Fisher and Ragunath v. Lalgudi* is also a timely reminder of the need for an applicant to show concretely that his invention has specific utility.[80] The claimed invention relates to five purified nucleic acid sequences that encode proteins and protein fragments in maize plants (commonly referred to as "expressed sequence tags" or "ESTs"). Claim 1 of the '643 application recites:

> "A substantially purified nucleic acid molecule that encodes a maize protein or fragment thereof comprising a nucleic acid sequence selected from the group consisting of SEQ ID NO: 1 through SEQ ID NO: 5".

The '643 application generally discloses that the five claimed ESTs may be used in a variety of ways, including:

(1) serving as a molecular marker for mapping the entire maize genome, which consists of ten chromosomes that collectively encompass roughly 50,000 genes;

(2) measuring the level of mRNA in a tissue sample via microarray technology to provide information about gene expression;

(3) providing a source for primers for use in the polymerase chain reaction ("PCR") process to enable rapid and inexpensive duplication of specific genes;

(4) identifying the presence or absence of a polymorphism;

(5) isolating promoters via chromosome walking;

(6) controlling protein expression; and (7) locating genetic molecules of other plants and organisms.

The examiner rejected claim 1 for lack of utility under section 101,[81] since the claimed ESTs were not supported by a specific and substantial utility but instead were generally applicable to any EST. For example, the examiner noted that any EST may serve as a molecular tag to isolate genetic regions. The claimed ESTs also lacked a substantial utility because there was no known use for the proteins produced as final products resulting from processes involving the claimed ESTs. On appeal to the Patents Board, the rejection was affirmed. On further appeal, the Court of Appeals for the Federal Circuit agreed that none of Fisher's asserted uses met the utility requirement of section 101. In its decision, the Court stated that its predecessor, the Court of Customs and Patents Appeal, have always required a claimed invention to have a specific and substantial utility to satisfy section 101 as espoused by *Brenner*.[82] The Court then went on to discuss the meaning of "substantial utility", referring to labels like "practical utility" and "real world" utility, which had been used interchangeably with "substantial utility". It concludes that "an application must show that an invention is useful to the public as disclosed in its current form, not that it may prove useful at some future date after further research. Simply put, to satisfy the "substantial" utility requirement, an asserted use must show that that claimed invention has a significant and presently available benefit to the public."[83]

As to "specific utility", the Court held that an application must disclose a use which is not so vague as to be meaningless. Terms like 'biological activity', 'biological properties' or 'useful for technical and pharmaceutical purposes' convey no explicit indication of the usefulness of the compounds and how to use them. Thus, in addition to providing a "substantial" utility, an asserted use must also show that that claimed invention can be used to provide a well-defined and particular benefit to the public.[84]

The United States approach to utility (industrial application) is instructive and is a timely reminder that inventions that have not reached the stage where the inventors are as yet able to specify "real world" use should not be granted any exclusive patent rights.

In recent years, the EPC has begun to adopt a utility-like approach to industrial applicability.[85] The move was brought about by European Union Directive 98/44 on the Legal Protection of Biotechnological Inventions, which was issued jointly by the European Parliament and Council of the European Union in July 1998 (Biotechnology Directive). The Biotechnology Directive states that Member States shall protect biotechnological inventions, and that human genetic material is patentable. The Biotechnology Directive is addressed to the national laws of the EU Member States.[86]

Article 3(1) of the Biotechnology Directive provides: "For the purposes of this Directive, inventions which are new, involve an inventive step and which are susceptible of industrial application shall be patentable even if they concern a product consisting of or containing biological material or a process by means of which biological material is produced, processed or used."[87] Thus biotechnological inventions such as genes, gene fragments and ESTs which satisfy the requirement of novelty, inventive step and industrial applicability are, in principle, patentable subject-matters. Article 5 of the Biotechnology Directive is addressed to the patentability of sequences or partial sequences of genes. Although Article 5(1) provides that "The human body, at the various stages of its formation and development, and the simple discovery of one of its elements, including the sequence or partial sequence of a gene, cannot constitute patentable inventions.", the impact of this provision, is, however, qualified by Article 5(2) of the Biotechnology Directive. This provides, "An element isolated from the human body or otherwise produced by means of a technical process, including the sequence or partial sequence of a gene, may constitute a patentable invention, even if the structure of that element is identical to that of a natural element."

More importantly for the purpose of this paper, Article 5(3) of the Biotechnology Directive provides that "The industrial application of a sequence or a partial sequence of a gene must be disclosed in the patent application."[88] Hence, in relation to the patenting only of nucleotide sequences of a gene, there is now a specific requirement to disclose the industrial application of the sequence in the patent application.

In September 1999, changes were made to the Rules in the EPC Implementing Regulations in order to incorporate the provisions of the Directive.[89] Rule 23b(1) of the EPC states that "the relevant provisions of the Convention shall be applied and interpreted in accordance with the provisions of this chapter. Directive 98/44/EC of 6 July 1998 on the Legal Protection of Biotechnological Inventions shall be used as a supplementary means of interpretation." Rule 23(e)(3) of the EPC further provides that "the industrial application of a sequence or a partial sequence of a gene must be disclosed in the patent application." Rule 27(1)(f) provides that "the description shall indicate explicitly, when it is not obvious from the description or nature of the invention, the way in which the invention is capable of exploitation in industry".

Following the amended rules, the Opposition Division of the European Patent Office was called upon to revoke a patent granted to ICOS Corporation relating to a DNA sequence encoding a protein on the ground, inter alia, of lack of industrial application.[90] The subject-matter of claim 1 relates to a purified and isolated polynucleotide encoding the amino acid sequence of V28 seven transmembrane receptor set out in SEQ ID NO: 28 or a fragment thereof possessing at least one ligand/antiligand binding activity or immunological property specific to said V28 seven transmembrane receptor. The opponents (SmithKline Beecham and Duphar International Research) argued, inter alia, that the lack of disclosure of a ligand of V28 7TM protein or the lack of disclosure of a specific involvement of said protein in a biological process precludes the industrial application of V28 7TM protein as required by Rule 23e(3) EPC concerning industrial application of a sequence. ICOS Corporation argued that according to Article 57 EPC the requirements for industrial application of an invention are satisfied "if it can be made or used in any kind of industry". It further argued that the specification discloses how to make the V28 protein and discloses also uses of V28 protein mainly as a receptor involved in immunological processes. SmithKline Beecham, Opponent 1, counter argued that the use of a newly identified protein in research is not equivalent to industrial application.[91] The Opposition Division disagreed with the proprietor's contention that the specification fulfilled the requirements for industrial application solely on the grounds that the specification showed that V28 could be made and could be used. It held that "in view of the requirements of industrial application as set in Article 57 EPC in conjunction with Rule 23b-23e EPC, the invention cannot be acknowledged as industrially applicable because industrial applications are not disclosed in the patent application."[92] According to the Opposition Division, "the potential uses disclosed in the application are speculative, i.e., are not specific, substantial and credible and as such are not considered industrial applications."[93] It is interesting to note that the language used by the Opposition Division is strikingly similar that that used by the American Courts.

In the *Max Planck*/BDPI case,[94] the Examining Division rejected the application in a suit which related to a Brain Derived Phosphatase (BDP I polypeptide), for inter alia, incapability of industrial application. On appeal to the Legal Board of Appeal, the Board stressed that "the requirement of Art.57 EPC that the invention "can be made or used" in at least one field of industrial activity emphasizes that a "practical" application of the invention has to be disclosed. Merely because a substance could be produced in some ways does not necessarily mean that this requirement is fulfilled, unless there is also some *profitable use* (emphasis by authors)[95] for which the substance can be employed.[96]

The Board made a distinction between two situations in relation to substances found in nature (for example, a protein, a DNA sequence, etc). The first, where the structure and function of the substance was elucidated and means were provided for extracting it or producing it in large amounts, industrial applicability existed in relation to the possibility to exploit the information and technical means disclosed in order to manufacture the substance and use it for some function related to its natural one or for some other previously unknown (now disclosed) function or as a starting material for making useful analogs or derivatives with some improved features. The Board said that if a function is well known to be essential for human health, then the identification of the substance having this function would immediately suggest a practical application in the case of a disease or condition caused by a deficiency, as was the case, for example, for insulin, human growth hormone or erythropoietin. In such cases, an adequate description would ensure in accordance with the requirements of Article 57 EPC that "the invention can be made or used in industry".[97]

The second, "in cases where a substance, naturally occurring in the human body, is identified, and possibly also structurally characterised and made available through some method, but either its function is not known or it is complex and incompletely understood, and no disease or condition has yet been identified as being attributable to an excess or deficiency of the substance, and no other practical use is suggested for the substance, then industrial applicability cannot be acknowledged."[98] The Board conceded that while the jurisprudence had tended to be generous to applicants, there must be a borderline between what could be accepted, and what could only be categorised as an interesting research result which per se does not yet allow a practical industrial application to be identified. The Board emphasized that even though research results might be a scientific achievement of considerable merit, they were not necessarily an invention which could be applied industrially."[99] In the present application, while the claimed BDP1 polypeptide was described as a substance found in the human body and as having unique properties, the question arose as to whether any disclosure or suggestion had been made as to how these properties of BDP1 might be exploited.

The meaning of "profitable use" alluded to in the *Max-Planck/BDP1 Phosphatase* case discussed earlier, and also "financial (commercial) gain" used in Decision T144/83,[100] is further explained by the Technical Board of Appeal in *Zymogenetics/Hematopoietic cytokine receptor*.[101] In the Technical

Board's judgment, the expressions tended "to convey the same idea: patents being an incentive to innovation and economic success, the criterion of 'industrial applicability' requires that a patent application describes its subject invention in sufficiently meaningful technical terms that it can be expected that the exclusive rights resulting from the grant of a patent will lead to some financial or other commercial benefit".[102] However, the need to show a "profitable use" is "not to be understood in the narrow sense of an actual or potential economic profit (i.e. generating more income than expenditure) or of a commercial interest (i.e. creating a new or increased business opportunity)." Rather, the Board considers that it "must be understood in the wider sense that the invention claimed must have such a sound and concrete technical basis that the skilled person can recognise that its contribution to the art could lead to practical exploitation in industry." The Board stressed that "it would be at odds with the purpose of the patent system to grant exclusive rights to prevent the commercial activities of others on the basis of a purely theoretical or speculative patent application. This would amount to granting a monopoly over an unexplored technical field."[103]

The Board further explained that the concept of "profit" should be seen in its wider sense of "benefit instead of its narrower sense of financial reward".[104] Hence the expression "profitable use" should be understood more in the sense of "immediate concrete benefit". This conveyed, in the words "concrete benefit", the need to disclose in definite technical terms the purpose of the invention and how it could be used in industrial practice to solve a given technical problem, this being the actual benefit or advantage of exploiting the invention. The essence of the requirement was that there must be at least a prospect of a real as opposed to a purely theoretical possibility of exploitation. Further, the use of the word "immediate" conveyed the need for this to be derivable directly from the description, if it was not already obvious from the nature of the invention or from the background art. It should not be left to the skilled reader to find out how to exploit the invention by carrying out a research programme. Not only was this the essence of the requirements of Rules 23e(3) and 27(1)(f) EPC, it also corresponded to the requirements of Articles 56 (the need to provide a non-obvious solution to a technical problem), 57 (the need to indicate how to exploit the invention), and 83 EPC (the need to provide a sufficient disclosure of the claimed invention). All those provisions reflected the basic principle of the patent system that exclusive rights can only be granted in exchange for a full disclosure of the invention.[105]

It is worth noting the Board's observation that "a product whose structure is given (e.g. a nucleic acid sequence) but whose function is undetermined or obscure or only vaguely indicated might not fulfill the industrial applicability criteria, in spite of the fact that the structure of the product per se can be reproduced (made). If a patent is granted therefore, it might prevent further research in that area, and/or give the patentee unjustified control over others who are actively investigating in that area and who might eventually find actual ways to exploit it."[106]

Although there is no equivalent of Rule 23(e)(3) of the EPC in the Malaysian Act or the Regulations, it is submitted that the new approach to industrial applicability applied by the European Patent Office jurisprudence could also be applied in Malaysia. In the first place, the Act contains in section 12 the definition of an invention as "an idea of an inventor which permits in practice the solution to a specific problem in the field of technology". If the applicant does not disclose any "specific, substantial and credible" use of the invention,[107] then there cannot be said to be a "solution to a specific problem", hence there is no invention which could be patented. Further, section 23 of the Act provides that "Every application for the grant of a patent shall comply with the regulations as may be prescribed by the Minister under the Act". Regulation 12(1)(f) of the Patents Regulations 1986 provides that the description shall "indicate explicitly, when it is not obvious from the description or nature of the invention, the way in which the invention is industrially applicable and the way in which it can be made and used or, if it can only be used, the way in which it can be used."[108] Non compliance with this requirement would lead to invalidation of the patent under section s. 56(2)(b) of the Act. It is therefore submitted that the Court would not be constrained in following the European or the United States approaches.

Conclusions and Suggestions for Reform

The chapter attempts to examine the various issues relating to the use of the patent system in protecting biotechnology-related inventions. If construed and implemented wisely, the patent system is indeed a viable system for this purpose. The following suggestions are made in the hope that it will provide more legal certainty in the use of the patent system for those who intend to use it to protect the fruits of their labour in relation to biotechnology-related inventions. It is also hoped that the suggestions summarized below will provide a better balance between the rights of the owners of these inventions on the one hand, and the rights of competitors and the public on the other.

1. The restriction against the patenting of plant and animal varieties should be removed. This will allow for legal certainty. The fact that there may, in certain situations, be overlapping protection for certain varieties of plant under the Protection of New Plant Varieties Act 2000 and the Patents Act 1983 should not be an obstacle to removing this restriction. Such overlapping protection is found in the United States system under the Patent Act, 35 USC, Chapter 15 Plant Patents and the Plant Variety Protection Act of 1970.
2. The requirements for novelty and inventive step should be strictly applied in relation to biotechnological inventions, bearing in mind that in view of the kind of technology involved in biotechnology, the attributes of a skilled person has to be reassessed and he should be deemed to have at least some measure of inventive capability, instead of being regarded as incapable of possessing any imaginative capacity at all.

3. The requirement for industrial Application / utility in relation to an invention should be tightened. Section 16 of the Patents Act 1983 states that "an invention shall be considered industrially applicable if it can be made or used in any kind of industry." This mirrors section 4(1) of the Patents Act 1977 United Kingdom and Article 57 EPC which states that an invention shall be considered as "susceptible of industrial application" if it "can be made or used in any kind of industry, including agriculture". To prevent excessively wide claims at a time when the usefulness of the invention has not be proved yet, it is suggested that Malaysia should adopt the approach in the United States. The applicant has to show both substantial utility and specific utility.

   Rule 23(e)(3) of the EPC further provides that "the industrial application of a sequence or a partial sequence of a gene must be disclosed in the patent application." Rule 27(1)(f) provides that "the description shall indicate explicitly, when it is not obvious from the description or nature of the invention, the way in which the invention is capable of exploitation in industry". This is to be contrasted with Regulation 12(1)(f), Patents Regulations 1986 (Malaysia), which inter alia, provides that the description indicates explicitly, when it is not obvious from the description or nature of the invention, the way in which the invention is industrially applicable and the way in which it can be made and used, or if it can only be used, the way it can be used.

4. Morality is a nebulous concept. The task for the decision maker is to search for a common morality code, not invent or impose one. It may be unreasonable to expect a patent examiner to decide on this question. It is proposed that a committee consisting of people experienced in the various disciplines of human endeavour to formulate a guideline on morality which

could be relied upon both by the examiners and the Court.

5. Section 13(1)(b) of the Patents Act should be amended. The present provision reads, inter alia, "... micro-biological processes and the products of such micro-organism processes could be patented". To ensure consistency in the use of terminology in this subsection, the present wording should be changed to "... micro-biological processes and the products of such micro-biological processes could be patented."
6. To ensure humans are not patented, regulations can usefully be drafted along the lines of the European Biotechnology Directive to specifically declare, *inter alia,* that processes for cloning human beings or processes for modifying the germ line genetic identity of human beings cannot be patented. Products of such processes should also be excluded.

Footnotes

1. Jeremy Rifkin, Biosphere Politics: A New Consciousness for a New Century, Crown Publishers, Inc, New York, 1991, Chapter 3, A Price Tag on Genes" at p 65.
2. Article 53: European patents shall not be granted in respect of:
(b) plant or animal varieties or essentially biological processes for the production of plants or animals; this provision does not apply to microbiological processes or the products thereof.
3. *Ciba-Geigy/propagating material* [1984] OJ EPO 112.
4. *Plant Genetic Systems/Glutamine Synthetase Inhibitors* (1993) 24 IIC 618 (Opposition).
5. *Plant Genetic Systems/Glutamine Synthetase Inhibitors* T356/93 [1995] EPOR 357 TBA.
6. *Novartis AG G 1/98* [2000] OJ EPO 111; [1999] EPOR 123, Enlarged Board of Appeal.
7. *Harvard/Onco-mouse* [1990] EPOR 4 - Examining Division.
8. *Harvard/Onco-mouse* T19/90 [1990] EPOR 501 TBA.
9. *Harvard/Onco-mouse* [1991] EPOR 525, on remittal, Examination Division.
10. *Harvard/Transgenic animal* (T315/03) 2005 EPOR 31.
11. *Harvard/Onco-mouse* [1990] EPOR 501, Appeal Board.
12. See *Harvard/Onco-mouse* [1991] EPOR 525, Remittal. Exam Division.
13. *Plant Genetic Systems/Glutamine Synthetase Inhibitors* T356/93 [1995] EPOR 357 TBA.

14. *Greenpeace UK v. Plant Genetic Systems N.V.* 24 IIC 618 (1993), Opposition Division of the EPO - 15/12/1992.
15. *Riddlesbarger Application* (1936) 53 RPC 57.
16. Note that beside the objection under section 31(1), further restrictions against patenting are found in s. 30A(1) – "If prejudicial to the interest or security of the nation", and s. 85, "If contravenes regulations made by the Minister". At present, no regulations have been made under s. 85.
17. *Plant Genetic Systems/Glutamine Synthetase Inhibitors* T356/93 [1995] EPOR 357 TBA.
18. For the equivalent provisions in the United Kingdom and the European Patent Convention, see section 4(2), Patents Act 1977 and Article 52(4), EPC.
19. *Occidental Petroleum's Application* (1986) 16 IIC 216.
20. *See-Shell/Bloodflow* T182/90 [1994] EPOR 320, para 2.1.
21. *See-Shell/Bloodflow* T182/90 [1994] EPOR 320, para 2.3.
22. *See-Shell/Bloodflow* T182/90 [1994] EPOR 320, paras 2.5 and 2.6. See also *Georgetown University/Pericardial access* T35/99 [2001] EPOR 21, at para 13.3. where the Technical Board of Appeal stressed that the concept of "'surgery' defines the nature of the treatment rather than its purpose".
23. *Unilever Ltd (Davis's) Application* [1983] RPC 219. See also *Schering AG's Application* [1971] RPC 337.
24. *Dysmenorrhea/ Rorer* T 81/84, 19 IIC 803 (1988).
25. *Diagnostic Methods G1/04* [2006] EPOR 15.
26. *BRUKER/Non-invasive measurement T385/86* [1988] EPOR 357.
27. *CYGNUS/Diagnostic method T964* [2002] EPOR 26.
28. *Diagnostic Methods* G1/04 [2006] EPOR 15.
29. For the equivalent provisions in the United Kingdom and in the European Patent Convention, see section 2(6), Patents Act 1977, United Kingdom, and Article 54(5), European Patent Convention.
30. *Schering's and Wyeth's Applications* [1985] RPC 545.
31. In effect, the claims were in the form of a "purpose-bound product claim", a product for use in a method of medical treatment.
32. In effect, the claims were for the "Use of a Product for a Method of Medical Treatment".
33. In effect, the claims were in the form of a ""Swiss claim", i.e., the use of a compound for the manufacture of a medicament for use in a method of medical treatment".
34. *Windsurfing International v. Tabur Marine* [1985] RPC 59, per Oliver J at p 77.
35. See section 14(1) and (2) of the Act. The corresponding provisions in the UK and under the EPC are found in section 2 and Article 54 respectively.
36. See, for example, *Humpherson v. Syer* (1887) 4 RPC 407.
37. See, for example, *General Tire and Rubber Co. v. Firestone Tyre* [1972] RPC 457 and *Merrell Dow Pharmaceuticals Inc and another v H.N. Norton & Co Ltd.* [1994] RPC 1 (Pat. Court); [1995] RPC 233 (CA), and [1996] RPC 76 (HL).

38. *Kirin-Amgen Inc v Hoechst Marion Roussel Ltd* [2005] RPC 9, House of Lords.
39. *Kirin-Amgen Inc v Hoechst Marion Roussel Ltd* [2005] RPC 9 (HL), per Lord Hoffmann at para 87. The essential difference between the EPO made by Amgen and GA-EPO was that the former was made by an exogenous DNA sequence coding for EPO which had been introduced into a host cell and the latter was made by an endogenous DNA sequence coding in a human cell into which an exogenous upstream control sequence had been inserted. The claims of the patent were for, inter alia, a DNA sequence for use in securing the expression of EPO in a host cell (claim 1); EPO which was the product of the expression of an exogenous DNA sequence (claim 19); and EPO which was the product of the expression in a host cell of a DNA sequence according to claim 1 (claim 26). … Claim 26 is to a product, namely a polypeptide which is the expression in a host cell of a DNA sequence in accordance with claim 1. Such a product is EPO.
40. *Kirin-Amgen Inc v Hoechst Marion Roussel Ltd* [2005] RPC 9, see para 88.
41. *Kirin-Amgen Inc v Hoechst Marion Roussel Ltd* [2005] RPC 9 (HL), Lord Hoffmann at para 88.
42. *Kirin-Amgen Inc v Hoechst Marion Roussel Ltd* [2005] RPC 9 (HL), Lord Hoffmann at para 91.
43. Ibid, at paras 98–101.
44. *Merrell Dow Pharmaceuticals Inc. and another v. H.N. Norton & Co. Ltd* [1995] RPC 233 (CA), per Sir Donald Nicholls, V.C. at 238.
45. Section 15, Patents Act, Malaysia. 35 USC s. 103(a) provides : A patent may not be obtained though the invention is not identically disclosed or described as set forth in section 102 of this title, if the differences between the subject matter sought to be patented and the prior art are such that the subject matter as a whole would have been obvious at the time the invention was made to a person having ordinary skill in the art to which said subject matter pertains. Patentability shall not be negatived by the manner in which the invention was made.
46. *Windsurfing International v. Tabur Marine* [1985] RPC 59, per Oliver J at 77.
47. *Windsurfing International v. Tabur Marine* [1985] RPC 59, per Oliver J at 73-74.
48. See, for example, *Bayer/Carbonless Copying* T1/80 [1979-85] B EPOR 250, the first published decision where the approach was first formulated by the Technical Board of Appeal, and *ICI/Containers* T26/81 [1979-85] B EPOR 362. See, however, the caveat of the Technical Board of Appeal in *Alcan/Aluminium Alloys* T465/92 [1995] EPOR 501, where the Board said that the "problem-solution" approach should be viewed as one of the many possible approaches that could be adopted when assessing inventive step, and that there is no reason why all cases involving inventive step should be "shoehorned' into a single approach. The problem-solution approach may not be appropriate where there is no close prior art from which to formulate the problem. This is especially so in cases involving newly created technology.

49. See *Graham v John Deere Co of Kansas City* 383 US 1 (Sup Ct 1966), per Justice Clark at 14-15.
50. *Gillette Safety Razor v. Anglo American Trading Co.* (1913) 30 RPC 465, Lord Moulton at 481.
51. *General Tire v. Firestone* [1972] RPC 457, per Sachs L.J. at 485. "If the art is one having a highly developed technology, the notional skilled reader to whom the document is addressed may not be a single person but a team, whose combined skills would normally be employed in that art in interpreting and carrying into effect instructions such as those which are contained in the document to be construed." See also *American Cyanamid v. Ethicon* [1979] RPC 215, per Graham J. at 245 and *Genentech Inc.'s (Human Growth Hormone) Patent* [1989] RPC 613, Pat Ct, per Falconer J at 619, and *Genentech Inc's Patent* [1989] RPC 147 (CA), Mustill LJ at 280.
52. *Technograph v. Mills and Rockley* [1972] RPC 346, per Lord Reid at 355.
53. *Genentech Inc.'s (Human Growth Hormone) Patent* [1989] R.P.C. 613, Pat Ct, per Falconer J at 619. See also *Valensi v British Radio Corp* [1973] RPC 337 at 377.
54. *Genentech Inc's Patent* [1989] RPC 147 (CA).
55. *Genentech Inc's Patent* [1989] RPC 147 (CA), Mustill LJ at 280.
56. *Genentech Inc's Patent* [1989] RPC 147 CA, Mustill LJ at 280.
57. *Graham v John Deere Co of Kansas City* 383 US 1 (Sup Ct 1966).
58. *Graham v John Deere Co of Kansas City* 383 US 1 (Sup Ct 1966), per Justice Clark at 14-15.
59. *Graham v John Deere Co of Kansas City* 383 US 1 (Sup Ct 1966), per Justice Clark at 19.
60. *The Standard Oil Company v American Cyanamid Company* 774 F.2d 448 (CAFC 1985), per Rich, Circuit Judge at 454. See also *Schneider (Europe) Ag and Schneider (USA) Inc v Scimed Life Systems, Inc* 1995 U.S. App. LEXIS 9754; 39 USPQ 2D (BNA) 1596 (CAFC 1995).
61. Cecil D Quillen, Jr in his paper presented at the Public Hearing on the Standard of Non Obviousness at the United States Patent and Trademark Office on July 20, 1994, at page 2..
62. According to Quillen, this requirement for 'motivation' is absent from the Supreme Court cases which assumed that the person of ordinary skill has sufficient imagination to consider collectively the teachings of relevant art, even if the references did not themselves suggest that they be considered together. The author felt that this change has lowered the standard by narrowing the scope of prior art which is considered in the statutory three-step analysis prescribed by Graham, and has rendered patentable inventions that once could not have been the subject of a valid patent. More than one commentator has suggested that the result is to have read section 103 out of the statute and to make patentable all inventions that are not "identically described or disclosed" in a single reference.
63. See, for example, *Re Dembiczak* 175 F 3d 994 (Fed Cir 1999), at 999, "Our case law makes clear that the best defense against the subtle but

powerful attraction of a hindsight-based obviousness analysis is rigorous application of the requirement for a showing of the teaching or motivation to combine prior art references. ... This is because 'combining prior art references without evidence of such a suggestion, teaching, or motivation simply takes the inventor's disclosure as a blueprint for piecing together the prior art to defeat patentability - the essence of hindsight."; *Pro-Mold & Tool Co v Great Lakes Plastics Inc* 75 F 3d 1568 (Fed Cir 1996) at 1572, "When obviousness is based on the teachings of multiple prior art references, the movant must also establish some "suggestion, teaching, or motivation" that would have led a person of ordinary skill in the art to combine the relevant prior art teachings in the manner claimed.; *Re Kotzab* 217 F 3d 1365 at 1371 (Fed Cir 2000) "Particular findings must be made as to the reason the skilled artisan, with no knowledge of the claimed invention, would have selected these components for combination *in the manner claimed.*"

64. *KSR International Co v Teleflex Inc* 127 S. Ct. 1727; 167 L. Ed. 2d 705 (Sup Ct 2007).
65. *KSR International Co v Teleflex Inc* 127 S. Ct. 1727; 167 L. Ed. 2d 705 (Sup Ct 2007) at 1734 and 715 respectively.
66. *KSR International Co v Teleflex Inc* 127 S. Ct. 1727; 167 L. Ed. 2d 705 (Sup Ct 2007), per Justice Kennedy at 1741 and 722 respectively.
67. *KSR International Co v Teleflex Inc* 127 S. Ct. 1727; 167 L. Ed. 2d 705 (Sup Ct 2007), per Justice Kennedy at 1743 and 724 respectively.
68. *KSR International Co v Teleflex Inc* 127 S. Ct. 1727; 167 L. Ed. 2d 705 (Sup Ct 2007), per Justice Kennedy at 1742 and 723 respectively.
69. *Re Deuel* 51 F 3d 1552 (Fed Cir 1995) at 1559, "'Obvious to try' has long been held not to constitute obviousness."
70. *KSR International Co v Teleflex* Inc 127 S. Ct. 1727; 167 L. Ed. 2d 705 (Sup Ct 2007), per Justice Kennedy at 1742 and 724 respectively.
71. *KSR International Co v Teleflex Inc* 127 S. Ct. 1727; 167 L. Ed. 2d 705 (Sup Ct 2007), per Justice Kennedy at 1741 and 722 respectively.
72. *KSR International Co v Teleflex Inc* 127 S. Ct. 1727; 167 L. Ed. 2d 705 (Sup Ct 2007), per Justice Kennedy at 1742 and 723 respectively.
73. *Genentech Inc's Patent* [1989] RPC 147 CA, Purchas LJ, at 214.
74. *In Re Durden,* 763 F.2d 1406, per Rich J at 1409-1410.
75. *In Re Durden,* 763 F.2d 1406, per Rich J at 1410.
76. *In Re Durden,* 763 F.2d 1406, per Rich J at 1410.
77. *In Re Durden,* 763 F.2d 1406, per Rich J at 1411.
78. Note: Footnote 5 to Article 27 of the TRIPS Agreement states: "For the purposes of this Article, the terms "inventive step" and "capable of industrial application" may be deemed by A Member to be synonymous with the terms "non-obvious" and "useful" respectively.
79. *Brenner, Commissioner of Patents v. Manson,* 383 U.S. 519; 148 U.S.P.Q. (BNA) 689 (Sup Ct 1966).
80. *Re Dane K. Fisher and Ragunath v. Lalgudi* 421 F.3d 1365 (Fed Cir 2005).
81. 35 USC Section 101 provides: "Whoever invents ... any new and useful ... composition of matter ... may obtain a patent therefor".

82. *Re Dane K. Fisher and Ragunath v. Lalgudi* 421 F.3d 1365 (Fed Cir 2005) at 1371.
83. *Re Dane K. Fisher and Ragunath v. Lalgudi* 421 F.3d 1365 (Fed Cir 2005) at 1371.
84. *Re Dane K. Fisher and Ragunath v. Lalgudi* 421 F.3d 1365 (Fed Cir 2005).at 1371.
85. See generally, Rob J Aerts, "The Industrial Applicability and Utility requirements for the Patenting of Genomic Inventions: A Comparison between European and US Law", EIPR 2004, 26(8), 349-360.
86. See Article 18 of Directive 98/44.
87. According to Art. 2 of the Biotechnology Directive, "biological material" is defined as "any material containing genetic information and capable of reproducing itself or being reproduced in a biological system".
88. See Recitals 23 of the Biotechnology Directive, "Whereas a mere DNA sequence without indication of a function does not contain any technical information and is therefore not a patentable invention" and Recital 24, "Whereas, in order to comply with the industrial application criterion it is necessary in cases where a sequence or partial sequence of a gene is used to produce a protein or part of a protein, to specify which protein or part of a protein is produced or what function it performs."Note that Recitals 23 and 24 of European Directive No. 98/44/EC have been incorporated into the EPC as of 1 September, 1999 by the introduction of Rules 23b -23e EPC.
89. See Implementing Regulations on the Convention on the Grant of European Patents of 5 October 1973, as last amended by Decision of the Administrative Council of the European Patent Organisation of 9 December 2004.
90. *ICOS Corp/(Transmembrane Receptor)* [2002] OJ EPO 293 (EPO) Decision of the Opposition Division dated 20 June 2001.
91. *ICOS Corp/(Transmembrane Receptor)* [2002] OJ EPO 293 (EPO) Decision of the Opposition Division dated 20 June 2001, para 8 of the Decision.
92. *ICOS Corp/(Transmembrane Receptor)* [2002] OJ EPO 293 (EPO) Decision of the Opposition Division dated 20 June 2001, para 8 of the Decision.
93. *ICOS Corp/(Transmembrane Receptor)* [2002] OJ EPO 293 (EPO) Decision of the Opposition Division dated 20 June 2001, para 9(i) of the Decision. "In more detail: The specification states that host cells expressing products of V28 7TM gene are useful in methods for the large scale production of V28 7TM protein (p. 3). Since the V28 protein is not disclosed to have any function (eg, biological which would implicate a therapeutic use nor as a marker which would implicate a diagnostic use), it cannot be seen why it would be useful to produce said protein on a large scale in industry. The specification states that antibody substances specifically reactive with V28 7TM protein are useful in complexes for immunisation to generate anti-idiotypic antibodies, for purifying V28 peptides and for identifying cells producing the V28 polypeptides (p. 4). Specific antibodies are not disclosed in the specification and may not even be possible to be generated due to high

sequence identity shared by a large number of proteins (see Table 1 of specification and above section 6(i)). Therefore, these proposed users are directed to a substance that has not been disclosed and can only be considered as speculative. The specification further asserts that antibodies, agonists or antagonists of V28 protein are manifestly useful in modulating ligand/receptor binding reactions involved in immunological and/or inflammatory events in vivo (p. 4). As discussed above (section 6(iii)), antibodies suitable for modulating ligand/receptor binding represent a special type of antibody which has not been exemplified in the specification. Furthermore, the involvement of V28 protein in immunological and/or inflammatory events in vivo has not been demonstrated either. The proposed use thus is directed to a potential interference of a speculative activity of V28 protein with a substance which has not been shown to be possible to prepare. Such a use lacks credibility."

94. *Max-Planck/BDP1 Phosphatase* T870/04. [2006] EPOR 14.
95. See later, endnotes 101-104 and accompanying text for amplification of the meaning of "profitable".
96. *Max-Planck/BDP1 Phosphatase* T870/04. [2006] EPOR 14., para 4, Reasons for the Decision.
97. *Max-Planck/BDP1 Phosphatase* T870/04. [2006] EPOR 14., para 5, Reasons for the Decision.
98. *Max-Planck/BDP1 Phosphatase* T870/04. [2006] EPOR 14., para 7, Reasons for the Decision.
99. *Max-Planck/BDP1 Phosphatase* T870/04. [2006] EPOR 14., para 6, Reasons for the Decision.
100. *Du Pont/Appetite Supressant* [1987] EPOR 6.
101. *Zymogenetics/Hematopoietic cytokine receptor* T898/05, Technical Board of Appeal [2007] EPOR 2.
102. *Zymogenetics/Hematopoietic cytokine receptor* T898/05, Technical Board of Appeal [2007] EPOR 2, para 4, Reasons for the Decision.
103. *Zymogenetics/Hematopoietic cytokine receptor* T898/05, Technical Board of Appeal [2007] EPOR 2, para 5, Reasons for the Decision.
104. *Zymogenetics/Hematopoietic cytokine receptor* T898/05, Technical Board of Appeal [2007] EPOR 2, para 8, Reasons for the Decision. In para 8, the Board explained that "a product which is definitely described and plausibly shown to be usable, e.g. to cure a rare or orphan disease, might be considered to have a profitable use or concrete benefit, irrespective of whether it is actually intended for the pursuit of any trade at all. Thus, although no particular economic profit might be expected in the development of such products, nevertheless there is no doubt that it might be considered to display immediate concrete benefits."
105. *Zymogenetics/Hematopoietic cytokine receptor* T898/05, Technical Board of Appeal [2007] EPOR 2, para 6, Reasons for the Decision.
106. *Zymogenetics/Hematopoietic cytokine receptor* T898/05, Technical Board of Appeal [2007] EPOR 2, para 7, Reasons for the Decision.

107. To borrow the phrase used by the Opposition Division in *ICOS Corp/ (Transmembrane Receptor)* [2002] OJ EPO 293 (EPO) Decision of the Opposition Division dated 20 June 2001.
108. Note that Rule 27(1)(f) EPC which provides that "the description shall indicate explicitly, when it is not obvious from the description or nature of the invention, the way in which the invention is capable of exploitation in industry" is in similar vein.

4

The Ethical Aspects of Biotechnology

Introduction

The march for biotechnology has resulted in a furor of research and products as well as therapies in many parts of the globe. Malaysia chooses not to be sidelined due to the many promises of enhanced quality and production of agricultural products, advanced medical research as well as production of pharmaceutical products, all made possible by the advent of biotechnology. In view of this, the Fourth Prime Minister of Malaysia, Dr. Mahathir Mohamed launched the New Biotechnology Policy on 28 April 2005 to *"give impetus to developing the biotechnology sector into a new economic engine to enhance prosperity and wellness of the nation by 2020"*. In line with this, the Malaysian Biotechnology Corporation (MBC) was created to spearhead the development of the sector. Prior to this, research in biotechnology had already taken place in a number of research institutions such as Malaysian Agricultural Research and Development Institute (MARDI), Palm Oil Research Institute Malaysia (PORIM) Malaysian Palm Oil Board (now MPOB) and Rubber Research Institute (RRI) Malaysian Rubber Board (now MRB) as well as at various universities in the country such as University Putra Malaysia (UPM), National University of Malaysia (UKM), University of Malaya (UM) and University Science Malaysia (USM).

Despite the many benefits to human lives, there remains a fear, that biotechnological research and products could have side effects, on humans, animals and the entire ecological system. No one can predict how present and future human life can be affected by the use and application of this powerful technology. Laws may be one mechanism to control the use of biotechnology, but in the Malaysian context the law lags ever so slowly behind the constant discoveries made through biotechnological research. Not only that, there are serious issues in enforcement. That is why many developed countries have chosen to rely on ethical concepts, as self governing mechanisms to ensure that any research and products will be safe for human consumption and do not pose a hazardous threat to the environment. This body of knowledge is now known as bioethics. It has been suggested that, legal and regulatory frameworks are not enough and that reliance on ethics and ethics committees would be a more practical approach to regulating biotechnological research and products.

Hence, this chapter seeks to discuss the ethical dimensions of research in biotechnology and any of its products, with special emphasis to the position in Malaysia. In doing so, this chapter is divided into four parts. The first part of the chapter discusses the meaning of bioethics and its relation to biotechnology. This part also briefly identifies the ethical issues raised when biotechnology is used in agricultural and health biotechnology. Meanwhile, the second part of the chapter looks at the role of bioethics committees and the importance of these committees in many parts of the developed world. Part three of the chapter continues the discussion on the position of bioethics committees in Malaysia. From here part four of the chapter looks into the influence of religion in bioethical considerations in Malaysia. Finally, the chapter seeks to provide some conclusions and recommendations that could address some of the problems that have been associated with biotechnology.

Bioethics and Its Relation to Biotechnology

Much of the local development in the area of bioethics is influenced by the development that has taken place in Western countries, especially the United Kingdom and the United

States. Western liberal thinking puts forward an array of ethical theories,[1] rules and principles[2] that have been used to resolve ethical dilemmas involving the use of technology in the life sciences, especially in the area of biomedicine.[3] This body of knowledge is now known as 'bioethics'.[4]

What is 'Bioethics'?

Western ethicists opine that it is difficult to depend on specific ethical theory, rule or principle because there are many variables that exist in real life situations. Beauchamp and Walters for example, cite three reasons why they think it is not feasible to adopt a single authoritative ethical approach to bioethics. First, no one has managed to convince philosophers of the existence of a single ethical rule, theory or principle that is ethically authoritative. Second, even though a person is convinced that there does exist such an authoritative ethical theory or principle, not everyone will share his views. They see this as an impediment to communicating and negotiating in the "midst of disagreements". This would result in a hostile approach to solving bioethical problems. Third, they do not believe that any single rule, theory or principle could be flexible and wide enough to accommodate a myriad of ethical problems. Due to these difficulties, many bioethicists believe that no rule, theory, or principles are, absolute. However, these rules, theories and principles could serve as power decision-making tools especially in the area of clinical medicine and biomedicine. Hence, the term "bioethics" is now commonly used to describe an area of study which analyses ethical issues arising from the biological and medical sciences.[5]

The study of bioethics involves the study of decision-making in cases which involve bioethical dilemmas and could be based on either traditional ethical theories or modern ethical theories and principles.[6] According to Beauchamp and Walters, among the well known traditional ethical theories are consequentialism,[7] which focuses on utilitarian[8] ethical theories and deontological[9] theories which look into the Kantian concept of the 'Categorical Imperative'.[10] On the other hand, the more modern ethical approaches consider not only traditional ethical theories as mentioned above but also include the 'Principle Based' approach,[11] virtue ethics,[12] the ethics of care,[13] and also the casuistry approach.[14] In an earlier work, Beauchamp and Childress had also included the liberal individualism approach which is based on the rights based theory.[15] To this list, another writer, Glannon, has also included feminist ethics,[16] metaethics,[17] contractarianism[18] and communitarianism[19] within his discussion on ethical theories influencing bioethics.

It must be noted that although the basis for bioethics differ from one theory or principle to the next, there are two things that most of these theories or principles have in common. The first is that bioethics must be grounded on pure reason.[20] Hence, religion is looked upon as an "orthodoxy" which places unacceptable limitations to ethical reasoning. This was largely due to the desire to break free from the medieval clutches of the conservative Roman Catholic Church and its political power that it wielded before the Reformation.[21] Although religion may play a role in bioethical decision- making, modern bioethics is essentially secular, pluralistic and multidisciplinary.[22] Secondly, many bioethicists agree on the need to also be free of cultural relativism.[23]

It must be emphasized that this represents a major problem in transplanting Western ethical conceptions to the Malaysian scenario. Despite being multi-racial, multi-religious and multi-cultural, Malaysian society puts a lot of emphasis on religious observances and cultural respect. This is especially prominent among the Malay-Muslim society.[24]

This chapter however will only focus on the 'Principle Based' approach as propounded by Beauchamp and Childress as the International Bioethics Committee (IBC) and many of the National Bioethics Committees in many parts of the world has chosen to abide by this ethical approach. Aside from that, these four principles closely blends in with the respect to religious ethics and respect for cultural observances that are still prominent amongst Malaysians.

The Principle Based Approach to Bioethics

Importance placed on individual autonomy is seen to be prevalent in the principle based approaches to bioethics. Nevertheless, particular attention must be given to the most popular principle based approach expounded by Beauchamp and Childress in their famous work, *Principles of Biomedical Ethics,*[25] known as the 'Four Principles' approach to bioethics. According to Beauchamp and Childress, their principle based approach emphasizes on principles of obligation.[26] Beauchamp and Childress concentrate on four main principles which begin with the respect for autonomy and followed by the duty of non-maleficence, beneficence and justice. Although Beauchamp and Childress discussed the application of the four principles approach to bioethics within specific settings, i.e. in the doctor-patient relationship, their approach has been the most oft referred concept when dealing with all types of bioethical problems.

It must be noted that the principle based approach is not exclusive to the four principles as expounded by Beauchamp and Childress. The four main principles have also been interpreted and applied in various ways. Macer for example emphasizes the use of "love" as an alternative method for interpreting the four main principles of bioethics as put forward by Beauchamp and Childress.[27] Macer uses "love" to describe how the four principles could be applied in people's lives. He uses the term "self love" to describe respect for autonomy, "love of life" to describe "non-maleficence", "love of good" to describe "beneficence" and "love of others" to describe "justice".[28] Views such as that held by Beauchamp and Childress as well as Macer commonly represent the Western liberal ethical belief that respect for individual autonomy should receive primary consideration in settling ethical dilemmas. Their discussions on the concept of respect for autonomy reflect the Western preoccupation with the need to give special regard to individual autonomy.

According to Beauchamp and Childress, autonomy may be interpreted in many ways.[29] Nevertheless, in the context of a theory, autonomy here means,

"…personal rule of the self that is free from both controlling interferences by others and from personal limitations that prevent meaningful choice, such as inadequate understanding."[30]

From the above, it could be seen that in order for autonomy to be complete, two essential requirements must exist, i.e. the liberty or independence from "*controlling interferences*" and also the capacity for intentional action. Hence, their explanation that merely being autonomous is not the same as being respected as an autonomous person.[31] Respecting the autonomy of a person would entail not only an obligation not to intervene in other people's affairs but also includes an obligation to "*maintain capacities for autonomous choices*".[32] The respect for autonomy can however, be legitimately limited by the rights of others. This is possible because Beauchamp and Childress make it a rule that all of their four basic principles have only prima facie standing, thus enabling considerations to be given to other competing moral interests.[33]

Here, Beauchamp and Childress have relied heavily on Mill's concept of 'individuality' whereby the limits to the respect of autonomy is set by the 'harm to others' principle. In this light, respect for autonomy would mean that persons should be allowed to develop according to their personal convictions so long as they do not interfere with the rights and freedoms of others. [34] Hence, the respect for autonomy operates in a setting where individuals can never expect to act autonomously without affecting others.[35]

Therefore, Beauchamp and Childress cite specific examples which can override respect for autonomy. These include:–

- Choices that endanger the public health,
- Choices that potentially harm innocent others,
- Choices that require a scarce resource for which no funds are available.

Under these circumstances and many others in the like manner, the exercise of individual autonomy may justifiably be restricted.

The respect for autonomy in the area of biotechnology would largely affect issues of informed consent in the conduct of research in biotechnology. This would mean that any research on human subjects must be with free and informed consent of the person subjecting himself to the research. This principle is largely in line with the Nuremberg Code, the Declaration of Helsinki, and more recently, the Universal Declaration on Bioethics and Human Rights, 2005. The report now turns to the Universal Declaration on Bioethics and Human Rights, 2005 which embodies all the four main principles of bioethics.

Nevertheless, attention must be given to the concept of responsibility when applying biotechnology to agriculture or health and medical research products. The concept of responsibility could also be inferred from the remaining three of the four principle based approach as laid down by Beauchamp and Childress. This can be done when consideration is also given to the principles of non-maleficence, beneficence and justice all of which are held to be of the same importance as respect for autonomy,

According to the second principle espoused by Beauchamp and Childress, there is the duty of each person to avoid harming others.[36] This principle asserts an *"obligation not to inflict harm intentionally"*.[37] Beauchamp and Childress explains,

"Obligations of non-maleficence are obligations of not inflicting harms and not imposing risks of harm."[38]

Like the principle of respect for autonomy, the principle of non-maleficence is also considered as prima facie and not absolute.[39] In applying the principle of non-maleficence, individuals should not only avoid causing harm to others but must also protect others against some types of harm.

If the principle of non-maleficence was given more regard, then any biotechnological research and products that could result in harming the public in any way would not be a justifiable, even if there is a possibility of obtaining some benefit from the technology. Since the principle of non-maleficence basically means 'do no harm', this would mean harm that is caused or can be caused "through acts or omission".[40] The original application of this principle is meant to ensure a high degree of responsibility from physicians towards their patients, it could, by analogy be applied to any cases where scientists, physicians or researchers are embarking on any type of research be it in the agricultural sector or in the health and medical sector.

Therefore, it would be the responsibility of the researcher or physician undertaking the research to ensure that the product or therapy would not harm the end users or the patients. In cases of clinical trials, the practice has been to explain the procedure to the patients and obtain a full written consent from those who have agreed to subject themselves to the clinical trials.

In relation to the effects of biotechnology on the environment, the principle of non-maleficence must also take into consideration the effects that the research or product will have on the environment and the eco-system.

The discussion on the principle of non-maleficence is closely connected to the principle of beneficence.[41] Attention given to the principle of beneficence would also lead individuals to consider respecting other people's interest. This principle requires individuals to not only avoid harming others but also do things that would "contribute to their welfare".[42] Here, Beauchamp and Childress divide beneficence into two types, positive beneficence and utility.[43] According to them,

"...positive beneficence requires the provision of benefits. Utility requires that benefits and drawbacks be balanced."[44]

In other words, the duty to do beneficence means there is an obligation on individuals to do actions for the benefit of others.

Beauchamp and Childress admit that many acts of beneficence are not obligatory, however, to them, the principle of beneficence asserts *"a moral obligation to help others further their important and legitimate interests"*.[45] Nevertheless, the application of this principle is somewhat different from the previous two principles in that if the principles of respect for autonomy and duty of non-maleficence operated as a prima facie obligation, this is not so for the principles of beneficence.

They consider positive beneficence as more of an ideal than an obligation.[46] They do consider certain circumstances where beneficence can be made obligatory. This arises in several instances. The first situation is when there arises the need to protect and defend the rights of others. In such a circumstance, an act of beneficence is no longer a mere ideal. In fact it becomes a duty or an obligation. Similarly, the second situation is when there is a need to prevent harm from occurring to others. The third situation that makes beneficence an obligation is when there is a need to remove conditions that will cause harm to others. The fourth situation where an act of beneficence becomes obligatory is when the situation requires an individual to help persons with liabilities. The fifth and final situation is when there arises a situation where a person is in danger and needs to be rescued.

Here, Beauchamp and Childress defend a 'reciprocity-based' justification for what they call as "Obligations of Beneficence".[47] Reciprocity here refers to the act of making an appropriate return for example returning benefit by proportional benefit.[48] What this means is that the obligation to act for the benefit of others is due to the fact that we have received or will receive beneficial assistance from others.[49] They nevertheless qualify the Obligation of Beneficence by noting that,

" *We…do not hold that persons devoid of reciprocal relationships of benefit never have an obligation to act beneficently.*"[50]

To them, such obligations of beneficence is more apparent in cases where the act will benefit the society.[51] As such, obligations of beneficence arise naturally out of the necessary 'give and take" of social life.

It would seem that the biggest challenge to the claim that there exists an obligation of beneficence is the accusation that to do so would result in paternalism. This is another evidence of how Western thinking abhors any tampering with individual autonomy. Beauchamp and Childress defends a *"version of paternalism that justifies strong paternalistic interventions under some conditions"*. According to them, there are many occasions where intervention is necessary in decisions for example in cases involving a non-autonomous dependent.[52] As beneficence involves a positive duty to do good or even the duty to prevent and remove harm,[53] then it too could be relevant in issues involving the use of biotechnology.

At this point, it must be noted that beneficence has usually conflicted with the respect for autonomy. In the realm of health care, doctors are often labelled as 'paternalistic' when they attempt to do good either against the wishes of the patient or acting without the patient's knowledge of a particular treatment.[54] Hence, this principle has largely been 'balanced' out by the principle of respect for autonomy, whereby the need for full and informed consent of the subjects is a necessity.

Finally, the principle of justice is also one key principle that must be given more consideration when discussing ethical principles in agriculture and health biotechnology. Whilst the extrapolation of the principle of autonomy, non-maleficence and beneficence was all encompassing and could be applied to a wide range of bioethical situations, the definition and application of the principle of justice has been rather narrow. It primarily concentrates on the discussion of fair distribution of resources. What could be taken from this principle nonetheless is their emphasis on the concept of equality that is the backbone of the concept of justice.[55]

The principle of justice can be "tightly constricted or broadly expansive".[56] If the libertarian interpretation to the principle of justice were applied, it would mean that the individual must be free to pursue whatever biotechnological research is necessary. Nevertheless, another way of looking at how the principle of justice could work differently. Usually, justice is looked upon as a tool in settling ethical disputes with regards to the distribution of goods in society.[57] However, if looked upon it in a broader light, the principle of justice when used in relation to advances in biotechnology operates in a way that ensures that justice must also be served to the public at large and the environment.

An example of how the concept of justice applies in this relation can be seen in Rendtorrf's interpretation of the principle based approach to bioethics. Although he too considers autonomy as an important principle,[58] he considers it an anomaly to only focus on autonomy or to put autonomy at the top of the hierarchy of principles. To do so, he maintains, would be *"forgetful of the fragile and vulnerable components of the human condition"*[59] which in reality requires care and respect to also be accorded to other human beings. Hence, he does not prescribe a hierarchical interpretation of the principle based approach to bioethics.[60] Instead, he suggests that a society built on responsible, autonomous decision-making does not mean a society without communitarian engagements and common values.[61] Thus, autonomy should not rule out the need to take into consideration relations with other human beings and therefore must take cognizance of other values.

Interestingly, it is his idea of a communitarian approach to autonomy that leads him to further suggest that there are situations in bioethics and bio-law where the principle of autonomy must give way to other more important principles.[62] Hence, to him, in certain cases, he puts forward the view that the principle of human dignity,[63] integrity[64] and vulnerability[65] would be more appropriate principles to apply. This is because, by giving ample considerations to these ethical principles, a balance could be struck between respect for individual autonomy and the other three principles, especially justice. From here, he views the application of the concept of autonomy as having very limited role in bioethics.[66]

If Rendtorff's views were to be applied in case where biotechnology is used, then to only those products or treatments which could benefit the public at large should be allowed to be carried out. Aside from the respect the right of the researchers and scientists to embark on various research projects, due regard must also be given to human dignity, integrity and justice. Clearly, Rendtorff places respect for autonomy in a situation where it must be considered hand in hand with other equally important principles.

Another writer, Mahowald has also developed an ethical concept that emphasizes the importance of equality which is compatible to an ethics of care as well as justice.[67] In doing so she has stressed on the concept of responsibility and avoided placing too much emphasis on the concept of individual rights. To her, the problem with much of the literature discussing rights is because people tend to view rights as "*the whole of the moral story*".[68] Mahowald thus argues that an explanation of rights must necessarily include "mutual or relation-based responsibilities".[69] She maintains;

> "*Although the terms duty, obligation and responsibility are often used interchangeably, I prefer the term responsibility because it is more suggestive (through its association with 'response') of interpersonal relationships as ground for moral judgments. Responsibilities arise not only because of impartially defined duties or obligations, but also because of ties formed by relationships or attachments among persons.*"[70]

Mahowald's position is interesting because to her, the need to focus on responsibilities is due to the importance placed on relationships with other people. Therefore, if the principles as laid down by Rendtorff and Mahowald are applied to cases of biotechnological researchers and products, all four principles must be considered as a whole and researchers as well as physicians must balance their right to conduct research with other important principles such as non-maleficence, beneficence and justice.

The next part of this Chapter discusses the ethical principles contained in the Universal Declaration on Bioethics and Human Rights, 2005.

The Universal Declaration on Bioethics and Human Rights, 2005

This Declaration aims at addressing the many ethical issues that arise due to medicine, the life sciences and any associated technologies which are applied to human beings[71]. It seeks to achieve this by providing a universal framework of principles and procedures to help guide countries who wish to legislate[72] and provide policies or instruments in the area of bioethics.[73] In doing so, the Declaration seeks to promote the respect for human dignity and protection of human rights whilst balancing it with the recognition on the importance of freedom in scientific research.[74] This means that although the Declaration recognizes the need for research in biotechnology due to its many benefits, such research and products must be done within a certain ethical framework, which is laid down in the Declaration.[75] The Declaration also seeks to ensure that the benefits of these technologies are made available equitably.[76] Aside from that it also seeks to protect and promote the interests of present and future generations.[77]

The four principles to bioethics was adopted by the Declaration in Articles 4, 5, 6 and 10. Article 4 maintains;

"In applying and advancing scientific knowledge, medical practice and associated technologies, direct and indirect benefits to patients, research participants and other affected individuals should be maximized and any possible harm to such individuals should be minimized."

This is in line with the principle of beneficence as outlined by Beauchamp and Childress. Meanwhile, Article 5 addresses the issue of autonomy and individual responsibility, the importance individual autonomy whilst such exercise must not cause harm to others. Articles 6 to 9 elaborate on the respect to individual autonomy whereby much emphasis is given to the role of informed consent. It provides that any type of medical intervention must be done with the expressed and informed consent of the person concerned.

Meanwhile, Articles 10 and 11 highlights the recognition given to all human beings as having dignity and rights and deserves to be treated equally and justly. This is to ensure that any research in biotechnology will not transgress boundaries of humanity. It seeks to avoid research on humans such as that done by the German Nazis when they targeted non-Germans as research subjects without any respect.

Article 16 of the Declaration must be given special attention. It recognizes that the results from any biotechnological research as well as its processes could very well leave an impact not only on present human lives but even future human lives. Therefore, the Article implores that due regard must be given to any impact that the "life sciences" might have on future generations. Nevertheless, it is submitted that the wording of the Article is rather mild, in that it only reminds governments and those who are involved in biotechnology to give "due regard" to the "impact of the life sciences on future generations". In view of the seriousness of the damage that could be caused, it is submitted that the wording needs to have more force. It would have sent a much more serious message if words such as, "serious attention" or "pertinent consideration" were to be used.

Similar wording is used in Article 17 of the declaration which seeks to highlight the importance of protecting the environment, the biosphere and biodiversity. It also recognizes the need to respect traditional knowledge. This Article has been largely abided by many countries, including Malaysia. This is largely due to international pressure whereby this Declaration echoes Principle 15 of the Rio Declaration on Environment and Development which led to the Convention on Biological Diversity together with its Protocol, the Cartagena Protocol on Bio-safety. Malaysia who is a signatory to this Convention and the Protocol has recently enacted the Bio-safety Act, 2007. A full discussion of this shall be made in Chapter Two and Five on agricultural biotechnology as well as Chapter Six which deals with research and processes in the biomedical sciences.

The recommendations of the Declaration are basic guidelines to researchers and governments all over the world. However, the responsibility to monitor any research in biotechnology, in all its areas falls on the government. As submitted before, there are two ways in which this could be done. One way is to enact specific laws seeking to control a specific area of biotechnology, its research, processes and products. Article 22 of the Declaration recognizes legislative measures as one of the measures taken by States in compliance with the Declaration. However, there are two weaknesses to this approach. Firstly, research in the area of biotechnology moves at a very fast pace. As such, it would be extremely difficult for governments to enact laws that would be in line with the developments. Secondly, even if there existed legislation, it would be very difficult to enforce the law in the absence of experts in the area. Due to these difficulties, another more manageable alternative is by establishing ethics committees, both at the national level as well as at the professional and/or at the clinical level. This has been the approach taken by many countries around the world today.

The Role of the Bioethics Committee

The importance of ethics committees has also been recognized by the Universal Declaration on Bioethics and Human Rights. Article 19 provides the following:

"Independent, multidisciplinary and pluralistic ethics committees should be established, promoted and supported at the appropriate level in order to:

(a) Assess the relevant ethical, legal, scientific and social issues related to research projects involving human beings;

(b) Provide advice on ethical problems in clinical settings;

(c) Assess scientific and technological developments, formulate recommendations and contribute to the preparation of guidelines on issues within the scope of this Declaration;

(d) Foster debate, education and public awareness of, and engagement in, bioethics."

Currently, at least thirty five countries have their own National Bioethics Committees.[78] These Committees play an important role of holding public forums and in collecting the views from the masses as to the ethical position of a particular biotechnological research, processes and products. In these countries, the advice of the ethics committee is often sought in establishing a policy on certain issues and further playing the role assisting in developing the legal and regulatory framework. These National Bioethics Committees also help to ensure that the government policy and regulatory bodies act in line with international declarations and conventions that had been ratified.

The Malaysian Position

Currently, Malaysia's attitude towards the ethical concerns in the area of biotechnology is mixed. Certain areas, such as agricultural biotechnology and the concerns for the safety of the environment have prompted the Malaysian government to amend the Food Act and enact the Biosafety Act, 2007. However, in many other areas of biotechnology, especially in regard to biomedical research and pharmaceuticals, especially those relating to humans, the Malaysian government has largely relied on ad hoc ethics committees or professional committees such as hospital ethics committees, committees appointed by the Ministry of Health and the Malaysian Medical Council. The country however does not have a National Bioethics Committee.

Malaysia has also been slow in ratifying international declarations and conventions. Malaysia still has not adopted the Universal Declaration of Bioethics and Human Rights, 2005, the Universal Declaration on Human Genetic Data, 2003, the Declaration on the Responsibilities of the Present Generations Towards Future Generations, 1997 and also the Universal Declaration on the Human Genome and Human Rights, 1997.

The next part of this Chapter provides an overview of the specific areas of biotechnology in Malaysia and the ethical concerns that come with it as well as how these concerns are addressed by the government.

Biotechnology in Malaysia

The Malaysian government has shown a keen interest in promoting biotechnology in the country. This could be seen from the 7th, 8th and 9th Malaysia Plans. During the 7th Malaysia Plan (1996-2000) the aim was to prepare the necessary infrastructures and technical support. In order to support developments and research in biotechnology, the Government had established the National Biotechnology Directorate (BIOTEK). The mission of BIOTEK is to lead the development of biotechnology in Malaysia through research and related activities directed at commercializing biotechnology and to establish Malaysia as a leading biotechnology industry. This is in line with Tun Dr. Mahathir Mohamad's wishes that:-

> *"...that biotechnology has great potential in Malaysia and it could be a catalyst for new growth areas in the country's economy as well as a*

source of new wealth and income for the people. Biotech is useful in many areas - agriculture, livestock farming, herbal industry and tradition and modern medicine."

The National Biotechnology Policy highlights three important areas that could benefit from biotechnological research:

- Agricultural Biotechnology;
- Healthcare Biotechnology; and
- Industrial Biotechnology.

For the purpose of this Chapter, concentration shall only be given to ethical concerns relating to agricultural biotechnology and healthcare biotechnology.

Agricultural Biotechnology

Biotechnology has been used to improve the production and sustainability of agricultural products in Malaysia. The main concern over the use of biotechnology in the agriculture sector may be summed up as follows:-

(a) *The Safety Issues:* Relating to the use of genetically modified organisms include the possible toxic or allergenic effects due to transgene products or products from interaction with host genes. Another concern is also the fact that increased use of toxic pesticide-resistant transgenic crops leads to pesticide related illness in farm workers and contamination of food and water.

(b) *Socioeconomic Impact:* This includes concerns over the marginalization of small farmers due to intellectual property rights and other restrictive practice associated with seed certification. There are also concerns over the substitution of traditional technologies and produce aside from the inherent genetic instability of transgenic lines resulting in crop failures.

(c) *Environmental Impact:* The environmental concerns relate to the spread of trangenes to related weed species which in turn creates super weeds. There are also concerns over the increased use of toxic, nondiscriminating herbicide-resistant transgenic plants which leads to large-scale elimination of indigenous agricultural and natural species. Another point of concern is the use of toxic herbicides which inadvertently destroys soil fertility and yield. This is also coupled with the problems with the use of bio-insecticidal transgenic plants which accelerate the evolution of biopesticide resistance in major insect pests. This results in the inability to rely on biopesticides used by organic farmers for years.

These are some of the concerns over the use of biotechnology in the agricultural sector. The Government enacted the Biosafety Bill 2007 and this has also led to the revision to the Food Act which will be further discussed in Chapter Five which deals with agricultural biotechnology.

In relation to the ethical issues in Malaysia, the Ministry of Science, Technology and Innovations (MOSTI) established the Genetic Modification Advisory Committee (GMAC) in 1996 under the auspices of the National Committee on Biodiversity (NCB). Its objective was to ensure that any risks associated with the use, handling and transfer of GMOs be identified and safely managed. In view of that, in January 1997, the GMAC had formulated the National Guidelines on release of GMOs into the Environment. The Guidelines require the establishment of an Institutional Bio-safety Committee (IBC) in all related research government institutions. It is the IBCs that will ensure that experiments undertaken by the institution conform to the provisions of the Guidelines. Due to this, many universities and government research institutions have established their own IBCs.

The only problem with this approach is in ensuring that all the research institutions in Malaysia abide by this Guideline. This is because the requirement for the establishment of IBCs in private institutions is not mandatory. Aside from that, these Guidelines are not law and therefore no penalties could be meted out for not following the Guidelines. Hence, there is still a need to rely on proper legal sanctions that can only be given with the promulgation of the proper legislations.

One Example - MARDI

Efforts were made by the Government to ensure the use of science and technology in agricultural products since 1969 whereby MARDI was established to develop and promote new and improved technologies in agriculture. This was to ensure that "these technologies will serve to increase productivity and efficiency, thus modernizing the agricultural sector as well as maximizing income farming". Biotechnology has been identified as one of the key technologies needed for the process of agricultural transformation. In view of this MARDI focuses on three main areas:

- Research in biotechnology including improvements made on plant, animal and micro-organisms through tissue, cell and gene manipulations. Research is also done in order to develop and apply bio-processing or bio-reactor and bio-sensing technologies for the agro-industry;
- Molecular biology and genetic engineering which focuses on the development of new crop varieties that cannot be easily produced through conventional breeding, especially those with pest and disease resistant abilities;
- Bio-processing which focuses on the use of biological materials such as micro-organisms and enzymes and even plant and animal cells to catalyze the conversion of raw materials to increase the value of food and non-food products.

It is interesting to note that aside from focusing on research towards improving and increasing agricultural products, MARDI is also concerned with safety issues. Hence, it also gives emphasis towards research in bio-diagnostics and bio-safety. This area of research focuses on the production and development of locally made diagnostic apparatus or the agriculture, food and environment sectors. Emphasis is given to the development of biosensors, immunodiagnostic and DNA-based diagnostic. All this is to evaluate the side effects of biotechnology on the human body and the environment.

Aside from that, MARDI also provides assessment of Genetically Modified Organisms used in food processing. However, there is no indication on the existence of an Ethics Committee. It is submitted that any type of research done must conform to the safety policy of the organization.

Aside from MARDI, other government related agencies were set up in various fields of agriculture such as the Malaysian Cocoa Board (MCB) established in 1988, the Rubber Research Institute of Malaysia (RRIM, the Malaysian Rubber Board, 1998, and the Malaysian Palm Oil Board(MPOB) 2000. These agencies also have their own IBCs.

Healthcare Biotechnology

The use of biotechnology to improve existing healthcare is the source of many ethical dilemmas. The use of biotechnology in healthcare can be divided into issues relating to use of human as test subjects, use of human tissues and genes to develop pharmaceutical products, stem cell research and therapy and issues in assisted reproductive technologies. It is in the healthcare sector that biotechnology has relied primarily on the four principles approach to bioethics in the decision making process.

However, again, due to the breadth of the subject matter, this report only concentrates on the ethical issues brought about by human embryonic stem cell research and therapy. Even then, it only discusses the use of human embryonic stem cells left over from ART treatments and will not even venture into the discussion of the ethical problems that surround the use of embryos that have been created by way of somatic cell nuclear transfer technology.

Ethical Issues in Human Embryonic Stem Cell Research and Therapy

Venture into the embryonic stem cell research must begin by considering why scientists are so keen in this area of research. Scientists consider embryonic stem cells as providing a promising avenue for finding new treatments for several diseases that were once thought to be incurable. Embryonic stem cells are said to be able to replace damaged cells and tissues thus curing the disease.[79] Among others it promises to be able to treat Parkinson's disease, diabetes and cardiac myopathy.[80] It has been submitted that research on embryos are necessary to allow scientists to develop and make available these therapies for those who need it. The emphasis on embryonic stem cells is primarily due to its pluripotent nature, whereby it could give rise to any type of cell type.

The main ethical problem when using human embryos for research would naturally be, the ethicality of conducting research on human embryos. Are embryos human? If they are, when can they be considered to be alive? If they can be considered as being alive, when does that life actually begin? If the embryos are humans should we allow scientists to conduct research on them?

This chapter puts forward three main ethical positions that have been adopted by different groups in relation to the human embryonic stem cell debate. These positions are known as the total respect position, the liberal position and the special respect position.

The total respect position sees the human[81] embryos as essentially human, and are essentially alive from the moment of conception.[82] According to them, the embryo is alive from the time of conception due to its ability to take up energy and self replicate and as the embryos originate from humans they are essentially humans. According to Sherley,

"The human egg endows the human genome with a special molecular program that sets the plan for complete development of a human being."[83]

Therefore, using embryos as subjects for research would be totally unacceptable and unethical as it would intentionally lead to the eventual destruction of the embryo. This is the position taken by many Christian groups as well as many other religious groups.

Meanwhile, the liberal position is the exact opposite of the total respect position. According to this position, embryos are not yet alive and cannot be considered as a person because it has not yet developed sentience and is not conscious and is not able to feel pain. Due to this, and due to the potential benefits that research on embryos promises, there is nothing wrong with conducting experiments on embryos.

The third ethical position is the special respect position which may be considered as the intermediate position between the first two positions mentioned above. According to this position, embryos deserve to be given special respect as they have the potential to become humans. However, this position also recognizes the potential benefits of conducting research on embryos. Therefore, in reconciling the problem, the position taken is that research on embryos should be permitted but only until 14 days after fertilization. The significance of the 14 day period is marked by the formation of the primitive streak which will later develop into the embryo's neural groove that will become the precursors to feeling pain and sensation.

The special respect position was the position adopted by the Warnock Committee in 1984 which became the basis for the 1990 Human Fertilization and Embryology Act in the UK.[84] This position has been followed in several countries such as Australia, New Zealand, Portugal, Finland, Greece, Slovenia, Estonia, South Africa and Canada. It is interesting to note that the United Kingdom however, recently opted for the liberal position.

International Ethical Positions on Human Embryonic Research

This part of the chapter examines several international documents in relation to embryonic stem cell research. The UNESCO Report by the International Bioethics Committee 2001 recognises the diverse opinions on the acceptability or non-acceptability of research on embryos as held by different nations. The UNESCO's stand on this is that countries should decide for themselves whether or not to permit research on embryos. Nevertheless, for countries that do allow such research to be conducted, they must put in force a regulatory framework which provides for the limits of the permissible. In all aspects of the research, importance must be placed on the respect for human dignity and the respect and principles in the UDHR (1948) as well as the Universal Declaration and the Universal Declaration on the Human Genome and Human Rights, (1997). The report also recommended that in considering what would be the appropriate guidelines and controls, states should put in the following guidelines:

- In cases where couples are asked to donate their left over embryos for research, they must be fully informed of the implication of the research and how the embryos will be used. Their agreement must be subjected to full, free and informed consent.
- The state should also continue to encourage new and alternative technologies for obtaining human stem cell lines - from adult stem cells.

Based on the UNESCO reports, it would be useful to look at the Convention on Human Rights and Biomedicine (Bioethics Convention) 1997. Article 18 of the said Convention specifically prohibits the creation of human embryos for research purposes. However, Article 18(1) does mention that should a state allow the creation of embryos in vitro, it shall ensure adequate protection of the embryo. This would suggest that the Convention, in essence does not consider use of embryos for research purposes as an act that would "protect" the embryo and would not allow research to be conducted on embryos. A reading of Article 21 also prohibits the use of the human body and its parts shall not give rise to financial benefit.

The Influence of Religion in Bioethical Considerations in Malaysia

Malaysia is a multi-racial society which also means that it is also multi-religious. The ethical aspects of biotechnology in Malaysia are influenced heavily by the religious positions on controversial issues brought up by the use of biotechnology and its products and outcomes. Nevertheless, the present Chapter shall concentrate mainly on the position of Islam due to the existence of JAKIM which has been able to document the various *fatawa* issued by the National Fatwa Committee.

There is a need to look into the stand of all the main religions in Malaysia that relates to the ethical issues brought up by the use of biotechnology. However, this needs to be done in another research due to the breadth of the subject matter.

In Malaysia, the National Fatwa Committee has played a very important role in issuing *fatawa* relating to the use of biotechnology in both agricultural and healthcare products. These *fatwa*[85] seek to protect the consumers especially Muslims. The importance of these *fatawa* has been recognized the Malaysian Government whereby the views of National Fatwa Committee will be sought after by the Government when formulating national policies and drafting legislations in specific areas of biotechnology.

The *fatawa* issued by the National Fatwa Committee relating to biotechnological issues may be divided into the following categories:

1. Agricultural Practices and Products - *fatawa* in relation to this area relates to the use biotechnological process and products, especially if it these processes and products are derived from sources that have been prohibited in Islam;
2. Food and Drink - *fatawa* in this area is similar to those in the area of agricultural practices and products. It too declares whether certain food or drinks that are derived from haram sources may be consumed by the Muslim public. The *fatawa* range from the use of alcohol as stabilizers in soft drinks to use of pigs DNA in any biotechnological process that are used in the production of certain types of food. However, these *fatawa* can sometimes be confusing as they are brief and does not provide the readers with explanations as to the reasoning behind the *fatawa*. For example, in the area of agricultural biotechnology, a 1981 fatwa on the use of processed food for chicken is rather confusing. It does not mention the type of technology used for the processing but it goes on to permit the use of cow's blood, pigs blood if it is mixed with other materials. This permission would go against the basic

tenant of Islam which specifically declares that the pig and anything that comes from it is *haram* which means prohibited. There is also a need for JAKIM not only play a reactive role but a more proactive role especially in educating the public on the Islamic position relating to research and products that would affect the Muslims in this country.

3. Medicine-General Therapeutics- The *fatawa* in the area of medicine is also concerned with the contents of certain medicine such as insulin which is derived from pigs and whether or not it should be permitted for Muslims. The general test of permissibility in such circumstances is darurah or necessity, wherein Shari'ah would allow the use of a prohibited item in cases where the life of a person is at stake.

However, of particular interest is the *fatwa* on stem cell research and therapies which was issued on 11th March 2002 and 22nd February 2005. The *fatwa* issued in 2002 was rather brief and only concentrated on human cloning. The Committee was of the view that human cloning for whatever purposes must be prohibited as it goes against the *fitrah* (nature) as humans. However, the Committee also issued a *fatwa* that the use of stem cell for research and therapy would be permitted so long as it does not originate from adult cloning technologies, and so long as the research does not affront the *hukum syarak*. The Committee however, did not elaborate further as to what acts could be considered as contrary to the *hukum syarak*.

The 2005 fatwa is specifically on therapeutic human cloning and research on stem cells. The Committee issued 7 *fatawa* on this subject matter:

1. Therapeutic cloning for medical treatment such as creating specific cells or replacing damaged organs while taking into consideration the limits set by the Shariah is permissible (*harus*);
2. It is *harus* or permitted to use frozen embryos or left over embryos from IVF for research purposes but only with the consent of the husband and wife who

underwent the IVF treatment. The research may only be done before the embryo reaches the *'alaqah* stage (implantation).

3. Once the embryos have been the subject of research, it must never be implanted in the womb of the wife or any other woman.
4. Research on changing the genetic traits of the embryo should be permitted if involving couples with a high risk of genetically transmitting the genetic problem to their offspring. However, the choice of the gender of the child is not permitted unless the gender factor is the one that establishes the genetic link which could lead to the death of the resulting child.
5. Research for commercial gain and which has no relation to the health of the mother or of the embryo is not permitted.
6. Research must be legitimate with clear research goals and must be conducted by qualified persons who are *amanah* and responsible.
7. The following sources are recognized as legitimate sources of stem cells:
   - Adult stem cells, provided consent is given and the procedure does not harm him;
   - From children with the consent from his parents and so long as the procedure does not harm the child;
   - From the umbilical cord of new born babies with the consent of the parents;
   - From fetuses which had been the subject of miscarriage or was aborted due to medical reasons and with the permission of his parents;
   - Creation of embryos for the purpose of harvesting stem cells, either through the fusion of the egg and sperm or through Somatic Cell Nuclear Transfer is not permitted as a means of stopping any possible misuse of the technology.

The *fatwa* makes it clear that the position of stem cell research and therapy for Muslims in Malaysia is permissive provided that it does not reach the *'alaqah* stage. Quite interestingly, this stage conforms to the position that allows research on embryos up to the 14 day period. Scientists have shown that it will take the zygote approximately 7 days to implant into the wall of the uterus and another 7 days for the formation of the primitive streak.[86] This position is the position adopted by countries who wish to benefit from the promises of stem cell research but at the same time recognise the need to respect the human embryo as a potential person.

The position taken by the Committee is rather permissive if compared to the position adopted by the international fatwa committees such as the *Majma' al-fiqh al-Islami* and the Committee of the Islamic Medical Sciences to the Islamic Academy. In 1990, the *Majma' al-Fiqh al-Islami*, in its 17th meeting forbade the creation of embryos that would be more than safe for implantation into the womb at a single treatment cycle. The main intention of this prohibition is to safeguard the embryo. Any embryo created is meant to be implanted and this will eliminate the problem of left over embryos. From here, it could be further deduced that in prohibiting the creation of access embryos, the *fatwa* would not permit any acts that would harm the embryos.

This protective position is also reflected in the *fatwa* issued by the Committee of Islamic Medical Sciences to the Islamic Fiqh Academy of Jordan, in its 5th meeting from 5th to 17th December, 1992. The meeting decided the following:

1. It echoed the Majma' al-Fiqh al-Islami *fatwa* that forbade the creation of access embryos but provided an exception - it allows the creation of access embryos only in special circumstances;
2. In case of death or divorce of the parties, the embryos must be kept until the end of the storage period and then allowed to perish. No embryo may be intentionally discarded, destroyed or donated.

A reading of this second *fatwa* would clearly prohibit the use of embryos for research purposes.

It is submitted that the Malaysian Fatwa Committee's stand in permitting the research on embryos provided it did not reach the *'alaqah* period as not being in line with the two main international fatwa mentioned above.

A look into the position of the embryo under traditional Islamic law could perhaps shed light on the position of the embryo under the Shari'ah. The discussion on the treatment of embryos have generally been made by classical jurists when discussing the criminal acts resulting in hurt to an unborn child and the legal position of unborn persons under the law of succession. According to Imam Abu Hanifah and Imam Shafie, if a person causes injury to a pregnant woman and causes her to miscarry, that person will be liable for the payment of compensation which is known as the "*ghurrah*". This shows that Islam does afford protection to the embryo even when it is still in the womb of the mother.

This position is further strengthened by the ability of the embryo to be subjected to the *faraidh* which means Muslim laws of inheritance rule. However, the embryo's right to inheritance may only be realised once it has been born. Perhaps, it could be argued that this protection should only be given to embryos which had implanted in the uterus. In vitro embryos should not be given the same treatment. This is especially so if the criminal position is taken against persons hurting the pregnant woman and inadvertently hurting the embryo. In vitro embryos are in glass and subjecting them to research would not hurt the mother in any way.

It is submitted that it would seem rather superficial to adopt that stand. This is because, the embryo, regardless of whether it is in vitro or in vivo, originates from the same source - i.e. the union of the sperm and the egg which is for all intents and purposes aimed at reproducing humans. To allow research done on embryos, even left over embryos would go against the very reason for which it was created in the first place.

It is also submitted that to allow research on embryos would also go against the concept of *Maqasid al-Shari'ah* which means the Main Objectives of the Shari'ah which among others emphasizes the protection of life and progeny. This would mean that once created, the embryo has a right to life, to be implanted, and to be born. It remains the progeny of a particular couple once it is created , regardless of whether or not it is born.

Conclusions and Suggestions for Reform

The foregoing discussions shows that the use of Biotechnology in the agriculture and healthcare sectors in Malaysia currently rely very heavily on ethical principles in attempting to deal with ethical issues that arise from the use of biotechnology. This is done primarily through the formation of ad hoc committees which are formed according to the relevant area of biotechnological use. Aside from that, there is also reliance on institutional Bioethics or Ethics Committees under different Government agencies.

Nonetheless, despite deep ethical concerns over the impact of biotechnology to human well being, health and the environment, Malaysia does not have a National Bioethics Committee to deal with these issues at the national level. As a result of this, move towards legislating and regulating many areas affected by the use of biotechnology is very slow. Reliance has to be made to existing foreign legislations as well as the ethical positions taken by National Bioethics Committees from foreign jurisdictions. It is submitted that this would not be in line with the ethical position that is prevalent amongst the Malaysian community and hence would be unsuitable for adoption.

It is therefore recommended that firstly, there is a need to strengthen the existing framework on reliance on ad hoc or institutional based Ethics Committees. This could be done with the setting up of a Bioethics Committee at the National level which will be responsible in formulating a comprehensive Guide for all professional Ethics Committees or institutional Ethics Committees.

Secondly, the National Bioethics Committee must be given the mandate and power to scrutinize all research applications as well as hear and decide on any unethical acts. They should also be given the power to provide some form of punishment in case of unethical acts done

Thirdly, reliance on the ad hoc and/or institutionalized Ethics Committees does not provide adequate safeguards. There is a need to properly legislate and regulate scientists and all those involved in biotechnological research and production of goods stemming from these researches.

Ultimately, the government needs to legislate specific areas of biotechnology according to the needs of the people and it must address the ethical concerns brought up by the use of biotechnology.

Footnotes

1. An ethical theory usually provides standards and principles of moral reasoning. For further reading see James Rachels, "Ethical theory and bioethics", in *Bioethics, An Anthology* edited by Helga Kuhse, and Peter Singer, (London: Blackwell Publishers, 2000), 15.
2. Principles are general action guides specifying that some type of action is prohibited, required, or permitted in certain circumstances. Rules also provide the same guides. However, principles are more general norms whereas rules are more specific norms. For further reading see James F. Childress, "A principle-based approach", in *Bioethics, An Anthology*, edited by Helga Kuhse and Peter Singer, (London: Blackwell Publishers, 2000), 61.
3. For further reading see Tom L. Beauchamp, and Le Roy Walter, (Eds.), *Contemporary Issues in Bioethics*, 16. See also Thomas R. McCormick, "Principles of Bioethics", in *Ethics in Medicine*,(Washington: University of Washington School of Medicine, 1998) available at <http://eduserv.hscer.washington.edu/bioethics/tools/princpl.html> (accessed on 14.10.2004). See also arguments put forward by Rachels along similar lines as that mentioned above. James Rachels, "Ethical theory and bioethics", 15, 19 and 20.
4. Helga Kuhse and Peter Singer, (Eds.), *Bioethics, An Anthology*, 1. There is another term that is also commonly used which has an approximate meaning to the term "bioethics", that is "biomedical ethics". Glannon has described it as a "study of issues pertaining to what ought or ought not to be done in biotechnology, medical research and medical practice". See Walter Glannon, *Contemporary Readings in Biomedical Ethics*, (Orlando: Harcourt College Publishers, 2002), 1. From here, bioethics is a study of how individuals need to respond to the effects of biomedicine in cases where there is a need to mediate between two or more competing interests. However, in this report, the term 'bioethics' shall be adopted.
5. This is how the term is defined by Helga Kuhse and Peter Singer, (Eds.), *Bioethics, An Anthology*,1. In the same volume, Rachels provide an interesting account of the role of ethical theories in shaping bioethics. To him bioethics sees an interplay between the use of ethical theories

and case study, see page 22 of the same volume. Another more simple definition of the word is provided by Macer, where he maintains that bioethics is "the study of ethical issues arising from human involvement with life". See Darryl Macer, "Ethics and Assisted Human Reproduction", *Pathways: The Novartis Journal,* (2000): 1, available at <http://www.biol.tsukuba.ac.jp/~macer/Papers/View.htm> (accessed on 15. 10.2004).

6. Beauchamp and Walters, *Contemporary Issues in Bioethics,* p. 12. There is no hard and fast rule which is employed by writers in making these classifications. While Beauchamp and Walters have divided their discussion based on the above classification, other writers such as Freeman, Glannon and Munson have provided their method of classifying the different ethical theories that form the basis of bioethics. Freeman for example has used the term 'absolute based approach' to describe Kant's categorical imperative and Catholic natural law. The absolute rule approach is actually a mix of Christian Catholic natural law theories and Kantianism. It puts forward the rule that there are "certain moral rules or precepts that are held to be without exception". For further reading see Michael Freeman, (Ed.) *Ethics and Medical Decision-Making,* (Aldershot: Ashgate Dartmouth, 2001), xxi. Glannon on the other hand has taken a sweeping approach and has discussed the different ethical theories under the headings Normative ethics and Descriptive ethics where further theories are included such as deontology, consequentialism, virtue ethics, feminist ethics, meta-ethics, communitarianism and contractarianism. For further reading see Glannon, *Contemporary Readings in Biomedical Ethics,* 2. Munson on the other hand discusses five ethical theories, also without any particular classification. He has considered utilitarianism, Kant's ethics, Ross's ethics, Rawls' Theory of Justice and the ethics of Natural Law and Moral theology. For further reading see Munson, *Intervention and Reflection. Basic Issues in Medical Ethics,* 4 – 31.
7. The core idea in consequentialism is to consider what makes an action or policy right is when it brings about better consequences than any of its alternative. For a detailed discussion on this theory see Glannon, *Contemporary Readings in Biomedical Ethics,* 11.
8. Utilitarianism is actually the best known version of consequentialism where the good is defined in terms of utility or the Greatest Happiness Principle. However, since consequentialism does not define the good solely in terms of utility, it is broader than utilitarianism. In short, utilitarianism can be considered a subset of consequentialism. For further explanation, see ibid.
9. Deontological theory specifies that the rightness or wrongness of actions does not depend on the consequences of the actions, but instead on a person's duty or obligation to act in a way that respects the rights, interests and claims of other persons. People in turn must be given due respect due to their intrinsic dignity and human worth. Glannon, *Contemporary Readings in Biomedical Ethics,* 12.

10. The most well known deontologist is Immanuel Kant (1724 - 1804) who 2came up with the categorical imperative as a fundamental principle or supreme morality. The categorical imperative consists of two main formulations, universality of rules and treatment of persons as an end instead of a means to an end. For further reading see ibid, 13.
11. Beauchamp and Childress' work on the 'four principles' approach to bioethics is the most well known principle based approach. However, there are also other writers who have different notions as to what principles should be relied on in settling bioethical issues.
12. Virtue ethics focuses on what sort of person is ideal, and so action is considered to have secondary importance. Here, the cultivation of virtuous traits is viewed as morality's primary function. For a more detailed discussion see Beauchamp and Walters, *Contemporary Issues in Bioethics*, 17. See also Glannon, *Contemporary Readings in Biomedical Ethics*, 17.
13. The ethics of care focuses on a set of character that people deeply value like sympathy, compassion, fidelity, love, friendship and the like. See Beauchamp and Walters, 18. Glannon has used the term 'feminist ethics' to describe the ethics of care. This is primarily because caring and compassion are generally considered as "feminine" virtues. However, in addition to ethics of care as extrapolated by Beauchamp and Childress, feminist ethics as described by Glannon concerns also the addressing of ethical issues that particularly affect women. Glannon,19.
14. Casuistry focuses on decision-making based on the usage of particular cases, where judgements reached rely on prior judgements in earlier cases. This is very much like the concept of binding precedent used in common law jurisdictions. In actual fact, casuistry is not an ethical theory but is actually seen as an alternative method to ethical decision-making. In fact casuists are sceptical of principles and theories, and prefer to resolve ethical problems based on a case by case basis. For further elaboration see Beauchamp and Walters, 19 – 21.
15. Tom L. Beauchamp, and James F. Childress, *Principles of Biomedical Ethics (4th Ed.)* (New York: Oxford University Press, 1994), 84.
16. Feminist ethics is important in giving basis to the fight for women's reproductive freedom in particular. It seeks to readdress the balance of power between men and women and put the women on an equal scale with an equal voice on all ethical issues affecting women. For further reading see Glannon, p. 19.
17. Beauchamp and Walters have also discussed meta-ethics but under the heading on non-normative ethics. Glannon is rather brief in discussing it as matters concerning the properties of ethics, whereas Beauchamp and Walters explains that meta-ethics involves the analysis of the meanings of central terms in ethics such as right, obligation, good, virtue and responsibility. For further clarification see Glannon, p. 9 and Beauchamp & Walters, p. 3.
18. Although initially based on the Hobbesian morality which insists of a set of rules that people come to accept for mutual benefit,

contractarianism later developed into a morality that consists of a framework of impartial principles or rules that people agree upon for the mutual benefit of cooperation. See Glannon, 20.

19. Communitarianism actually is the opposite of the liberal understanding of ethical perceptions. It rejects liberal individualism that many ethical theories have in common and focuses more on the idea that individual conceptions of the good cannot be divorced from the values of community in which individuals live. As social beings, ethical conceptions must be raised within a common social framework. For further reading see Glannon, 23.
20. Many bioethicists consider religion and culture as factors which could not influence rational decision-making. According to Munson for example, "Rational persuasion alone is regarded as the basis for justification". See Munson, *Intervention and Reflection,* p. 4.
21. Rebecca J. Cook, Bernard M. Dickens, and Mahmoud F. Fathalla., *Reproductive Health and Human Rights. Integrating Medicine, Ethics and Law,* (Oxford: Clarendon Press, 2003), 64.
22. Cook, Dickens, and Fathalla, *Reproductive Health and Human Rights. Integrating Medicine, Ethics and Law,* 65.
23. There are writers who have tried to 'bridge' this gap. Segun for example opined that through transcultural bioethics, the universality of bioethics could be achieved without having to undermine distinct cultural identities. For further reading, see Segun Gbadegesin, "Bioethics and cultural diversity", in *A Companion to Bioethics* edited by Kuhse, and Singer, , 24.
24. This is evident especially in the approach to science and technology. For further reading see Mohd Hazim Shah, "A Tale of Two Scenarios in the Development of Science and Technology in Malaysia", in *Public Policy, Culture and the Impact of Globalisation in Malaysia,* edited by Mohd Hazim Shah and Phua Kai Lit, (Kuala Lumpur: Malaysian Social Science Association, 2004), 59 at 60.
25. Tom L. Beauchamp, and James F. Childress, *Principles of Biomedical Ethics (4th Ed.),* (Oxford University Press: New York, 1994).
26. In their approach, they have united the principle based and common-morality ethics. Common-morality relies heavily on ordinary shared moral beliefs for its content rather than relying on pure reason, natural law, a special moral sense etc. It is also the source of the principles in their approach to bioethics. For further understanding see Ibid, at 100 – 101, and 104.
27. Darryl R.J. Macer, "Ethics and Assisted Human Reproduction", in *The Novartis Journal,* Vol.1 (2000): 40 – 43. Retrieved from <http:www.biol.tsukuba.ac.jp/~macer/Papers/View.htm> (accessed on 15. 10. 2004).
28. Macer, "Ethics and Assisted Human Reproduction", 41.
29. They give examples of the possible meanings of autonomy, "'self-governance, liberty rights, privacy, individual choice, freedom of the will, causing one's behaviour and being one's own person". See Beauchamp and Childress, *Principles of Biomedical Ethics,* 120.

30. Beauchamp and Childress, *Principles of Biomedical Ethics*, 121.
31. *Ibid*, 125.
32. *Ibid*.
33 This is one of the major differences between Beauchamp and Childress' approach to bioethics if compared with the more traditional utilitarian and deontological theories. While utilitarian and deontological theories rely on one absolute theory that is binding and supports all actions, their principle based approach is only prima facie binding and may even be subject to revision. According to them, this leaves room for compromise in case of conflicts and opens the door to various methods of negotiation and mediation. For further reading see Beauchamp and Childress, 105.
34. *Ibid*, 126.
35. *Ibid*, 270.
36. Beauchamp and Childress, *Principles of Biomedical Ethics*, 189.
37. It is associated with the maxim *Primum non nocere* which means "Above all, do no harm" which is one of the first principles of the Hippocratic Oath. See ibid.
38. *Ibid*, 194.
39. *Ibid*.
40. Thomas R. McCormick, "Principles of Bioethics", in *Ethics in Medicine*, (Washington D.C.: University of Washington School of Medicine, 1998), retrieved from <http://eduserve.hscer.washinton.edu/bioethics/tools/princpl.html> (accessed on 14.10.2004), p. 4.
41. There are writers such as William Frankena, as noted by Beauchamp and Childress, who treats the principle of beneficence as also including non-maleficence, where one is considered to do good when one avoids from doing harm to others. In Frankena's words, "Beneficence is where one ought not inflict evil and ought to prevent evil, remove evil and do good" See Beauchamp and Childress, 190.
42. Beauchamp and Childress, *Principles of Biomedical Ethics* , 259.
43. *Ibid*.
44. *Ibid*, 260.
45. *Ibid*.
46. Beauchamp and Childress, *Principles of Biomedical Ethics*, 261.
47. *Ibid*, 269.
48. *Ibid*.
49. *Ibid*.
50. Beauchamp and Childress, *Principles of Biomedical Ethics*, 270.
51. *Ibid*, 270.
52. *Ibid*, 273.
53. Mabie, *Bioethics and The New Medical Technology*, 9.
54. For example in the case of the Jehovah's Witness.
55. Beauchamp and Childress, *Principles of Biomedical Ethics* , 329.
56. Mabie, *Bioethics and Modern Medical Technology*, 13.
57. McCormick, "Principles of Bioethics", 3.
58. He explains the tendency that bioethicists have in giving attention to the principle of respect for autonomy is due to the fact that autonomy is

central to the idea of liberal democracy. It is viewed as essential to the possibility of self-realisation and self-development. See Jacob D. Rendtorff, "Basic Principles in Bioethics and Biolaw", in *Bioethics and Medical Ethics*, retrieved from <http://www.bu.edu/wcp/Papers/Bioe/BioeRend.htm.>(accessed on 14.10.2004).

59. *Ibid*, 4.
60. Rendtorff, "Basic Principles in Bioethics and Biolaw", in *Bioethics and Medical Ethics*,, 3.
61. *Ibid*, 4. Incidentally, this is not too far from Beauchamp and Childress' approach to bioethics whereby they too formulated their four principles approach from common morality.
62. *Ibid*, 6.
63. The principle of human dignity is also an influential concept in Western tradition. It signifies that human beings have a special position that places them over the natural and biological position in nature. Since human beings have the capacity of moral reasoning, humans are endowed with dignity which carries with it their value and responsibility over their fate and the fate of other beings in this world. Human dignity is also closely related to autonomy as a person is autonomous, he is able to choose whether to protect his dignity or let it fall low and follow his desires. Ibid. It is a concept that is prevalent in the Universal Declaration on the Human Genome as well as the basis for policy making mechanism adopted by the United States President's Council on Bioethics.
64. Rendtorff's principle of integrity is rather confusing. It seems to bear great similarity to his concept of human dignity. He maintains that integrity concerns the "untouchable core of the personality that must not be subjected to unwarranted external intervention". Ibid, 7.
65. The principle of vulnerability is about the expression of the human condition. The fact that humans are vulnerable creatures manifests itself in laws that seek to protect vulnerable human beings. Recognition of this fact helps formulate the principle of vulnerability which forms the foundation for ethical notions of responsibility and care towards others. Recognizing the importance of this principle is crucial in considering the ethics concerned for the "fragility of the human condition". Ibid, 9.
66. Rendtorff, "Basic Principles in Bioethics and Biolaw", 9.
67. Mary Briody Mahowald, "Fertility Enhancement and the Right to Have a Baby" in *Contemporary Readings in Biomedical Ethics*, edited by Glannon, 169.
68. Mahowald quoting Joan Callahan and Patricia Smith, "Liberalism, Communitarianism and Feminism," in *Liberalism and Community*, edited by Noel Reynolds, Cornelius Murphy and Robert Moffat, New York: Edwin Mellen Press), at the time of her writing the article was forthcoming. Cited in her article at 169. Other writers have also noted this. Hursthouse also notices that "current philosophical literature on reproductive issues is largely limited to a vocabulary of rights and little attention is paid to the social and familial contexts in which reproductive decisions are usually made". See Rosalind Hursthouse, "Reproduction

and Ethics", in *Routledge Encyclopaedia of Philosophy,* edited by E. Craig, (London: Routledge, 1998), retrieved from http://www.rep.routledge.com/article/L083. (accessed on 21.1.2004).

69. Mahowald, *ibid.*
70. Mahowald, "Fertility Enhancement and the Right to Have a Baby," 170.
71. Article 1, Universal Declaration on Bioethics and Human Rights, 2005.
72. Article 2(a), Universal Declaration on Bioethics and Human Rights, 2005.
73. Article 2(c) and (d).
74. Article 2(d).
75. Article 2(f).
76. Article 2(g)
77. See Appendix 1, p. 9 for a list of the countries that have National Bioethics Committees.
78. John A. Robertson, "Human Embryonic stem cell research: ethical and legal issues", *Journal of Science and Society,* January 2001, Vol.2, 74.
79. *Ibid.*
80. "What else can they be", J.L. Sherley, "The importance of valid disclosures in the human embryonic stem cell research debate", Cell Proliferation, 2008, 41(Suppl. 1) 57 - 64, at p. 58.
81. *Ibid.*
82. *Ibid.*
83. Derek Morgan & Robert G. Lee. *Human Fertilization & Embryology Act 1990.* 1991. Blackstone Press: Oxford, p. 2.
84. This is the plural of the word fatwa which means a religious ruling that is issued by a group of jurists after they have done the necessary research and deliberations which is known as the exercise of their ijtihad. These jurists consider new situations which have not been mentioned in the Qur'an and Sunnah and issue a decree or ruling that will be followed by the public. In Malaysia, the institution of fatwa has been formally recognized whereby the National Fatwa Committee is given the power to deliberate and decide on matters brought to them and any fatwa issued will then be published so that it could be followed by all Muslims in Malaysia.
85. Morgan, p. 64-65. It is at this point that the Warnock Committee considered as the crucial transformation from molecular matter to a potential human being is established.

5

Legal Framework in Agricultural Biotechnology in Malaysia

Introduction

Biotechnology has emerged as a powerful technology that has a big potential for a number of economic sectors, including agriculture. Various basic human needs such as food, cloth, medicines, cleaner environment and pharmaceuticals have been fulfilled through biotechnological means. The convergence of these new technology platforms with the powerful information technology provides a greater understanding of the biology of plants, animals, humans, and microorganisms at the molecular level, enabling us to develop better strategies and approaches to deal with current and future challenges.[1] In Malaysia, the primary production or the upper stream is a shared responsibility of various government agencies such as the Department of Agriculture (DOA) for the production and supply of various agricultural produce, Department of Fisheries (DOF) for fish and related products and Department of Veterinary Services (DVS) for animal and animal based products.

The discussion in this chapter will be divided into three parts. Part one concentrates on the use of biotechnology in animal and animal products which is under the direct supervision of Department of Veterinary Services (DVS) which includes the application of the Animal Ordinance 1953, Animal Rule 1962 and application of various states enactments that regulate the licensing requirements for animal farming. The second part of this chapter continued on the use of biotechnology in fish and fisheries product which falls under the jurisdiction of the Department of Fisheries. Discussion is made on the laws, standards and the Code of Practice (Good Aqua Practice) adopted by the Department to ensure fish farmers are more responsible towards the consumers and the environment. The last part of the chapter deals with use of biotechnology in agriculture. The main discussion of this part is on the use of genetically modified plants and seed, its control and labeling of genetically modified foods.

Animal & Animal Products: Department of Veterinary Services (DVS)

The animal industry has become a fully integrated commercial sector producing quality food from animal products towards national self-sufficiency and export. The Department of Veterinary Services is committed in its objective to ensure the growth of a sound animal industry to supply quality and safe food from animal products for national consumption and exports. The department is responsible to promote the growth and development of a sound animal industry; to ensure that foods of animal origin are clean, wholesome and fit for human consumption; to promote the growth and development of the animal feeds industry and to ensure the welfare and well being of all animals. In doing so the department is bound to follow the various laws enacted on animal production.

The Animal Ordinance 1953[2] was enacted to amend and to consolidate the laws to prevent the introduction and spread of animal diseases within the Federation; to control the movement of animals, the slaughter of animals, and for the general welfare, conservation and improvement of livestock in the federation. It also covers the import and export of animals and birds. Section 33 to section 37 of the Ordinance generally governs the use of animal drugs. However, the Animal Ordinance 1953 does not provide for the use of GMO in animal feed.

The Animals Rules 1962 was drafted under section 86 of the Animal Ordinance 1953. The Rule addresses matters related to the import and export of animals and birds, control and licensing of breeding farms, control and licensing artificial insemination centres and poultry processing plants. The Animals (Importation) Order 1962 requires that all meat and livestock imported into Malaysia to be *halal*, safe and disease free. For purposes of human consumption, section 3(2) of the Order provides that importation must be subjected to the restrictions set out in the Second Schedule.

The Federal Animal Quarantine Station (Management and Maintenance) By-Laws 1984[3] was enacted to regulate the quarantine of animals imported into this country. It is a requirement under section 7 of the By-Laws that no animal should be admitted into the quarantine station unless an import licence of the animal has been obtained.

Apart from the Federal law, there are various states enactments that have been enacted to govern matters related to animal production. Part III, section 6(1), (2) of the Control and Licensing of Poultry Farming and Poultry Related Activities (Negeri Sembilan) Enactment 1996, provides that no person shall carry out poultry farming or any poultry related activity unless within licence issued under the Enactment. Section 9 further provides that any person who operates or carries out any poultry farming or any poultry related activity without licence is committing an offence. Similar licensing requirement is imposed by section 6(1), (2) of Control and Licensing of Poultry Farming (Johore) Enactment 1997.

Besides, various State Enactments have been passed to control and regulate pig-farming activities. Since this is within state jurisdiction, certain states, for instance Selangor, imposed strict requirements. It is a requirement under section 6(1) of the Control of Pig Farming Activities (Selangor) Enactment 1991[4] that the State Authority will, by notification declare any area in the State as a "Pig Farming Area".

Biotechnology in Animal Farming/Production

The Department of Veterinary Services (DVS) is responsible for ensuring the safety, wholesomeness, and accurate labeling of meat, meat food products, and poultry products under the Animal Ordinance 1953, the Animals Rules 1962, and the

Animals (Importation) Order 1962. However, none of these regulations address the issue related to the biological products for administration to animals.[5] There is an active legal framework for animal biotechnology. A good example is the issue of gene improvement under section 51 of the Animal Ordinance 1953. Although regulated, it is still limited in terms of enforcement.[6]

The Department of Veterinary Services also plays an important role in controlling the import and export of 'technology' for purposes of research. This includes the import and export of semen, and other biological materials. The importer or exporter must comply with certain requirements such as to apply for a veterinary health certificate and to declare the 'species and health status of that animal. The main objective of the import and export control is to curb or to prevent animal diseases. Nevertheless it does not include the import and export of live animals that has gone through genetic engineering.

To date, for the purpose of animal production for human consumption, the technology used is still at a very basic level i.e. cross-breeding between a local animal and an imported animal that has big potential to increase productivity. Currently, there is no biotechnology that involves the molecular level or extraction of DNA that requires laboratory research.[7]

Meanwhile, in terms of food safety, animal welfare and use of growth promotants, antibiotics and animal drugs in animal feed, references will be made to the Food Regulations 1985. In addition, it is also said that use of biotechnology in animal production for human consumption does not face any serious or fundamental legal issues. There is no urgent need to have a separate Act to regulate biotechnology in animal production in this country. It is perceived that the existing Animal Ordinance 1953 and Food Regulations 1985 provide adequate legal provisions to the present situation. Aside from that the Biosafety Act 2007 does not in any way affect the present practice of biotechnology in animal production for human consumption and food security in this country.[8]

DVS Import and Export Control

The following chart shows a simplified version of how the DVS controls the import and export of animals and birds.

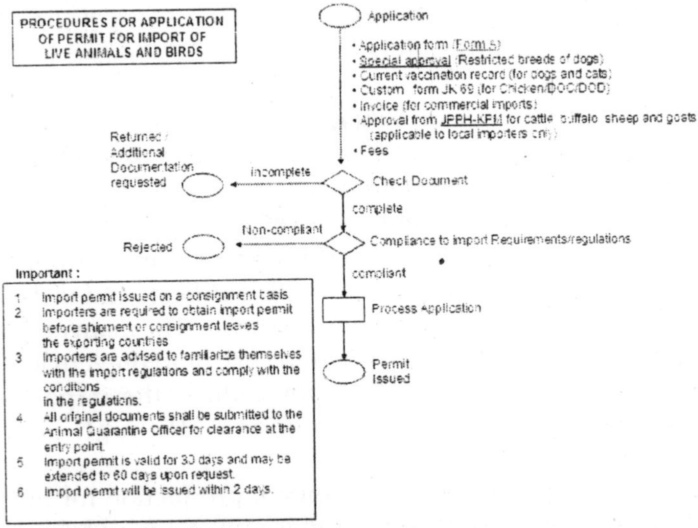

Jabatan Perkhidmatan Veterinar
Department of Veterinary Services Malaysia

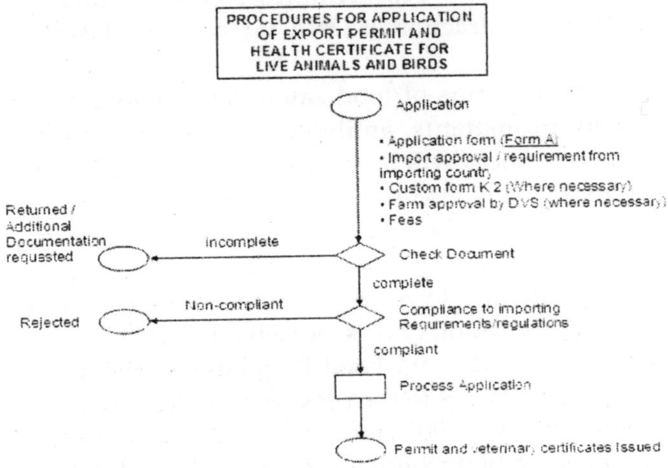

1. Veterinary certificate to be issued within seven (7) days of export
2. Permit and veterinary certificate issued within 3 days of application

Fish and Fisheries Product: Department of Fisheries (DOF)

The Fisheries Act 1974 governs various matters relating to fishing and fish products in Malaysia. Section 4(2)[9] empowers the Lembaga (Board) to regulate the marketing of fish, the licensing of wholesalers, retailers, fish-processors, importers and exporters; to prescribe and regulate the packing, grading, weighing and storing of fish; to establish, regulate and if necessary, manage any area where wholesale fish market is to be carried out; to regulate the processing of fish; to prohibit, regulate or control the movement of fish, and etc. In addition, the Fish Marketing Regulations 1973[10] provides for the licensing of the sale of fish within a controlled area, the packaging of fish for sale within a controlled area and also the grading of fish before sale.

Part IV of the Fisheries Act 1985[11] provides the general licensing provision for fishing activities allowed to operate in Malaysia. For riverine fishing and turtles which are within the jurisdiction of the States, various state laws have been passed to adopt the provisions of the Fisheries Act 1985.[12]

In addition, the Department of Environment is empowered under section 25 (restriction on pollution of inland waters) and section 27 (prohibition of discharge of waste into Malaysian waters) of the Environmental Quality Act 1974, to control pollution of inland waters and discharge of waste into Malaysian waters. The scope of duties of the DOF does not directly deal with the use of biotechnology in fishing practices or in increasing and processing of fish products.

Standards/Guidelines: Good Aquaculture Practice (GAqP)

A voluntary scheme is managed by the Department of Fisheries for aquafarmers to promote Good Farming Practices, (i.e. more responsible and environmental friendly practices) at the farm level to ensure product quality and safety, consistency in production and remain competitive in the global market. Important elements incorporated into the scheme are ISO 9002, SSOP (Standard Sanitary and Operating Procedures), Product Standards and Specifications, compliance with the COP and Good Aquaculture Practices (GAqP) and other terms and conditions as determined by the Department of Fisheries Malaysia.

Objectives of the Programme are as follows:

1. To improve the product safety and quality;
2. To make the industry more responsible, more eco-friendly to ensure sustainable development for the future;
3. To prevent the occurrence of fish diseases and pollution;
4. To encourage the Good Aquaculture Practices based on Aquaculture's Code of Practice (COP);
5. To enhance the marketing;
6. Preparation for the implementation of HACCP for aquaculture products "voluntarily" by the fish farmers; and
7. To control the use of pesticides and dangerous chemicals in fish farming.

***Code of Conduct for Responsible Fisheries* (CCRF)**

The CCRF provides various aspects for the conduct and management of fisheries in Malaysia. There is no specific clause that governs the use of biotechnology in fisheries production. However, clauses 12.1 and 12.2 of CCRF states that the state should be responsible for the scientific development in fish and fisheries production and should do whatever is necessary to promote research in various areas including biology, ecology, environmental science, and other areas. This could be presumed to have also included the use of biotechnology in enhancing fisheries in Malaysia.[13] It is further stated that states should establish an appropriate institutional framework to determine the applied research which is required and its proper use.[14]

Although the Department of Fisheries has conducted various programmes at farm levels nevertheless none of these programmes spell out the requirements for the use of feeds that may contain GMOs, neither do the programmes prohibit fish farming using biotechnology. In addition, all the regulations are silent on the usage of biotechnology in fish farming in this country.

Regulatory Issues[15]

To date, the Fisheries Research Institute is getting involved in DNA Profiling, vaccine development for treatment of fish diseases, molecular genetics for the purpose of identifying the gene quality and probiotics collection of microbes for water treatment.

Based on the interview conducted, to date there is no problem involving gene manipulation in the fisheries industry in Malaysia. It is the stand taken by the government not to allow gene manipulation for fish produce for human consumption in order to avoid any possible controversy.[16] However, there has been a small practice of gene manipulation for ornamental fish but only at a very minimum level.

Bio-safety Act 2007 and Fisheries Activities

In the interview it was said that although the Bio-safety Act 2007 does not contain any specific provision for the use of biotechnology in fisheries for human consumption, nevertheless the Act 2007 is sufficient for the present situation. It was further added that the Act 2007 does not in any way affect fisheries activities for human consumption. In addition, there is no necessity to have a specific Act to govern fishing activities in Malaysia.

Agricultural Produce: Department of Agriculture (DOA)

Malaysia has dedicated a sizable proportion of land area to agriculture. As of 2006, Malaysia had more than 4.1 million hectares planted with oil palms and more than 1.2 million hectares planted with rubber trees. In addition, Malaysia dedicated more than 681,000 hectares to rice cultivation and more than 141,000 hectares to coconut plantations. In total, more than 6.2 million hectares or 19 percent of Malaysia's total land area is dedicated to the production of 11 major crops. When other minor crops and pasture and rangeland are taken into account, Malaysia's total land area dedicated to agriculture approaches 30 percent. Malaysia relies heavily on its agriculture sector for foreign revenue as well as for domestic consumption and therefore places strong emphasis on monitoring and preserving agricultural biodiversity.[17]

Agricultural biodiversity includes all components of biological diversity of relevance to food and agriculture. It also includes all components of biological diversity that support the ecosystems of which agriculture is a part of (agro-ecosystems): the variety and variability of animals, plants and micro-organisms, at the genetic, species and ecosystem levels, which are necessary to sustain key functions of the agro-ecosystem, its structure and processes. Thematic areas includes genetic resources for food and agriculture, including cultivated or domesticated species and their wild relatives, the components of agricultural biodiversity that support the provision of ecosystem services upon which agriculture is based, a biotic factors, which have a determining effect on agricultural biodiversity, such as physical landscapes within which agriculture occurs, or the way in which agriculture manages landscapes in order to manage agricultural biodiversity, and the socio-economic and cultural dimensions since agricultural biodiversity is largely shaped by human activities and management practices and large numbers of people depend on agricultural biodiversity for sustainable livelihoods.[18]

Malaysia signed the United Nations Convention on Biological Diversity on the 12th of June 1992, and ratified it two years later on the 24th of June, 1994. As a signatory to the convention, Malaysia is committed to sustainable development, management, and conservation of all her natural resources. As part of Malaysia's commitments under the convention, Malaysia has set up a Clearing House Mechanism (CHM) to facilitate reporting and the transfer of biological diversity and conservation-related information, both nationally and internationally. The Clearing House Mechanism (CHM) provides links to more than 70 informative web pages. Among these are links to national policy documents, national reports to various Multi-lateral Environmental Agreement (MEA) bodies, biological inventory databases, curated collections, directories of resource individuals and pertinent government ministries, departments and agencies.

Protection of New Plant Varieties Act 2004

Since the early 19th century, the introduction of new varieties in agriculture and forestry has been an essential component to maintain and sustain good and high crop productivity and quality. New varieties are constantly being bred for higher yields, for better agronomic traits like taste, for resistance against pest or diseases, and for tolerance to saline or drought conditions, etc. The Department of Agriculture (DOA) has been registering fruit clones since the early 1930's and was officially made the National Registrar of Varieties in 1994 by the Ministry of Agriculture. The responsibility of implementing the PNPV Act 2004 has been entrusted to the DOA Malaysia.

The Malaysian government has realised the importance of Plant Varieties Protection (PVP) for the development of the country. Malaysia, is a member of the World Trade Organization (WTO) and a signatory to the TRIPS Agreement, which under Article 27.3 (b), stipulates that member countries shall provide for the protection of plant varieties by a patent or by an effective *sui generis* system or by any combination thereof. As such, Malaysia is able to fulfill its obligation under Article 27.3 (b) of the TRIPS Agreement with the introduction of the PVP legislation.[19]

Under this PNPV Act 2004, the scope of a breeder's right extends to acts carried out on a commercial basis including producing or reproducing, conditioning for the purpose of propagation, offering for sale, marketing, exporting, importing and stocking the material for the earlier activities. Hence, unauthorised conduct of such acts will constitute an infringement under the PNPV law.[20] The rights of plant breeders are further expanded by the Protection of New Plant Varieties Regulations 2008 (PNPV).[21]

Plant Quarantine Regulations 1981

Regulation 4(1) (a) of the Plant Quarantine Regulations 1981[22] states that plants imported into this country must be inspected, and if found to be diseased or infested, may be treated or destroyed. This regulation is meant to curb plant diseases from being brought into this country.

Food Regulations 1985

To ensure safe food production, it is necessary that soil and water used for irrigation in the primary production is free from any contamination. Under the Farm Accreditation Scheme Malaysia (SALM), the Department of Environment is given the task to monitor that the use of soil and water in primary production is in compliance with the Environmental Quality Act 1974.

Use of Genetically Modified Seed or Plant

Good Agricultural Practice (GAP): This is a national programme implemented by the Department of Agriculture to recognise and certify farms which adopt good agricultural practices (GAP), operate in an environmentally friendly way and yielding products that are of quality, safe and suitable for human consumption. It prescribes the minimum standard of conditions that must be fulfilled before certification is given. The standards of condition constitute the minimum most praiseworthy and commendable conducts of farming a farmer should adopt. In fulfilling the conditions, farmers are discouraged from using any genetically modified planting materials. Farms conforming to the stipulated conditions will receive a certificate of official recognition, which allows the producer to affix seals of quality on their products destined for domestic and international markets. This would work as a marketing tool for their produce.

Use of GMO Agricultural Seed: The use of GMO seeds, or specifically, any GMO planting materials, is discouraged under the Good Agriculture Practice Scheme Malaysia (SALM).

Under the scheme the farm must satisfy the following conditions:

1. The farm is a legal entity.
2. The farm has a soil inspection report.
3. The soil and terrain is suitable for the intended crop.
4. The farm is situated at an elevation less than 1000 meters above sea level.
5. The farm practices sound soil conservation measures.
6. The farm maintains up-to-date records of activities.
7. Sewage or industrial sludge is not permitted for fertilisation.
8. Genetically Modified planting materials are not permitted.
9. The pesticides used are legally registered by the Pesticides Board.
10. The farm practices integrated pest management (IPM).
11. The farm posses a proper storage for pesticides and fertilisers.
12. Farm workers use personal protective clothing when applying the pesticides.
13. The farm possesses a proper waste disposal plan.
14. The farm practises good harvesting techniques, handling and transport.
15. The farm employs workers that are legal aged more than 16 years old.
16. Pesticides residues in farm produce are less than the MRL of Schedule 16 of the Food Act 1985.
17. Contents of heavy metals are below permissible limits of Schedule 14 of the Food Act 1983.[23]

Although the scheme prohibits the usage of GM seeds, nevertheless there is no policy statement developed by DOA that requires mandatory compliance with the scheme. To date this programme is on voluntary basis. As a result not all farms in Malaysia will adhere to this condition. Thus there could be many unregistered farms that use GM seeds which could not be identified by the Department of Agriculture. Hence, a big volume of genetically modified agricultural produce may have entered the local supply chain.

SJPM - 1/2001, Malaysia Standard MS 469: 1993 - Specification for Rice (Oryza Sativa) Seed For Planting

This Guideline is used for the purpose of producing high seeds of high quality and standards according to current conditions and demand. It was formulated based on a few standards such as Indian Minimum Seed Certification Standards (March, 1971), Department of Agriculture, New Delhi, Minimum Seed Certification Standards (1960),Provincial Department Of Agriculture And Forestry, Taiwan, Quality Declared Seed, Technical Guidelines For Standards And Procedures (1993) FAO Plant Production And Protection, Paper 117-ROME, and Minimum Seed Certification Standards (1991). This standard is silent on the use of GMO seed in padi (rice) farming in Malaysia. It is more for the purpose of ensuring food security for national consumption. Although it contains labeling specifications but it is meant for seed identification purposes.

GMF Labelling and Food that Contains GMOs

Ever since genetically modified food (GMF) came into the chain of food production, it has become a world issue to provide labelling for GMF. In Malaysia, there is no requirement to label the GMF but there is a real need to consider this matter seriously by the government on the grounds that some food may not be taken by some consumers due to religious, medical or health reasons. Furthermore, there are foods that may contain animal genes and this is not supposed to be taken by vegetarians. In addition, consumers make decisions about what they eat for a wide variety of religious, health, ethical, philosophical and emotional reasons. Most major world religions have some rules or traditions as to food. Jews and Muslims do not eat pork; Christians often avoid meat on Fridays or during Lent and many Buddhist are vegetarians.[24]

To date, the Food Regulations 1985 only provides for the compulsory labelling of cultured milk or fermented milk.[25] Aside from that, regulation 26A provides for the compulsory labelling requirements for the use of bifido bacteria in food items in order to assist the appropriate storage for this food.[26] In this respect, bifido bacteria is treated as a food additive and nutrient supplement that enhances the health benefits of that particular food item. Generally the Food Regulations contain comprehensive labelling requirements for fruit and fruit products,[27] vegetable and vegetable products such as tomato puree, tomato pulp, vegetable juice and soya bean products,[28] tea, coffee and its related products,[29] cocoa and cocoa products,[30] jam fruit jelly, marmalade[31] and others. Nevertheless none of these provisions require the labelling of GMOs/GMF even when it is present in the product.

The European Union (EU) has introduced regulations requiring labelling of all GMF. In the U.S., where genetically engineered corn, soybeans and potatoes are being grown commercially, repeated public opinion surveys show consumers overwhelmingly want labelling.[32] A survey sponsored by Novaritis found that more than 90% of Americans want labelling.[33] The United States Food and Drugs Authority (USFDA) announced new rules governing the testing and labelling of GMF. The Food and Drugs Authority (FDA) plans to publish a proposed rule mandating that developers of GMF and animal feeds notify the agency at least 120 days before they intend to market such products.[34]

In Australia, the labelling requirements for food containing genetically modified organisms came into force on 7th December 2001. It was agreed that, although genetically modified food sold in Australia has had to firstly pass a rigorous safety assessment, nevertheless, there are consumers who have objections to genetically modified food. Therefore, it is crucial that GMF is properly labelled to enable people to make an informed choice about the products they choose.[35]

Similarly, in Hong Kong, consumer movements have suggested an identification standard of 0.1% (that means manufacturers must label any food that contains at least 0.1%

GMF). It was also suggested that for illiterate and senior citizens who are not able to read the tiny characters on a label, presenting labelling information with graphic symbols would be helpful. In such cases, the Chief Executive of the Hong Kong Consumer Council commented that, steps taken by the Malaysian law regarding the special lettering requirements for certain food, such as diabetic, margarine, milk and milk products, are good practices to be followed.[36]

In Japan, it has been reported that the largest Japanese corn buyer announced to the American Corn Growers Association (ACGA) that U.S. corn farmers exporting to Japan must segregate their GM crops from non-GM crops. The Manager of the Feed Grain Department for Murubeni America Corporation is reported to have said that the segregation is required for food crops, as Japanese consumers are growing increasingly wary of GMF.

In addition, in 1998, Jean Halloran and Michael Hansen from the Consumer Policy Institute/Consumer Union, U.S, identified eight reasons why genetically engineered food must be labelled. Among those are; GMF is different and not 'substantially equivalent' with the original food; GMF can cause toxic effects as shown by one of the very first products introduced into the market in the late 1980s, whereby Showa Denko company of Japan began making tryptophan (an amino acid used as dietary supplements) by a new process, using genetically engineered bacteria and selling it in the U.S. Within months, thousand of people who had taken the supplement began to suffer from eosinophilia myalga syndrome, which included neurological problems. Eventually at least 1500 were permanently disabled and 37 died;[37] GMF can cause allergic reactions;[38] GMF can increase antibiotic resistance. For instance, the genetically engineered Bt maize plant from Novartis, includes an ampicillin-resistence gene. Ampicillin is a valuable antibiotic used to treat a variety of infection in people and animals. A number of European countries, including Britain, have refused to permit the Novatis Bt corn to be grown, because of concern that the ampicillin resistence gene could move from the corn into bacteria in the food chain, making ampicillin a less effective weapon against bacterial infections.[39]

Therefore, based on the above findings, and for the general interest of consumers, it is strongly proposed that there should be a proper labelling of GMF under Malaysian law. Additionally, being a multiracial country with a big population of Malay, Chinese and Indians who are generally classified as Muslims, Buddhists and Hindus, food is taken not only to satisfy hunger but also according to religious obligations. For instance, food injected with animal genes such as pig or frog is prohibited for the Muslims and food with animal origin is not to be taken by the vegetarians. Thus apart from food safety, it is also a social responsibility of the producers to label the ingredients accordingly.

Bio-safety Act 2007

Although the Malaysian laws are silent on the use and labelling of GMF in form of finished products, nevertheless in 2007 the Biosafety Act was enacted with the main objective to regulate the release activities and import activities involving living modified organisms.

The Bio-safety Act 2007 is the basis for regulating the biosafety aspects of biotechnology. It sets forth a number of procedures and rules regulating the release, importation, exportation and contained use of living modified organisms and the release of such products of such organisms; in order to protect the human, plant, and animal health, the environment and biological diversity. The National Biosafety Board is tasked with the duty to oversee that the procedures and rules are complied with (*see Section 4 and 5*); and generally acting under the recommendation of the Genetic Modification Advisory Committee and various other governmental agencies.

Part III of the Act regulates all release and import activities involving living modified organisms. "Release activities" means the intentional introduction of living modified organisms or products of such organisms into the environment through the activities or for the purposes specified in the Second

Schedule.[40] The Second Schedule list down details of the activities that would fall under the scope of "release activities". It includes research and development purpose in all field experiments; supply or offer to supply for sale or placing on the market; offer as gift, prize or free item; disposal; remediation purposes, and any other activity which does not amount to contained use. All release and import activities which involve living modified organisms must be approved by the National Biosafety Board. The approval process itself is rigorous and demanding in nature; requiring the industry players to submit scientific risk assessment and management and also an emergency response plan.[41] In addition, the Board and the Advisory Committee have the right to request additional information at any stage of the application as they see fit. The reports would be scrutinised and assessed by the Advisory Committee - a body which consists of science-based experts and experts from other relevant disciplines - and the Advisory Committee would then forward its recommendations to the Board for consideration. The Board would then grant the application by issuing a certificate of approval or refuse the application on such terms and conditions as it thinks fit. The governmental agencies and the public would be consulted as well; although the extent of public participation in the process is limited by section 59 of the Act which protects industry players from disclosing confidential information. Neverthless, the extent of the effect of Section 59 in obstructing public participation is yet to be seen.

The dawn of biotechnology brings with it many great benefits as well as great concerns over the impact that living modified organisms might have on the environment and on the safety of consumers' food. The Bio-safety Act 2007 mandates that the industry players seeking approval for the release and import activities by submiting a report on risk assessment and the proposed measures that shall be undertaken to prevent, minimise or control the risks and adverse effects the living modified organisms on human, plant, and animal health, the environment and biological diversity. The National Bio-safety

Board and the Advisory Committee would formulate their views based on the science-based risk assessment and management report. Presumably the public has access to these documents in order to scrutinise the potential impact one given activity might have on the human and animal health and the environment. In the light of the theoretical drawbacks and the tangible benefits of biotechnology, the risk assessment and management report are the only ways for the governmental agencies, the public and any academic institutions to formulate their views objectively. The right of the public to voice their opinions may promote greater accountability amongst the industry players; as they are the industry's target group.

An emergency response plan should come together with the risk assessment and management report.[42] It enumerates the safety measures and procedures for protection of human and animal health and the environment in the event of an emergency. The approved person shall coordinate any emergency relief operation together with the relevant governmental agencies and the costs of any mitigated action shall be borne by the approved person.[43] In addition, section 36(2) of the Act dictates the approved person must comply with any minimum risk management measures as determined by the Board after consultation with the Advisory Committee.

Malaysia, being a party to the Cartagena Protocol on Bio-safety, has reaffirmed and reiterated the precautionary approach stated in, among others, the preamble of the Bio-safety Protocol, by enacting section 35 of the Bio-safety Act. Under the provision, the Board or Minister may take appropriate action where there is lack of scientific certainty due to lack of scientific data, information, analysis, or knowledge as to the extent of potential damage any living modified organisms might have on human, plant, and animal health, the environment and biological diversity. It is said that the section validates the Board's or the Minister's decision 'to err on the side of caution'. The same section allows the Board or the Minister to take into account socio-economic considerations in reaching a decision.

Exportation/Contained Use of Living Modified Organisms/ Importation for the Purpose of Contained Use of Living Modified Organisms

The rules for the exportation of living modified organisms are enumerated in Part IV of the Bio-safety Act. Generally, any person seeking to export any living modified organism must notify his intention to the National Bio-safety Board. This duty can be discharged by conforming to the rules and regulations of importing countries and to inform the Board of such requirements. The exporter must comply with the rules and regulations of the importing party for the purpose of ensuring the safe movement and handling of products containing living modified organisms. This is, again, a reaffirmation of the Advanced Informed Agreement contained in the Cartagena Protocol on Bio-safety which, in effect, requires an exporter to seek consent from importing countries before any shipment of any living modified organism meant to be introduced into the environment.

For the activities of contained use and importation for the purpose of contained use, any person involved must give prior notification to the Board. "Contained use" is interpreted under section 3 of the Bio-safety Act as any operation including research and development, production or manufacturing operation involving living modified organisms, or storage of living modified organisms, undertaken within a facility, installation or other physical structure such that it prevents the contact and impact of the living modified organisms on the external environment. The notification must be accompanied by an emergency response plan; the specific measures to be taken; and other information as specified by the Board.[44] The Director General of the Board would then issue an acknowledgement of receipt of notification and the approved person may proceed to undertake such activities subject to any order by the Board under subsection 30(3).[45] The Advisory Committee is entitled to make recommendations on notification to the Board after assessing the paperwork. Upon the issuance of an acknowledgement of receipt of notification, the Board may make further appropriate order if it is satisfied that there is a risk posed to human, plant, or animal health, the environment and biological diversity; or where the approved person fails to comply with any term and condition imposed on the notification; or failure to comply with the order of the Board; or where the approved person has contravened the provisions of the Bio-safety Act or any regulation made thereon regardless of any prosecution; or where the approved person has been convicted for an offence under the Bio-safety Act or any regulation made under it.[46]

Liability

The Bio-safety Act also addresses liability committed by a body corporate and individual. Section 64 of the Act reiterates the duty of care that a director owes to the company which he is responsible for including the day-to-day management of and conduct of the company. The Act makes them liable for the offences committed under the Act or any regulation made thereunder.

As to the liability of the individual, he shall be liable to any penalty prescribed for a particular offence under the Act or any regulations made thereunder. If the offence was committed by his agent, partner, or servant, then he can avoid responsibility if he proves that the offence was committed without his knowledge, consent or connivance and he has taken all reasonable precautions and exercised due diligence to prevent the commission of the offence.[47]

Administrative Framework/National Policy on Biotechnology

Malaysia's Clearing House Mechanism (CHM)

The primary objective of the CHM is to provide a mechanism for the efficient exchange of information on biological diversity in Malaysia between involved persons and institutions. In addition, the CHM portal facilitates international access to information on the status of biodiversity studies and biodiversity management in Malaysia. In line with the CHM philosophy, the system will collate information from a variety of different sources, provide easy access to and make available for public circulation, information, databases and other relevant material, provided by the various stakeholders.

National Strategy for the Conservation of Malaysia's Biological Diversity

The Convention also provides an important framework for Malaysia's integration of natural resources and environment and biodiversity management policies. Article 6 of the Convention obliges all parties to develop and implement the National Biodiversity Strategy and Action Plans.

The principles clearly state that the utilization of biological diversity, including the development of bio-technology, and the principles and practice of biosafety should be adhered to by all parties.[48] It is also stated in the principles that the Malaysian government is duty bound to formulate and implement the policy framework for sustainable management and utilization of biological diversity in close cooperation with scientists, the business community and the public.[49] In addition, it is the objective of Malaysia's National Biodiversity Policy to emphasise on biosafety considerations in the development and application of biotechnology.[50]

Support of Capacity Building Activities for the Implementation of the Cartagena Protocol on Biosafety[51]

This project was aimed at assisting Malaysia to fully implement the obligations under the Cartagena Protocol to matters related to transboundary movement of LMOs. This includes the assessment, management and long term monitoring of the risk to the sustainable use of biodiversity and to human health potentially posed by the introduction of LMOs. This could be achieved through the strengthening of the national biosafety framework with the necessary regulations, enhanced technical capacity and enforcement and monitoring capacities as well as the existence of a well managed information and coordination network.

Under this programme several activities have been planned as follows:

- To organise a series of workshops to formulate guidelines for the establishment of an Institutional Biosafety Committee;
- To organise a series of workshops to formulate guidelines and Standard Operating Procedures (SOPs) for research on GMOs in contained trials and laboratories;
- To organise a series of consultative workshops to review forms and the whole process for notification on GMO research;
- To organise a series of consultative workshops to review the proposed application forms, the application and approval processes for release of LMOs (R&D trials and for commercial purpose);
- To review process for exemption, identify products to be exempted from AIA (Advanced Informed Agreement) and the appropriate application regimes;
- To review the utility of a "User Guide in making an application" for a user-friendly application process;
- To organize workshops for biosafety officers who will serve in their respective IBCs (Institutional Biosafety Committee) to review research proposals on GMO research to check for proper risk assessment and that management procedures are in place for contained use;
- To organise a special workshop for enforcement officers to acquire basic knowledge in investigation skills or procedures; LMO identification and sampling procedures; documentation; AIA procedures; and risk management;
- To organise a "hands-on" workshop for GMAC (Genetic Modification Advisory Committee) members on handling requests and applications for release of LMOs, using real dossiers and administered under the proposed Biosafety Act;

- To organise workshops for biosafety officers who will serve in their respective IBCs to review research proposals on GMO research to check for proper risk assessment and that management procedures are in place for contained use.

It is expected that the said project could achieve the following outputs:

1. Enhanced management capacity at the national level.
2. Implementation of the national risk management regime.
3. Enforcement of laws and regulations under the Biosafety Act.
4. Better coordination between different enforcement agencies.
5. Better cooperation and partnerships between public and private sectors.
6. Increased capacity for focused research in biosafety.
7. Increased capacity in risk assessment, for implementation and enforcement of a national risk management programme, as the officers trained under this proposed project would be able to train others in their respective fields; and
8. Increased awareness and understanding on biosafety issues among government-officials and policy makers.

Conclusion and Suggestions for Reform

Animal Products

The Department of Veterinary Services (DVS) has not published a formal policy governing new gene transfer technologies when applied to food-producing animals. For instance, it was presented that the statutory food safety requirements for animal drug residues in genetically modified animals are the same as those for other animal drugs. Basically, the food products produced from genetically modified animals must be as safe as those from non-transgenic animals; and the sponsor of the transgenic animals must demonstrate safety of the animal products before the animal can enter the food supply.

Secondly, the Department of Veterinary Services should consider the development of a comprehensive, risk-based Animal Feed Safety System (AFSS) describing how animal feeds (individual ingredients and mixed feeds) should be manufactured and distributed to minimise risks to animals consuming the feed and people consuming food products from animals. To date there is no act that requires ingredients used in animal feed to be listed on the product label.

Preference could be made to various practices implemented by other countries. For instance, in the United States, the Federal regulations require ingredients to be listed on the product label by their common or usual name in descending order of predominance according to weight.[52] There is only one exception to the requirement to list the common or usual name on the label, that is when the ingredient is part of a collective name. Regulation 21 CFR 501.110 describes the use of collective names. The following are acceptable collective names: animal protein products forage products, grain products, plant protein products, processed grain byproducts and roughage products. These collective names may be used in the ingredient list for livestock and poultry feeds, but not pet foods.[53]

Thirdly, although use of growth promotants, antibiotics, and animal drugs are governed by the Food Regulations 1985, nevertheless both Food Regulations 1985 and Animal Ordinance 1953 are silent on the use of animal feed that contains GMOs. It is strongly believed that legal provisions must be enacted to provide for the administration and safe use of animal feed that contains GMOs.

Fourthly, both import and export control exercised by the Department of Veterinary Services impose no restriction or control over import or export of live animal produced through biotechnology or transgenic animals. Thus, it is suggested the import and export control should also include the necessary requirements for the import and export of GM products. For example, the importer must get a declaration from the relevant authority of the country of origin that the imported animals are transgenic animals or the animal products containing GMOs.

Bio-safety

It was admitted in the Malaysia's National Policy on Biological Diversity that the creation, transportation, handling and release of genetically modified organisms (GMOs) carry certain environmental, safety and health risks that are still inadequately understood. For instance, the introduction of GMOs could have adverse effects on ecological stability in forests and farms, in unintended or unpredictable ways, if the process is not properly controlled. Genetically modified plants may interbreed with their wild relatives and their progeny could become pests. The release of GMOs may have adverse natural feedback as our knowledge of their population dynamics is limited. Biosafety concerns should thus receive high priority. In the development of biotechnology, especially genetic engineering, there must be corresponding development of an adequate regulatory framework for bio-safety.

Food Labelling

The Bio-safety Act includes a mandatory labelling of products containing living modified organisms.[54] "Products of such organisms" means any product derived from a living modified organism or part of a living modified organism if the product contains detectable recombinant DNA; or where the profile, characteristic or properties of the product is or are no longer equivalent to its conventional counterpart irrespective of the presence of recombinant DNA. Thus, the question of whether to label GM products or not has been replaced with how to label them. To date, Malaysia has yet to reconcile the provision with the Food Regulations 1985 or issue any implementation guidelines. The Cartagena Protocol on Bio-safety did not address the issue of labelling, as its mandate is to address the issue of bio-safety. The issue of consumer safety and preference was not part of the negotiation.

Until then, the question remains as to possible exemption that may be granted to the mandatory labelling if the amount of detectable recombinant DNA is negligible or extremely small and the product is similar to its conventional counterpart. For instance, Regulation (EC) No. 1830/2003 exempts labelling requirement for products containing less than 0.9% of genetically modified organisms, if such traces are adventitious or technically unavoidable.

And then there is the question of the need for a specific designation for products containing living modified organisms, apart from the traditional labelling of nutritional content and value found in food. In the United States of America, the Food and Drug Administration discouraged manufacturers from labelling their products as "GM free" as they considered it misleading, denoting the meaning that such food is more superior than GM food. In Malaysia, the Food Act 1983 prohibits misleading labelling (Section 16) and the Section 18 of the Food Regulations 1985 prohibits labelling of unnecessary matters. A designation such as "Biotechnology Product" is generally considered to be more appealing than the designation "May Contain Genetically Modified Organisms".

It has been said that legislators should be prudent in balancing the interests of the consumers and industry players as unnecessary stringent rules and regulations would burden the industry players and also discourage consumers from purchasing such products. Ultimately, retailers will refuse to stock GM products and this will spell the doom for the entire biotechnology industry in Malaysia; the very industry Malaysia is trying to champion.

Transportation

The Bio-safety Act 2007 did not explicitly regulate the issue of transportation of living modified organisms or products containing such. Presumably, the issue of transportation and safety movement of LMO would be considered for safety evaluation during the application and notification process under Part III and Part IV of the Bio-safety Act respectively.

Guidelines could be made, however, to the Cartagena Protocol on Bio-safety. Article 18 of the Protocol addresses these issues.

Proper documentation is also seen as crucial in ensuring safe trans-boundary movement of living modified organisms under the Protocol. Any LMO which is intended to be released into the environment of the importing party must identify the shipment as containing LMO as well as its traits and characteristics. The documentation must also include requirements for safe handling, storage, transport and use, the name and address of the exporter and importer as well as a declaration that the movement is in conformity with the Protocol. A contact point for further information must be included as well. A similar requirement of documentation is to be applied to shipments of LMO for contained use.

Shipments of LMO intended for direct use as food or feed or for processing must be included in the documentation, that the shipment "may contain" LMO and is not intended for intentional introduction into the environment. A contact point for further information must be included.

Suggestions for Reform

GM Labelling: Consumers have a right to be informed about the products that they buy. Indeed some ethical aspects of GMOs fall within the context of the right to adequate food which is derived from the Universal Declaration of Human Rights.

> "The availability of food in a quantity and quality sufficient to satisfy the dietary needs of individuals, free from adverse substance, and acceptable within a given culture; the accessibility of such food in ways that are sustainable and that do not interfere with the enjoyment of other human rights."
>
> (E/C.121/1999/5)

Hence, in order to ensure consumers protection it is suggested that the relevant authority should require the manufacturer or producer to provide or comply with adequate labelling of Genetically Modified Food (GMF). For instance, for processed meat product that contains meat (60%), reconstituted textured soy protein*, water, wheat flour, soy protein*, dehydrated potato, salt, beetroot powder, onion powder, mineral salts (450), black pepper, lecithin* should be labeled as OR Wheat flour, water added, yeast, soy flour *(Genetically modified)*, vegetable oil, sugar, emulsifiers (471,472E), preservatives (282), enzyme amylase should be labeled as **Genetically modified*

Nevertheless, certain GM foods may be exempted from labelling as GM product if;

- Highly refined foods where the effect of the refining process is to remove novel DNA and/or novel protein;
- processing aids or food additives where novel DNA and/or novel protein is not present in the final food;
- flavours which are present in the food in a concentration of no more than 1g/kg (0.1%);
- foods, ingredients or processing aids in which the genetically modified food is unintentionally present in a quality of no more than 10g/kg (1%) per ingredient;
- food intended for immediate consumption that is prepared and sold from food outlets, caterers or self-catering institutions. In this situation the consumers have the right to ask the proprietor what is the food being purchased and whether it is from Gm source.

Negative Labelling of GMF: Some manufacturers may have decided to introduce negative labeling of GM food. For example, certain fruit drinks, juices, soy sauce etc include the words *"GM Free"* on the packaging. Although this may be possible, but practically this should not be encouraged unless there exists an adequate tracing system, especially so if it involves import products.

Footnotes

1. Hassan Mat Daud, The Current and Future Outlook of Agricultural Biotechnology in Malaysia, MARDI, Kuala Lumpur, Malaysia.
2. The Animal Ordinance 1953 was amended by Animal (Amendment) Ordinance 1953 but does not further extend the scope of Animal Ordinance 1953. Later, it was amended by the Animal (Amendment No.2) Ordinance 1953, which came into force on 1st January 1954.
3. Enacted under s. 81 of the Animal Ordinance 1953.

4. See also Control of Rearing of Pigs (Pahang) Enactment 1998, Control of Rearing of Pigs (Negeri Sembilan) Enactment 1981, Control of Rearing of Pig (Malacca) Enactment 1980, Control of Rearing of Pig (Perak) Enactment 1992.
5. Under the USFDA, Virus Serum, Toxin Act (VSTA) the term "biological products," also refers to biologics, biologicals, or products, and shall mean all viruses, serums, toxins (excluding substances that are selectively toxic to microorganisms, e.g., antibiotics), or analogous products at any stage of production, shipment, distribution, or sale, which are intended for use in the treatment of animals and which act primarily through the direct stimulation, supplementation, enhancement, or modulation of the immune system or immune response. The term "biological products" includes, but is not limited to vaccines, bacterins, allergens, antibodies, antitoxins, toxins, immunostimulants, certain cytokines, antigenic or immunizing components of live organisms, and diagnostic components, that are of natural or synthetic origin, or that are derived from synthesizing or altering various substances or components of substances such as microorganisms, genes or genetic sequences, carbohydrates, proteins, antigens, allergens, or antibodies.
6. Soh Tian Siong, Enforcement Officer, Enforcement Division, Department of Veterinary, Putrajaya.
7. Hafizal Ahmad, Veterinary Officer, Animal Health Division, National Institute of Animal Biotechnology, 27000 Jerantut, Pahang.
8. *Ibid.*
9. Fisheries Act (Amendment) Act 1974.
10. Enacted under s. 4 (2).
11. Enacted under Article 74 (1) of the Federal Constitution.
12. Among those are Fisheries (Adoption) Enactment (Perlis) 1988, Fisheries (Adoption) Enactment (Kelantan) 1986, Fisheries (Adoption) Enactment (Johore) 1989, Fisheries (Adoption) Enactment (Negeri Sembilan) 1989.
13. Department of Fisheries Malaysia, CCRF, Clause 12.1 States should recognise that responsible fisheries require the availability of a sound scientific basis to assist fisheries managers and other interested parties in making decisions. Therefore, States should ensure that appropriate research is conducted into all aspects of fisheries including biology, ecology, technology, environmental science, economics, social science, aquaculture and nutritional science. States should ensure the availability of research facilities and provide appropriate training, staffing and institution building to conduct the research, taking into account the special needs of developing countries.
14. Department of Fisheries Malaysia, CCRF, Clause 12.2. states should establish an appropriate institutional framework to determine the applied research which is required and its proper use.
15. Ismail Ishak, Q52 (Researcher), International Coordinator, Institute Penyelidikan Perikanan (Fisheries Research Institute (IPP), Jalan Batu Maung, 11960, Batu Maung, Pulau Pinang. Telephone conversation held on Tuesday, 10/2/2009 at 4.30pm-4.45pm.

16. The practice is not based on any protocol.
17. http://www.frim.gov.my/CHM/thematic_issues_1a.html
18. *Ibid.*
19. With the PVP legislation, growers are in a better position to have access to new and improved varieties for commercial growing. Temperate flower growers in Malaysia, for example, are facing problems in getting new varieties from Netherlands and other countries which breed these varieties. The extension of rights to harvested material further complicates the issue. The objective of the Act is to provide for the protection of the rights of breeders of new plant varieties, and the recognition and protection of contribution made by farmers, local communities and indigenous people towards the creation of new plant varieties; to encourage investment in and development of the breeding of new plant varieties in both public and private sectors; and to provide for related matters.
20. Persons who may apply for registration of new plant variety and the grant of a breeder's right are breeders, the employer of the breeder, the successor in the title of the breeder, a farmer or group of farmers, local community or indigenous people who have carried out the functions of a breeder and any government or statutory body which has carried out the functions of a breeder. However, if the applicant's ordinary residence or principal place of business is outside Malaysia or if the applicant is a group of farmers, the applicant should appoint an agent who is a resident or who has a registered office in Malaysia. Besides that, if the applicant is a local community or an indigenous people, the authority representing the local community or indigenous people shall be the agent.
21. Made under section 60 of the Protection of New Plant Varieties Act 2004.
22. Plant Quarantine Regulations 1981 was enacted under s. 23 of the Plant Quarantine Act 1976.
23. http://www.doa.gov.my. Under the programme, each farm registered with the Department of Agriculture will be evaluated on three basis: 1.Environmental Setting of Farm: Legality of farm, Altitude above mean sea level (a biodiversity consideration), Previous use or history of the land, Slope and terrain of farm, Soil erosion risk factor, Source and quality of irrigation water and farm use, Source and distances from pollution centers. 2.Verification of Farm Practices: Farm records of activities undertaken, Soil and substrate preparation and management (including soil fumigation, if any), Selection of planting (variety, root stock, clones etc), Crop nutrition or fertilizer program, Crop pest management system (pesticides usage, IPM, etc), Harvesting techniques and field transport, Post harvest treatment, grading and packaging, Storage of farm inputs and products, Farm waste disposal system (empty pesticides containers and other non-degradable products), Farm workers legal status, welfare and safety training of farm operatives: 3. Safety of Farm Produce: Physical and chemical analysis of ex-farm gate produces covering: Physical quality of produce such as appearance, infestation from pests and taste, Levels of pesticide residue in the produce covering groups such as

dithiocarbarmates, organo-chlorine, organo-phosphates and synthetic pyrethroids, Contamination of heavy metals such as arsenic, lead, mercury and cadmium.

24. Halloran, J, Hansen, M, *Why We Need Labelling of Genetically Engineered Food*, London, Consumers International, April, 1998, at 2-11.
25. Regulation 113(4), Food Regulations 1985.
26. Regulation 26A, Twelfth A Schedule.
27. Regulations 225-245,
28. Regulations 209-222
29. Regulations 260-273
30. Regulations 274-281
31. Regulations 246-251
32. *Ibid.*
33. Feder, B.J., "Biotech Firm to Advocate Labels on Genetically Altered Products," *New York Times*, 24 February, 1997, in Halloran, J, Hansen, M, n. 65.
34. Ms. Kathryn, Clements Gilje, Mr. Alexei Monsarrat, *LABELS*, Volume 4, No.3, Minneapolis, Institute for Agriculture and Trade Policy for the Consumers Choice Council, May, 2000, at 2.
35. For more information on labeling of GMF in Australia see ANZFA, " The Hon Trish Worth, 4th Annual Food Composition and Labelling Standards," at http://www.anzfa.gov.au/mediareleasepublications/speechs/speechthehontrishworl539.cf> viewed on 18 June 2002, 2.
36. See "Looking Beyond the Label," *The Star*, 30 September, 2002/ Section 2/ 7. For special lettering requirements see for example regulation 91 (4); regulation 391 (10) (a); regulation 390 (10) (a) and regulation 389A (12) (a), Food Regulations 1985, above, n. 28.
37. Mayeno, A.N. and G.J. Gleich, "Eosinophilia Myalgia Syndrome and Tryptophan Production: A Cautionary Tale", 1994, *TIBTECH*, at 346-352. *(n.p).*
38. Sampson, H.A., Mendelson, L. and J.P.Rosen, "Fatal and Near-fatal Anaphylactic Reactions to Food in Children and Adolescents", *The New England Journal of Medicine*, 1992, 327:380-384.
39. Additionally, GMF can alter nutritional value; genetic engineering can alter nutritional value of foods in positive ways.
40. Section 3, Biosafety Act 2007
41. Section 36 & 37, Biosafety Act 2007
42. Section 37 Biosafety Act 2007
43. Section 62 Biosafety Act 2007
44. Section 24, Biosafety Act 2007
45. Section 25, Biosafety Act 2007.
46. *Ibid*, section 33.
47. Section 65 of the Biosafety Act 2007.
48. Malaysia's National Policy on Biological Diversity (Official declaration: Thursday, April 16 1998, Kuala Lumpur, Ministry of Science, Environment and Technology), p.2, Principles (xi).
49. Malaysia's National Policy on Biological Diversity, Principles (vi).

50. *Ibid,* p. 3.
51. UNDP in Malaysia/Support to Capacity Building Activities on Implementing Cartagena protocol on Biosafety, Project Number: 00051229, Period of Project: March 2007-March 2010, http://www.undp.org.my/cartagena-protocol-on-biosafety. Malaysia signed the Cartagena Protocol Biosafety in the year 2000 and it was ratified on the 3rd September 2003 and was enforced on 2nd December 2003. In 2007 the Biosafety Act (11th July 2007) was passed which states that before Living Modified Organism (LMOs) or its products can be imported, prepared, and placed in the market, it shall go through a scientific assessment before its approval by the National Biosafety Board (NBB).
52. FDA, (21 CFR 501.4).
53. FDA, (21 CFR 501.4).
54. *Ibid,* section 61.

6

Legal and Regulatory Framework of Health and Medical Biotechnology in Malaysia

Introduction

Beginning from the Eighth Malaysia Plan (2000-2005), Malaysia has introduced fiscal and industrial policies to develop biotechnology as an industrial priority sector. It is in Malaysia's aspiration that with her rich biodiversity and natural resources and the right initiatives, she is poised to be a biotechnology hub.

Generally, the development of healthcare biotechnology in Malaysia has been centred mainly on:

- Vaccines and therapeutics
- Contract research and contract manufacturing
- Medical devices, diagnostics and drug delivery technology.

Since then, Malaysian companies are undertaking R & D and/or manufacturing activities for various products in the biotechnology healthcare industry. The products include bio-fertilisers, tissue culture of palm oil planting materials, rapid bio-diagnostic kits for typhoid fever, standardised herbal extracts, animal vaccines, industrial enzymes and nuclide acids (DNA & RNA) extractions, pro-biotics and animal feeds, the manufacture of microbials and pro-biotics, bio-enzymes, enzymatically modified sweetener and bio-diagnostic kits, toxicology services and breeding of animal activities and research in drug discovery from natural resources. Some of the market players are already making a strong entrance by introducing major health products such as Inno Biologics, a company owned by the Ministry of Finance Incorporated, that is developing a biological based treatment and diagnosis of colorectal cancer. The company is also making head way in the research of cell therapy and stem cell. Other successes include the commercial production of several diagnostics kits for dengue, several diagnostic kits for other infectious tropical diseases and a bio-enhanced formulation of artemisinin, an anti malarial drug.

Being one of the world's top 12 mega biodiversity centres, naturally Malaysia is keen to tap the natural resources for medicinal potential. The already developed traditional use of plants and herbs would further assist the venture to turn jungle herbs into commercial drugs.

This articles forays into the existing legal landscape surrounding the health biotechnology industry in Malaysia. The article commences with a peep into the initiatives introduced by the government to boost the biotechnology sector. The article then continues with a survey of the existing current legal and regulatory framework with a view of assessing its relevance, applicability and later adequacy to cover all the needs of the health biotechnology industry.

Legal Framework

Biotechnology basically involves three main stages, research; product development; and commerciali-sation. As a result, biotechnology becomes subject to the general scope of laws and regulations governing the respective stages. Graph 1 itemises some of the legal issues that arise from the stage of research, to product development till commercialisation of biotechnology health products. As can be seen, different legal issues appear at different stages with the exception of ethical issues which are relevant to all stages.

Despite all the ambitious plans, unfortunately, not much attention is paid to the establishment of a legal regulatory

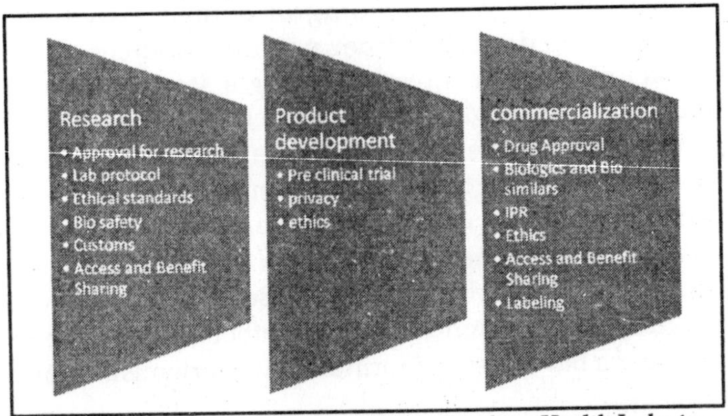

Graph 1: Legal Issues Relating to Biotechnology Health Industry

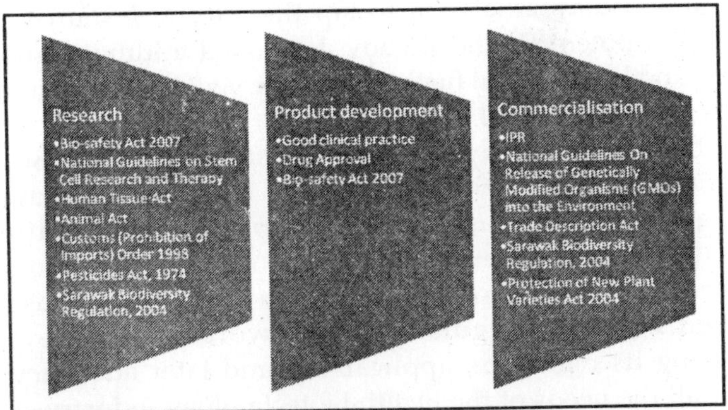

Graph 2: The Various Laws Applicable to Biotechnology Health Industry

environment that is supportive of the health biotechnology industry. Most of the laws that were passed predates the biotechnology era and little has been done to revise them to accommodate developments that took place in the biotechnology industry. The only law that was passed recently at the Federal level is the Bio Safety Act 2007 but the scope of the Act is very restricted. Another relevant piece of legislation is the Sarawak Biodiversity Centre Ordinance 1997[1] that was passed to deal with issues such as ethnobotany, traditional knowledge, access and benefit sharing and the rights of the indigenous people. The Regulation is however a state legislation with no corresponding law at the Federal level.

In general, biotechnology activities fall within the scope of other legislations that regulate various aspects of biotechnology developments like research, development and marketing. The legislations are either substantive/enabling or subsidiary/procedural. The legislations are listed below and an attempt is made to briefly examine their relevance to related stages of biotechnology.

Research

Several regulatory issues can be examined under the aegis of research starting from procurement of research materials to the safety of research employees.

Sourcing of Research Materials from Outside the Country

Critical research materials, equipments and implements are sourced from outside the country. The production of stem cells, for example, require the ready supply of stem cell lines, either from human or animal (such as rabbits) from outside the country. Easy access to these imported research materials is therefore crucial. Currently, there is no single legislation that gives due regard to this. Two pre-biotechnology era legislation, i.e. the Customs Act 1967 and the Pesticides Act 1974, could have limited application to the sourcing of research materials from outside the country.

Customs Act 1967 (Revised-1980): The Act deals with the importation and exportation of products in and out of Malaysia. Section 31 of the Act empowers the Minister to prohibit certain imports and exports of goods or certain classes of goods, either absolutely or subject to conditions. Armed with this power, the Minister passed the Customs (Prohibition of Imports) Order 2008.

The provisions of this Order would be relevant to the procurement of materials that may be used in research activities relating to biotechnology.

The Fourth Schedule to the Order contains a list of goods that may not be imported into Malaysia without import license from the relevant government institutions issued in accordance with the Order. The list consists of domestic animals, live or dead or any part thereof; pests including any invertebrate or vertebrate animal, fungus, bacterium, virus, viroid, mycroplasma like organisms, weeds, or other organisms which are capable of being injurious to plants and including any dangerous pests; any invertebrate animal (including the eggs of such animals) fungus, bacterium, virus, or any other organisms which are beneficial to agriculture and which are not capable of being injurious to plants; any animal or bird, other than a domestic animal or fowl–dead or alive.

There is nothing in the Order that relates to the importation of genetically modified organisms. This is probably because the importation of living modified organisms does not require import licence from the Customs, but upon approval from the National Bio-safety Board. However, the Order would be relevant if the resource materials required for genetic modification involves transgenic pathogen as it may fall within the definition of 'bacterium, virus or other organism' as spelt out in the Order.

One area which is conspicuously missing from the Order is live human cells and tissues.

Pesticides Act 1974: The Act contains provisions that are relevant for research and development, particularly in the area of pesticides. The Act creates a Pesticides Board which is responsible for the control of manufacture, importation, sale and storage of pesticides. Most importantly, Section 13 of the Act contains a prohibition as to the importation and manufacture of pesticides except under licence.

The function of the Board is to grant permits for the manufacture and registration of pesticides that have effects on plants, animals and fruits in Malaysia. It also covers research and development of pesticides and approves the importation of samples for research purposes, etc.

The Act has no application to plant pesticides where plants have been modified to contain parasite resistant traits such as Hessian fly, Cereal cyst nematode or Lepidoptera. Plant pesticides would fall within the definition of living modified organisms and would therefore be governed under the Bio Safety Act 2007. The definition adopted in the Act in relation to "pest"[2] and "pesticide"[3] excludes any possible extension to plant pesticides.

The Sourcing of Human Biological Materials

The only legislation that deals with the use of human body parts is the Human Tissues Act 1974. As regards the use of human embryos for research, the Ministry of Health's guidelines on Assisted Reproductive Technology (2000) and the National Organ, Tissue and Cell Transplantation Policy (2007) would be relevant.

Human Tissues Act 1974: As is made clear in the preamble itself, the Act is confined to the use of parts of human bodies of deceased persons for therapeutic purposes and for purposes of medical education and research. The Act, which only contains five sections, deals primarily with the usage of cadaveric organs for organ transplantation. Section 2 of the Act for example, allows the removal of bodily organs for therapeutic as well as research purposes. This Act which is passed before the age of biotechnology does not address the latest medical advances where live tissue samples and bodily cells are taken from humans for research and therapeutic use.

Code of Practice on Assisted Reproductive Technology[4] : In Malaysia, a Code of Practice was formulated to provide guidance to physicians and hospitals involved in Assisted Reproductive Technologies ('ART').

Part IV(b) of the Guidelines are important as it relates to storage of gametes and embryos. According to this part, anyone consenting to the storage of their gametes or of embryos produced by them must:

- specify the maximum storage (maximum three years);
- dispose off the gametes or embryos if they die or are incapable of varying or revoking their joint consent.

Emphasis is made for the attainment of consent from the couple undergoing the ART treatment concerning the storage and disposal of embryos or for research[5]. A couple undergoing ART should be asked for instructions concerning the storage and disposal of embryos. Specific instructions must be obtained from the couple and informed consent duly obtained. It is further provided that no research or experimentation shall be performed on or using any human oocyte[6].

Part V of the Guidelines meanwhile specifies that the termination and disposal of gametes and embryos must refer to the couple's written consent. In the absence of instructions, the embryos are then stored for a maximum period of three years before they are destroyed. If the couple consents to it, the Guideline also allows research on left over embryos provided that the research does not exceed the 14 days requirement.

The Code of Practice acknowledges that the human embryo is given special status. Hospitals and private healthcare centres are to decide carefully whether or not to dispose, how to dispose and whether to use it for research purposes. The Centre then should decide the culture period, the method that is to be used to terminate development and the procedure to ensure that embryos do not continue to develop after 14 days or after the appearance of the primitive streak. The Code stipulates that all research must have licence from the Ministry of Health. Licences will only be granted for the following types of research projects:

- to promote advances in the treatment of infertility;
- to increase knowledge about causes of miscarriage;
- increase knowledge on causes of congenital disease;
- develop better contraceptives;
- develop methods for detecting presence of gene or chromosome abnormalities before implantation;
- increase knowledge about serious diseases;
- allow such knowledge to be applied in developing treatments for serious disease.

The Code of Practice contains several specific prohibitions[7]. First, the keeping or using of an embryo after the 14 day period or after the appearance of the primitive streak is not allowed. So is the placing of an embryo in a non-human animal and replacing a nucleus of a cell of an embryo with a nucleus taken from the cell of another person, another embryo or a subsequent development of an embryo altering the genetic structure of any cell while it forms part of an embryo. It was also specifically mentioned that embryos that have been appropriated for research must not be used for any other purposes[8].

National Organ, Tissue and Cell Transplantation Policy[9]*:* In 2007, the Health Ministry introduced guidelines for stem cell research in Malaysia[10]. Among the policies is that the Ministry of Health will undertake to encourage and promote stem cell research in Malaysia. Second, all stem cell research must pass through an institutional review board and an institutional ethics committee to prevent unethical research and unethical use of stem cells. Third, research on stem cells derived from adult stem cells is allowed in accordance with existing guidelines. Fourth, the use of fetal tissues from legally performed termination of pregnancy is also allowed in accordance with existing guidelines. Fifth, the use of non-human stem cell lines is also allowed (mice and primates). Sixth, the use of embryonic stem cell lines (from 64 cell lines) for therapeutic purposes should be allowed. Seventh, the creation of embryos either from ART or SCNT specifically for the purpose of scientific research is presently prohibited.

The Health Ministry Guidelines were formulated taking into consideration a National Fatwa that has also been released on Therapeutic Human Cloning and Stem Cell Research in 2005[11]. The Fatwa states:

(a) That therapeutic human cloning is permitted (*diharuskan*) if for–medical treatment–through the creation of certain cells or replacing damaged organs "taking into account the limits permitted by the *Shari'ah*.

(b) The use of embryos left-over from IVF for research purposes is permitted (*harus*) on two conditions:
- The couples had consented;
- Before the embryo reaches the stage of *'alaqah*.

(c) Research on pre-embryo for purposes other than for therapeutic purposes is also permitted provided that–
   - The couples consented;
   - The embryo is not implanted into any womb.

(d) Research on pre-embryo to detect any predisposition to any genetic diseases for high risk couples is allowed and only embryos that were determined to be clear from any of such diseases could be implanted in the womb of the mother during the marital term.

(e) Any genetic treatment on pre-embryo to change the natural characteristics of the pre-embryo such as hair, hair colour, intelligence, height including sex determination is not allowed. However, sex determination is allowed if it is linked to predisposition to fatal genetic diseases.

(f) Any type of research for commercial gain or that which has no relation to the health of the mother or the feotus is not permitted.

(g) Research done must be–
   - Legal with a clear research proposal;
   - For scientific purposes;
   - Carried out by qualified research personnel who are trustworthy and responsible.

(h) Sources of stem cell permitted–
   - excess embryos (consent obtained from parents);
   - aborted fetus as a result of natural abortion or from medical treatment that is allowed under the *Shariah* and is carried out with the consent of the family members; not from aborted fetus that is carried out deliberately without any causes accepted by the medical fraternity and *Shariah*.

(i) Stem cell created from SCNT (somatic cell nuclear transfer technology) is not permitted based on *sadd al-zara'i* (blocking the means of evil)

With this Fatwa, one could infer that there is no blanket approval for stem cell research as the Malay word "*diharuskan*" refers to "*mubah*" in Arabic which means "something which is permitted" and not "something which is promoted or encouraged". Secondly, it would appear that the Research must be for therapeutic purposes only - which must be on legitimate grounds and not for commercial purposes. Thirdly, the Malaysian Fatwa Council requires that such research must be legal and conducted in a responsible manner. However, the first statement allowing therapeutic cloning would have to be made more consistent with the last stand on the creation of stem cell through somatic cell nuclear transfer. If the latter practice is not allowed, the first statement in relation to the permissibility of therapeutic cloning would have to be clarified further.[12]

Bio-prospecting

Rules that govern bio-prospecting would be important as it determines the mechanism in which biological resources could be mined for research purposes. The following legislation has provisions touching directly on the issues:

Fisheries Act 1985 [Act 317]: This Act relates generally to the conservation, management and development of fisheries, turtles and riverine fishing in Malaysia. The Act provides for optimum utilisation of fishery resources based on sound conservation and management principles and in accordance with national policies, development plans and program.

The Act prohibits a foreign vessel from fishing (or attempting to fish) or conducting techno-economic research or survey within Malaysian waterways except in the following circumstances:

(a) the vessel is authorized to do so under an international fishing agreement concluded either between the government of Malaysia and another country or between the government of Malaysia and an international organization to which the vessel belong or with which the vessel is registered,

(b) under a permit issued under section 19 of the Act,

(c) where subject to the general direction of the Minister, techno-economic research or survey is conducted under the following conditions

- pursuant to an agreement between a Malaysian citizen and such person to whom such foreign fishing vessel belongs;
- the conduct of such research or survey shall be under the general directive of the Deputy-General; and
- any data and findings of such research or survey shall be made available to the Deputy General as frequently as he may prescribe.[13]

In addition, a foreign fishing vessel shall not load, unload, supply or transship any fish in Malaysia fisheries waters without the written permission of the Deputy-General.[14]

The Deputy-General may consult with a State Authority for the purpose of promoting development and rational management of inland fisheries. In this regard, he may initiate

(a) the conduct or co-ordination of research;

(b) the provision and maintenance of experimental and demonstration aquaculture stations, fish-breeding stations and training centres;

(c) the provision of advice and technical assistance to the appropriate authorities of the State;

(d) the provision of publicity and demonstration facilities and other connected services; and

(e) the provision of advice on measures for the prevention of fish diseases.[15]

Some observations could be drawn from the provisions. Firstly, though the term 'fishing' could give the impression that it covers the catching of fish for consumption purposes, the definition of "fishing" under section 2 suggest that it could cover research purposes. Under the said provision, the term 'fishing' is defined to mean-

(a) the catching, taking or killing of fish by any method;

(b) the attempted catching, taking or killing of fish;

(c) engaging in any activity which can reasonably be expected to result in the catching, taking or killing of fish; or

(d) any operation in support of, or in preparation for, any activity described in paragraph (a), (b) or (c) of this definition;

Secondly, equally broad is the definition of fish that may include transgenic fish.[16] Thirdly, it is possible for the state authorities to indulge in research for the purpose of the development of inland fisheries. This could pave the way for research in the genetic modification of fish including for medicinal and pharmaceutical purposes.

Worldwide projects involving the creation of transgenic fish include:

- Inserting genes for increased growth rates and increased resistance to disease in Rainbow trout, tilapia, catfish, grass carp, mollusks, and prawns. These genetic modifications are intended to increase aquaculture productivity for human food consumption.
- Inserting human clotting genes into Tilapia for possible pharmaceutical application.
- Inserting the "anti-freeze" gene into goldfish for research purposes and to add consumer appeal as household pets.
- Algae are being genetically engineered for use as a bioremediation tool. Genetic modification is increasing the algae's ability to absorb higher levels of toxic heavy metals.[17]

Finally, though the preamble of the Act talks of conservation of fisheries, it only makes it an offence to fish or take, or remove any aquatic plant or part thereof from marine parks and reserves.[18] Obtaining fish sample in deep seas, rivers or any other open water resources would not be an offence. This Act is of little use for bio-prospecting purposes.

Protection of Wild Life Act 1972: The main focus of the Act is protected wild animals, reserved forests and reserved lands, wild life reserves and wild life sanctuaries.

Section 4 of the Act deals with the procedure for the granting of permits to enter a reserved forest, wild life reserve and sanctuary. Section 51A of the Act deals specifically with the conduct of research or study in these areas. This provision requires the attainment of a written permission from the Director General for Wild Life and National Parks for those who intend to do research or study of a wild animal or wild bird or any part thereof. Section 81 and 82 further makes it an offence for anybody to enter a wild life sanctuary and wild life reserve without a permit.

The Protection of Wild Life Act is certainly an important legislation that controls access to forests, wild life reserves and sanctuaries. The main limitation of the Act is that the list of protected animals is limited to those gazetted under the accompanying schedules. The applicability of the Act to microorganisms, fungi or any other unicellular living things is not certain.

This Act's main concern is clearly illegal poaching and the protection of endangered wild life.

National Forestry Act 1984: This Act was passed for the purpose of the management and conservation of forests and forestry development within the States of Malaysia. The term 'forest produce' is broadly defined as to include:

(a) the following when found in or brought from a permanent reserved forest:

guano, peat, rock, sea-sand, river-sand, sea-shells, shell-sand and surfaces oil;

(b) the following when found in or brought from a permanent reserved forest or State land:

- trees and all parts or produce not hereinafter mentioned of trees;
- plants including climbers, creepers and grasses, and all parts or produce of such plants;
- silk, cocoons, honey and wax and edible bird's nests;

(c) the following whether found in or brought from a permanent reserved forest, State land, mining land, reserved land or alienated land: timber, fuelwood, charcoal, getah, getah taban leaves, wood oil, bark, extracts of bark, damar and atap.

The Act regulates certain activities involving permanent reserved forest through two types of permits. The first type is the use permits that are required for the occupation of, or carrying out activities upon, permanent reserved forest prohibited as required under section 32. The 'use' permits however could not be used for the purpose of taking forest produce[19] unless in certain circumstances[20].

The second type of permit is the removal licence which is required for the removal of forest produce from four types of lands:

(a) Alienated land;

(b) Land held under temporary occupation licence;

(c) Mining land; or

(d) Reserved land.[21]

This Act is clearly passed to govern deforestation and its main concern is to control illegal logging. As listed in the schedule the major forest produce relates to timber; charcoal and rattan.[22] It is not so concerned with bio-prospecting[23]. As the Act is passed before the biotechnology era, this is not surprising.

However, it is our view that the existing permit system could be extended to control access to biological resources for bio-prospecting purposes.

Customs (Prohibition of Exports) Order 2008: The Order created three categories of prohibition:

- Absolute prohibition which falls under the first schedule[24],
- Conditional prohibition except under an Export Licence as listed under the second schedule[25]
- Conditional prohibition except in the provided manner as listed under the third schedule[26]

The exportation of genetic resources would be falling under either the second schedule or the third schedule. For example, it is forbidden to export any species of plant or any parts thereof which is alive and can be propogated including the stem, branch, tuber, bulb, corn, rhizome, stock, budwood, cutting, layer, slip, sucker, root, flower, fruit, seed or any other part like pollen, spores, meristem, tissue, callus tissues in culture medium or cryogenically preserved without an export permit from the Department of Agriculture[27]. It is also wrong to export any animal or bird, other than a domestic animal or domestic fowl, whether alive or dead or any part thereof, including all animals and birds specified in any written law in Malaysia without an export permit from the Wildlife Department or the Department of Veterinary Services[28].

If our biological resources are considered as capable of being usurped by others for research purposes, there is then a need for the Customs (Prohibition of Exports) Order 2008 to be revised. This Order deals with the prohibition of specified animals/plants and parts of live animals/plants to other countries falling either under the Second Schedule or the Third Schedule of the Order.

Sarawak Biodiversity Centre Ordinance, 1997 and Sarawak Biodiversity Regulations 2004: The Sarawak Biodiversity Centre Ordinance, 1997 was passed to establish the Sarawak Biodiversity Centre and the Sarawak Biodiversity Council. The Ordinance is a pioneer in Malaysia on access and benefit sharing, biodiversity[29] and traditional knowledge.

The core function of the Sarawak Biodiversity Council is to regulate access to biological resources[30] from Sarawak. The Sarawak Biodiversity Centre's main task is to manage a sustainable utilization of biodiversity of the State.

The Sarawak Biodiversity Regulation, 2004 is a subsidiary legislation made pursuant to Sarawak Biodiversity Centre Ordinance, 1997. The Regulation provides within its framework the condition and procedure for collection and use of biological resources from state land, forest, forest reserve, protected forest, natural plant, nature reserve and wild life sanctuary. The scope of the Regulation is the combined effect of the federal legislation, namely, the Protection of Wild Life Act 1972 and National Forestry Act 1984.

It makes it unlawful to collect or use such biological resources for research or propagation to support such research unless a permit has been issued by the Sarawak Biodiversity Council[31]. A permit for this purpose is issued upon application made in a prescribed manner and to which the Chief Executive Officer of the Centre has no objection[32]. To successfully obtain a permit under this Regulation, an applicant is basically required to complete an agreement with the Government of Sarawak[33]. The terms of the agreement are to be dictated by the State government and they include the agreement on the place or institution in which research is to be carried out; the right of government to access reports; the right of government to patents and intellectual property to or over any discoveries resulting from the research undertaken and, where appropriate, the sharing of such rights with other parties to the agreement. In particular, it is made clear in the Regulations that there can be no application for intellectual property over any research discovery without the consent in writing of the Chief Executive Officer[34].

In the Regulations, some of the key terms are further clarified to ensure that none of the biological resources needed for bio-prospecting are left out. The term "aquatic life" for example, is defined in the Regulations to include "fish and any aquatic animals or plant life, sedentary or not, and all species of finfish, crustacean, mollusca, aquatic mammals, or their eggs or spawn, fry, fingerling, spat or young, and any marine or freshwater organisms, and the derivatives or parts thereof". The clarification is understandable, as it is meant to ensure that even derivatives and parts of "aquatic life" are covered. Secondly, the usage of "aquatic life" is much clearer and broader than "fish" under the Federal Fisheries Act 1985 to cover organisms that could be potential resource material for genetic engineering.

The term "biological resources" is also redefined to include any extracts, whether in liquid or solid form, tissues, by-product or derivative or synthesized form thereof and where the context so admits, protected resources". This is to ensure that even the by product, derivative or synthesized form of biological resources is included, including its genomic form.[35]

The Sarawak State Government has also learnt from experience the difficulty in controlling the taking of biological resources. It is hard to monitor tourists coming into contact with biological resources and taking them back home by just pinching or removing 'one twig', leaf or roots of a particular plant. Thus, it is important to have a set of laws that reflects the reality that bio-prospecting can also occur by just taking a small sample of a particular specimen. Thus the term "specimen" in relation to biological or protected resources, includes any sample, extract, part, derivative, components, representation or by-product of any plant, insect or aquatic life.

The new definition of "export" reflects this. Thus, the term "export" in relation to biological resources, means removing, shipping or taking away by any means the same out of the State for research or purposes relating to pharmaceutical or biotechnological developments.

Of most important is the term "ethno-biology". The interest in biological resources brings with it interest in ethno-biology especially the medicinal knowledge of the indigenous people. The term "ethno-biology" is thus defined to mean "the knowledge or information pertaining to the uses by the natives of the State of biological resources for medicinal, food, health or other purposes including the classification, indigenous nomenclature, conservation techniques and general sociological importance of such biological resources to them".

Research on known herbal plants used by the indigenous people of Sarawak would also be subjected to the permit system. Section 29 of the Regulations makes it clear that no person can undertake ethno-biological research except with a permit issued by the Council. "Ethno-biological research" means the search or study, based upon ethno-biology, on traditional medicinal materials with potential constituents from which new curative agents or compounds may be created or found for modern pharmaceutical, biotechnological or other commercial development.[36]

For ethno-biological research, it is a requirement that the permit holder make payments to the natives as reward for the knowledge or information provided by them in connection with the ethno-biological research undertaken under the permit, regardless whether the research results in the commercial development of any medicinal or other products. Where the research results lead to any intellectual property, it is imperative that the rights to the intellectual property are shared with the natives who supplied the knowledge or information.[37]

In 2003, the principal Ordinance was amended to clarify that research would also include the therapeutic properties of biological resources.[38] For that purpose, Section 21 and 22 of the principal ordinance was also amended.[39]

Conduct of Research

Some regulatory oversight for the conduct of research itself could be derived from existing legislation such as Animals Act 1953 and possibly, Radiation Protection (Basic Safety Standard) Regulation, 1988.

Animals Act 1953: This Act covers the aspect of procurement of materials for research especially in so far as prevention of the introduction and spread of animals' diseases within Malaysia is concerned. It prohibits cruelty to animals, controls the movements of animals in Malaysia, and promotes the conservation and general welfare of animals. The Act defines animals to include horses, cattle, sheep, goats, swine, dogs, cats and any four-footed beast kept in captivity or under control, of any age or sex. The scope of the Act also covers bird which the Act interprets to include domestic fowls, ducks, geese, turkeys, and guinea.

The Act empowers the Minister to make an Order specifying countries from which importation of animals, birds or their products is approved or prohibited. In any case, importation of animals and birds can only be done pursuant to a licence issued by the Minister under the Act. In addition, imported animals or birds may not land in Malaysia unless it has been examined with satisfaction by a Veterinary Officer and he issues a permit to that effect. If the veterinary officer is of the opinion that an imported animal, bird or carcass is infected with disease he may refuse to permit its landing, and cause it to be destroyed and disposed off at the expense of the owner, or quarantined. Export of animals is also subject to similar statutory preconditions and actions by the Veterinary Officer. Under the Act, no one is entitled to possess live cultures or vaccines unless he is licensed by the Deputy General. Similarly, prior written permission of the Deputy General is required for the importation or possession of any living noxious insect, living pest, living disease germ, virus or bacterial culture that is naturally harmful or dangerous to animals or birds. In all cases, the failure to obtain the requisite permission constitutes a punishable offence. Unfortunately, the Act has nothing to say on the importation and exportation of genetically modified animals or live cultures.

Cruelty to animals is a punishable offence under the Act. Cruelty is broadly defined to include 'beating, kicking, ill-treating, overriding, overdriving, overloading, torturing, infuriating or terrifying any animal'. The word 'animal' in this part means any living creature other than a human being and it includes any beast, bird, fish, reptile or insect, whether wild or tame. Unfortunately, the Act deals with inhumane treatment to animals but does not touch on the use of animals in laboratory testing or research.

As the Act was passed before the advent of biotechnology, there is nothing in the Act that relates to genetic modification of animals.

Radiation Protection (Basic Safety Standard) Regulation, 1988: The provisions of this Regulation concern research facilities, exposure of persons to radiological radiation and impacts on both human and environmental health. Under the Regulation, a person is required to obtain a license to operate a radiological examination centre. A person can be made the subject of radiological examination only if there is justification to do so and the benefit accrues to the person. A licensed operator of a radiological centre is obliged to classify working areas into three; clean areas; supervised areas; and controlled areas. In addition, he is obliged to monitor controlled areas and keep records of workers' exposure to radiation.

Under the Regulation, an operator is obliged to conform to basic scientific principles, design and performance in experimental protocols. He must carry out an assessment of predictable risks and show respect for rights of a subject. A subject must be provided with adequate information on the nature of experiment and his prior informed consent must be obtained. His right to withdraw consent must also be observed.

The Regulation allows doctors to combine medical research with professional care and thus to use new therapeutic and diagnostic measures etc.

The scope of the Regulation is restricted to the running of a radiological centre and the conduct of radiological examination. With the current advances in bio-diagnosis and DNA profiling, diagnosis of diseases through DNA analysis are routinely done by microbiologist in labs. There is thus a need to come up with new regulations that could cover this.

Pathology Laboratory Act 2007: This Act was passed to provide for the regulation and control of pathology laboratories. Under the Act, no one can set up and maintain a pathology laboratory without licence in Malaysia.[40] Under the Act, a pathologist is defined to mean a registered medical practitioner who possesses the qualifications, training and experience in the discipline of pathology as approved by the Director General.[41] The confinement of pathology to only registered medical practitioners[42] defies the reality that molecular diagnosis and genetic testing is routinely done by a molecular biologist in research laboratories in Malaysia. In particular, the existing DNA testing done by research institutes fall within the definition of 'pathology services' and is not legitimately done if not endorsed by a pathologist as that is the only analysis of human tissues recognised under this Act. This is because the term "pathology services" is broadly defined to mean "any services in the analysis and examination of samples of human tissue or fluid or any other product of the human body or for assessing any change in the physiological state of human beings for the purposes of preventing, diagnosing or treating diseases in human beings".[43]

Clinical Trials

Control of Drugs and Cosmetics Regulation, 1984: The main legislation that regulates clinical trials is the Control of Drugs and Cosmetics Regulation, 1984 made under the powers conferred by section 28(1) of the Sale of Food and Drugs Act 1952. Under the Regulation, the term clinical trial is defined as "any investigation or series of investigations on persons conducted by or under the supervision of persons with scientific training or experience for the purpose of finding about or determining the safety, effectiveness and other effects of any product."

Under the Regulations, guidelines were passed for application to conduct drug-related clinical trials in Malaysia. Under the guidelines, application to conduct clinical trials could be approved by institutional in-house research review committee (RRC) and medical research ethics committee (MREC). The Research Review Committee (RRC) reviews the scientific merit of each proposal while the Medical Research Ethics Committee (MREC) reviews the ethical aspects of the study to safeguard the rights, safety and well being of all trial subjects. The guidelines also contain the flow chart for the approval of clinical trials in the various institutions in Malaysia.

Risk and Disease Control

Destruction of Disease Bearing Insects Act, 1975 [Act 154]: The scope of the Act is restricted to destruction and control of disease bearing insects and for the medical examination and treatment of persons suffering from insect-borne diseases and for matters connected therewith. Section 11 of the Act mandates that approval be obtained for operations likely to propagate or harbour disease-bearing insects. Section 14 of the Act further provides for the prohibition on breeding etc. of disease-bearing insects without permission. This Act has limited application to biotechnology research. It may, however, be useful as a control mechanism as it creates offences not only to the owner of the premise but also any possible occupier and servants of the premise. Furthermore section 15 of the Act prohibits the creation of conditions likely to propagate or harbour disease-bearing insects. This provision could constrain research activities that involve disease bearing insects.

Prevention and Control of Infectious Diseases Act, 1988 [Act 342]: This Act deals with the prevention and control of infectious diseases and provides for other matters connected therewith. Section 9 of the Act deals with the importation or exportation of human remains and pathogenic organisms or substances. The scope of the prohibition of import and export of such materials are quite broad as it covers:

- any human remains, human tissues or part thereof, or
- any pathogenic organism or substance or part thereof.

The term 'pathogen' is relevant as it could potentially cover genetically modified virus, bacteria or other recombinant micro-organisms. It is not clear how pathogen could currently be imported into Malaysia.

"pathogenic organism or substance" includes-

- any animal;
- any noxious insect;
- any living germ, microbe, bacteria or virus;
- the culture of any germ, microbe, bacteria or virus; or
- the product of any germ, microbe, bacteria or virus, capable of causing any infectious disease[44];

It could possibly extend to the importation and exportation of human tissues for research on infectious disease. To what extent this Act is being used to control the importation and exportation of pathogenic organisms or substances is not clear.

Plant Quarantine Act 1976: This Act relates to the use, control, import and export of pests, beneficial organisms, plants and soil present in Malaysia. The Act enables the direct removal, destruction or treatment of any pest, plant, land or tool which appear to be either diseased in a manner that affect others or is in a condition favorable to the introduction or spread of a disease.

Again, as the Act pre dates biotechnology, there is no reference to genetically modified plants that may contaminate the environment. However, under the National Guidelines on Release of Genetically Modified Organisms (GMOs) into the environment set by the Genetic Modification Advisory Committee (GMAC), the Plant Quarantine Act 1976 is recognised as an existing mechanism that could be utilised in implementing the Guidelines.

Environmental Control

Environmental Quality Act 1974: The Environmental Quality Act was passed to cater for the need to conserve the environment in the midst of massive physical development. The Act establishes an Environmental Quality Council whose function is to coordinate activities relating to the discharge of wastes, and general control of the environment[45]. Among the Council's power is to advise the Minister generally on all issues relating to the environment. With the passing of the Act, a licence system was set up. The Director General is empowered under the Act to issue of licences[46] for activities that may cause danger to the environment such as pollution, emission, discharge or deposit of wastes.

Generally, the Act deals with waste and pollution control and have little to do with release of living modified organisms to the environment which falls under the scope of the Bio Safety Act 2007.

Bio-Safety Act 2007

The Bio-Safety Act makes provision for the protection of human, plant and animal health as well as the environment and biological diversity[47]. It serves the goals by regulating the release, importation, exportation and contained use of Living Modified Organisms and products of such organisms. The Act establishes the National Bio Safety Board with the power to administer and enforce its provisions, to promote research and facilitate the collection, storage and dissemination of data on Living Modified Organisms ('LMO'), products of such LMO and bio safety. The Act also gives recognition to the Genetic Modification Advisory Committee's role to provide scientific and other technical advice to the Minister of Environment and the Board in respect of their functions under this Act.

More fundamentally, the Act is to be read together with other laws relating to the import and export of biological resources, human, plant and animal health, the environment and biological diversity. The Act is passed specifically to answer the needs arising from the application of modern biotechnology.[48] The main focus of the Act is living modified organism[49] and products of such organisms[50]. One would wonder why the Act would be referring to LMOs and not GMOs?[51] This is probably because the fear of contamination and cross breeding between species is more real in the context of LMOs and not GMOs.

The term "living organism" is defined to mean any biological entity capable of transferring or replicating genetic material, including sterile organisms, viruses and viroids. From this definition, stem cells thus could potentially be classified as living organisms as it is capable of transferring genetic material. However, stem cells could not be classified as living modified organisms as they are extracted from human in its natural form and could not be considered to be modified in any manner.

Consistent with the focus of the Act on bio-safety, the Act mandates any release activity[52] and import activity involving living modified organisms to be done with prior approval of the National Bio-safety Board.

Such approval could only be conferred when a risk assessment report and an emergency response plan has been submitted to the Board. The requirement for approval is however not extended to products containing such living modified organisms. In particular, the risk assessment report must contain an assessment of the risk and adverse effect that such living modified organisms and products of such organisms will have or are likely to have on human, plant and animal health, the environment and biological diversity and the proposed measures that are undertaken to prevent, reduce or control those risks and adverse effect.

The emergency response plan must provide:

(a) Safety measures and procedures for the protection of human, plant and animal health, the environment and biological diversity against harm or damage caused directly or indirectly by living modified organisms or products of such organisms; and

(b) All necessary measures to be taken in the event of an emergency.

The Act clearly covers the conduct of field trials of living modified organisms as it would fall under the definition of 'release activity'. However before such field trial could be carried out, a risk assessment has to be carried out first and a clear report would have to be submitted to the Board.

The Board has powers to review approvals particularly when there is evidence of risk posed to human, plant or animal health, the environment or biological diversity[53]. In such an instance, the Board may revoke the approval, impose a temporary cessation order or impose additional terms and conditions.

Part IV of the Act deals with the exportation and contained use activities involving living modified organisms and importation of living modified organisms for purposes of undertaking a contained use activity. To that extent, the Act is a mandatory compliance for researchers in the field of biotechnology as it includes "any operation including research and development, production or manufacturing operation involving living modified organisms, or storage of living modified organism, undertaken within a facility, installation or other physical structure such that it prevents the contact and impact of the living modified organisms on the external environment".

For such activities to take place, it is necessary that the Board is notified first. The notification must also include an emergency response plan and any specific measures to be taken in contained use.

For exportation of LMOs, there must be compliance with the requirements of the importing country. The exporter must also submit a notification to the Director General of his intention together with an emergency response plan.

Section 61 of the Act imposes labeling requirement on all living modified organisms, items containing LMOs and the products of such organisms.

It is clear that the main concern of the Act is living modified organisms. However, it is not clear whether the Act covers genetically modified plants, animals or human cells, tissues and cellular and tissue based products.

The Genetic Modification Advisory Committee (GMAC) was established much earlier within the ambit of the National Committee on Biodiversity of MoSTE.[54] In 1997 the GMAC released a National Guidelines on Release of Genetically Modified Organisms (GMOs). The guidelines cover GMOs at all stages of research, development, use, release and placing on the market. It covers, but is not limited to, genetically modified plants, animals (including for example, insects, mollusks and fish) and microorganisms and products consisting of or containing GMOs. The Guidelines thus clarify that the scope of powers of GMAC does not go beyond LMOs as defined under the Biosafety Act 2007 only. Under the Guidelines, a detailed outline of factors to be considered when there is release of transgenic[55] plants, animal and GMOs could be found. The Guidelines mandate the establishment of an institutional biosafety committee whose task is to ensure that experiments relating to genetic modification and release undertaken by the institution conform to the provisions of the Guidelines.

The Guidelines however only covers the general scientific and technical aspects of the release of GMOs into the environment. The Guidelines are only administrative in nature and unaccompanied by legislation to ensure compliance.

Commercialisation

For the sale and commercialisation of bio-pharmaceutical products, several legislations could be relevant. The legislation could cover aspects such as the drug approval process which is critical for any development, sale and manufacture of drugs. Other important issues include labeling, breeder's right, bio-safety and the development of standards.

The Drug Approval Process

Biological products include a diverse range of substances such as vaccines, blood and blood components, allergenics, gene therapy, cellular and tissue-based components, recombinant therapeutic proteins, and xeno-transplantation products. Bio-diagnostics kits for the early detection of typhoid fever using monoclonal antibodies would equally fall within the definition of 'drug'. Therefore, biological products may meet the definition of a drug, and thus, may be subject to the approval process through the procedure set under the Regulations.

Unfortunately, it is not clear whether there is any special provision for the approval of biological products for sale and manufacture in Malaysia. It is also not clear whether there is any special provision for the approval of bio-medical products for animal use. The same position could be extended to the whole array of bio pharmaceutical products including recombinant protein, bio-markers, stem cell lines, etc.

The Drug Regulatory System

Admission of new prescription (ethical) pharma-ceutical drugs (both in-patent or generic), and over-the-counter (OTC) drugs into the domestic market is usually subject to control for reasons of quality, safety and efficacy. Before these products could be imported or manufactured locally, the importer or manufacturer would have to apply for a product registration. The products would only be registered after clinical trials, laboratory testing and approval. On registration of the product, a separate licence would have to be issued to the importer, manufacturer or wholesaler.[56]

Regulated Drugs

Biotechnology related Pharmaceutical Products: Approvals for such products are required under the Sale of Drugs Act 1952 (Revised 1989). Under this Act, "drug" is defined very widely to include "any substance, product or article intended to be used or capable, or purported or claimed to be capable, of being used on humans or any animal, whether internally or externally, for a medicinal purpose". The phrase "medicinal purpose" means any of the following purposes:

- alleviating, treating, curing or preventing a disease or a pathological condition or symptoms of a disease;
- diagnosing a disease or ascertaining the existence, degree or extent of a physiological or pathological condition;
- contraception;
- inducing anesthesia;
- maintaining, modifying, preventing, restoring, or interfering with, the normal operation of a physiological function;
- controlling body weight;
- general maintenance or promotion of health or well-being.[57]

Further, the word "appliance" includes the whole or any part of any utensil, machinery, instrument, apparatus, or article used, or intended for use, in or for the making, keeping, preparing or supplying of any drug. [58]

The Minister is given wide powers under the Act to make regulations to implement the Act, in relation to, inter alia, the following purposes:[59]

- to prescribe the standard of strength, weight, quality, or quantity of any drug or of any ingredient or component part thereof;
- to prohibit any modes of manufacture, preparation, or preservation of any drug;
- to secure the cleanliness and freedom from contamination of any drug in the course of its manufacture, preparation, storage, packing, carriage, delivery, or exposure for sale or sale and the cleanliness of places, receptacles, appliances, and vehicles used in such manufacture, preparation, storage, packing, carriage, or delivery, exposure for sale or sale and to secure the proper conduct of places in which the

preparation or sale of drugs is carried on and for these purposes to require any person to submit to a medical examination;

- to provide for the licensing or registration of premises used for, or persons engaged or occupied in the manufacture, preparation, storage, packing, carriage, delivery, exposure for sale or sale of any drug and for these purposes to require photographs of persons registered or licensed;
- to prescribe the mode of labeling drugs sold in packages or otherwise and the matter to be contained or not to be contained in such labels;
- to prohibit or regulate the manufacture, sale, advertisement for sale, supply, importation or exportation of any articles of drugs and for this purpose to establish any body or authority;
- to require all ingredients contained in any medicine, proprietary, secret or otherwise, to be disclosed in the prescribed manner and form and with the prescribed particulars at or prior to the sale thereof.

Establishment of the Drug Control Authority: Pursuant to the above powers, the Control of Drugs and Cosmetics Regulations 1984 (CDCR) was promulgated.[60] The main function of the Regulations is to control the manufacture, sale, supply and importation of drugs. Drugs can only be commercialised upon registration and the attainment of licence from the Drug Control Authority of the Ministry of Health Malaysia. Registered products can only be manufactured, processed, packed, labeled and tested in premises which comply with standards set by the authorities.

Regulation 3 of the CDCR established a Drug Control Authority (DCA) to function as the licensing authority. (set up in 1985) The DCA is managed by the Director General of Health, Director of Pharmaceutical Services, Director of the National Pharmaceutical Control Laboratory, and seven other appointed members. The main responsibility of the DCA is to ensure the safety, quality and efficacy of pharmaceuticals in

Malaysia. The National Pharmaceutical Control Bureau (NPCB) of the Ministry of Health, Malaysia serves as the secretariat of the DCA, The NPCB is responsible for the daily operations of drug registration and cosmetic notification, together with the attendant monitoring and surveillance activities.[61]

Registration and Licensing Requirements: Part III of the CDCR provides for the registration and licensing of certain products.[62] Regulation 7(1) provides that except as otherwise provided in these Regulations, no person shall manufacture, sell, supply, import, possess or administer any product unless –

- the product is a registered product; and
- the person holds the appropriate licence required and issued under these Regulations.[63]

The CDCR defines a "product" as:[64]

- a drug in a dosage unit or otherwise, for use wholly or mainly by being administered to one or more human beings or animals for a medicinal purpose;
- a drug to be used as an ingredient of a preparation for a medicinal purpose; or
- a cosmetic.[65]

The definition of "products" in the CDCR has to be compared with the definition of "products" in the Sale of Drugs Act, where the word "article" is also mentioned. The omission of "article" in the definition of "product" in the CDCR would mean that diagnostic agents and test kits for laboratory use; non-medicated medical and contraceptive devices; non-medicated bandages and surgical dressings; and instruments, apparatus, syringes, needles, sutures and catheters etc. are as yet not subject to the registration and licensing requirements.[66]

Registration and Licensing of Products

Registration: Provisions relating to the procedures for registration a product are laid down in Regulation 8. Regulation 8(2)(d) provides that every application for the registration of a product shall be accompanied by "such documents, items, samples, particulars or information as the Authority may require."

Procedure for Processing New Applications: Three types of applications for a new product registration are available:[67]

(i) Application for an innovator product (NCE–new chemical entity which *has not been registered by the DCA*)/Biotech)

This relates to products containing:

- a new chemical entity or a biological entity;
- a new combination of existing chemical/biological entity(s);
- existing chemical or biological entity(s) in a new dosage form; or
- existing chemical or biological entity(s) for use by a different route of administration.

(ii) Application for a generic product[68]

Such products could related to controlled poisons or non-controlled poisons under the Poisons Act 1952.

(iii) Application for product registration via the abridged procedure

This procedure is applicable for certain categories[69] of OTC products and also for traditional medicines.

The data required to support an application is divided into four parts:[70]

- administrative data (Part I);
- data to support product quality (Part II);
- data to support product safety (Part III); and
- data to support product efficacy (Part IV).

The type of data to be submitted will be based on each application type as follows:

Innovator product	Parts I to IV (except for existing chemical or biological entity(s) in a new dosage form which will require only Parts I & II, together with pharmacokinetic data).

Generic product[71] Parts I & II
Abridged procedure Part I only

Application Review and Timeframe: The DCA's application review process follows a queue system, which is divided by product type: New Chemical Entity (NCE), biotechnology products, generic products, abridged applications and traditional products. However, if a product is used to treat a serious or life-threatening disease, the DCA may expedite the review process for that particular product.[72]

Period of Registration: Upon compliance with all the requirements of the DCA, especially with respect to safety, efficacy and quality of the product, a product will be registered. The period of registration of a product shall be as specified in the registration certificate issued under sub-regulation (8) and where so specified the registration shall be valid till the end of the specified period.[73] Where the period of registration of a product is not specified the registration shall be valid until it is cancelled[74].

Licensing: The licensing provisions are found in Regulation 12. The types of licences that could be issued are:[75]

- a manufacturer's licence, authorising the licensee to manufacture the registered products in the premises specified in the licence and to sell by wholesale or supply the products;
- a wholesaler's licence, authorising the licensee to sell by wholesale or supply the registered products from the address of the business premises specified in the licence,
- a clinical trial import licence, authorising the licensee to import any product for purposes of clinical trials, notwithstanding that the product is not a registered product;[76]
- an import licence, authorising the licensee to import and sell by wholesale or supply the registered products from the address of the premises specified in the licence.

Labeling

Trade Descriptions Act 1972: The general policy of the Act is to prohibit the application of false trade descriptions in the course of a trade or business. It makes it an offence to apply any false description to any goods or to supply or offer to supply any goods to which false trade description has been applied.

Under section 4, 'trade description' is interpreted to mean the indication, by whatever means (direct or indirect), of certain matters with respect to any goods or parts thereof. The indication may relate to physical characteristics (like nature or designation of the goods; its quantity, size or gauge; method of manufacture, production, processing or reconditioning; composition; fitness for purpose, strength, performance, behavior or accuracy; the standard of fineness of articles made of precious metal; any other physical characteristics). It may also relate to its quality (as where the goods are presented to have been tested by a particular person and to be results thereof; to have been approved by any person or to be in conformity with a type approved by any person). It may be an indication of a place or date of manufacture, production, processing or reconditioning or of a person by whom it is manufactured, produced, processed or reconditioned. It may relate to other history, including previous ownership or use.

Where animal is the subject matter of trade indication that may relate to sex, breed or cross breed, fertility or soundness. If indication relate to semen, the matters of trade description include the identity and characteristics of the animal from which it was taken and measure of dilution. The word "quantity" is used in the Act to include length, width, height, area, volume, capacity, weight and number.

The Act does not have express reference to any declaration as to whether a particular product is free from genetically modified organisms. This is unfortunate as any imposition of labeling requirements would have to comply with the general legal policies on trade description.

Environmental Control

National Guidelines On Release of Genetically Modified Organisms (GMOs) into the Environment: As is mentioned earlier, the guidelines cover GMOs at all stages of research, development, use, release and placing on the market. It covers, but is not limited to, genetically modified plants, animals (including for example, insects, mollusks and fish) and microorganisms and products consisting of or containing GMOs. However, there is not much in the guidelines that covers any aspects of regulation on commercialisation of products containing GMOs in the market.

Breeders' Right

Protection of New Plant Varieties Act 2004: The Protection of New Plant Varieties Act 2004 came into force on 1st January 2007. The accompanying Regulations were passed on 20th October 2008. The Act regulates the registration of new plant varieties[77] developed through traditional means as well as through bio-technology. An application of a new variety developed through genetic modification would have to be supported by documents relating to the compliance of any law regulating activity involving genetically modified organisms in cases where the development of the plant variety involves genetic modification.[78] It is also a requirement that such applications must be supported by documents relating to the compliance of any law regulating access to genetic or biological resources.[79] For new varieties developed through genetic engineering, they would have to comply with the DUS requirement; i.e. distinct, uniform and stable like any variety developed through traditional means.[80]

More importantly, two of the grounds for the prohibition of registration and grant of breeder's right would be relevant to varieties developed through genetic engineering. The grounds are:

- Which may affect public order or morality; or
- Where there is reasonable ground to believe that the cultivation, reproduction or any use of that plant variety may produce a negative impact on the environment.

These two grounds are also the grounds of opposition to an application for registration of a new plant variety and grant of breeder's right.[81]

Under section 31 of the Act, a holder of a breeder's right is conferred the right to carry out all or any of the following acts on a commercial basis:

- Producing or reproducing;
- Conditioning for the purpose of propagation;
- Offering for sale;
- Marketing, inclusive of selling;
- Exporting;
- Importing;
- Stocking the material for the purpose mentioned in paragraphs (a) to (f).

The availability of plant variety protection ('PVP') for recombinant plants could bring enormous benefit to the industry. Given the number of new varieties created with improved traits and gene, such as male BT corn, Flavr Savr, Round up Canola, and virus resistant papaya, PVP protection would increase the commercial value of such varieties tremendously.

Establishment of Standards

Standards of Malaysia Act 1996 (Act 549): Section 13 of the Act establishes the Standards and Accreditation Council. The Act focuses on standardisation policies, programs and schemes. It promotes industrial efficiency and consumer protection. Under the Act, the Minister is empowered to provide standard specifications for commodities, practices and processes. The scope of the Act extends to approval of voluntary standards, accreditation of testing laboratories, calibrating laboratories and organisations engaged in conformity assessment or training of personnel for conformity assessment.

To expand the reach of this Act to the biotechnology industry, there is a need to expand the scope of its provisions to products bearing GMOs and Non LMO labels and be read together with the Bio Safety Act 2007 on the labeling of products containing LMOs or non LMO product. This step is necessary especially so that Malaysia is poised to introduce biotechnology products with GM label and *halal* certification. It has also been said Malaysia wants to tap the non LMO market. Having a simple labeling standard would assist Malaysia in this effort.

Gaps Identified in the Existing Legal Framework

From the previous discussion, most of the legislations and by laws that would be relevant to the conduct of research in the field of medical and pharmaceutical biotechnology has been identified. With the exception of the Bio-Safety Act 2007, all of the laws pre date biotechnology and has not been refined to reflect changes in technology.

In relation to the regulatory framework for the sourcing of research materials from outside the country, one finds that critical research materials for biotechnology have not been dealt with. The Customs (Prohibition of Imports) Order 1998 does not deal with the importation of animal and human tissues, cells, blood samples, genes, embryos, cellular and tissue-based products, etc. The position of pathogen[82] and bioremediation[83] is also not clear. Though the Bio-Safety Act 2007 has answered some of the needs, the Act only covers living modified organisms. Whilst pathogen could possibly be falling under the definition, it remains an issue whether genetically modified products from human biological materials could be classified in the same manner.

The Pesticides Act 1974 has been instrumental in controlling research of pesticides. This Act is of little relevance to plant pesticides as the definition of both 'pest' and 'pesticide' as defined under the Act would exclude any possible extension to them.

Sourcing of human biological materials is becoming more crucial in the development of vaccines, bio-diagnostic kits and other biological based treatments. Yet the only relevant legislation on this, the Human Tissues Act 1974, has not been updated to cover the extraction of live tissues, blood, cells, gene and gene samples from a human being. Critical in the research of stem cell is the extraction of embryonic stem cells. The permissibility of the act depends on the legitimacy of conducting research on human embryo in the first place. To this end, the Ministry of Health Code of Practice on Assisted Reproductive Technology (2002) and the National Organ, Tissue and Cell Transplantation Policy would be relevant. The former enables research on excess human embryo if licensed by the Ministry. The latter, goes further, to allow research on human embryonic stem cell lines; though the act of extraction of embryonic stem cells from the human embryo is not allowed. Though the Code and the Policy would be useful in guiding stem cell research in Malaysia; yet the fact that they are unaccompanied by laws passed by Parliament would be a cause to question the effectiveness of their enforcement in Malaysia.

Bio-prospecting is one crucial area in dire need of fresh injection of policy and legislative guidelines. The existing laws; Fisheries Act 1985, Protection of Wild Life Act 1972, and the National Forestry Act 1984, have created a permit system for various usage of genetic resources. The Protection of Wild Life Act 1972, mandates the attainment of a permit to enter wild life sanctuary and wild life reserve. The National Forestry Act 1984 creates a permit system for the use and removal of forest produce. All these permit systems could have been reinforced to cover bio-prospecting. Equally relevant is the Customs (Prohibition of Exports) Order 2008. This Order could have been reinforced to regulate the taking of natural resources without the proper permit. All these laws could have been easily amended following the experience of the Sarawak Biodiversity Centre in controlling bio-prospecting.

In relation to conduct of research, two legislations, the Animals Act 1953, and the Radiation Protection (Basic Safety Standard) Regulation, 1988 would be relevant. The Animals Act 1953 talks generally of cruelty to animals but have nothing to do with the use of animals for experimentation. The Radiation Protection (Basic Safety Standard) Regulation, 1988 sets the basic standard for the running of radiation laboratories but has little to do with bio-diagnostics. Further, the Pathology Laboratory Act 2007 confines the diagnosis of human tissues in the hands of pathologists who in turn must be registered medical practitioners. This is in stark contrast to reality where molecular diagnosis and genetic testing is routinely done by a molecular biologist, who is a scientist and not necessarily medical practitioners, in research laboratories in Malaysia. In practice, the result of the genetic and DNA testing need to be endorsed by a pathologist to be recognised under the law.

Little has also been done in relation to the conduct of clinical trials for recombinant vaccines or biologics in general under the Control of Drugs and Cosmetics Regulation, 1984. The guidelines on the conduct of drug related clinical trials sets the flow chart for the approval of any clinical trial in Malaysia. Of most importance is the provision on ethics whereby any ethical decision is to be borne by an institutional research ethics committee. This raises the concern that in biotechnology research in particular, where ethical issues could be more complex, there may be a need for a National Bioethics Committee.

For risk and disease control, three legislations could be important; i.e. the Destruction of Disease Bearing Insects Act, 1975, the Prevention and Control of Infectious Diseases Act, 1988 and the Plant Quarantine Act 1976. The first Act is concerned with the control of disease bearing insects, the second with the control of infectious diseases and the third with the control of pests or diseased plants. These three legislation are instrumental in controlling infectious diseases, or causes to infectious diseases in the form of living plants, pathogen or insects. As the definition of pathogen could potentially cover genetically modified virus, bacteria and other recombinant micro-organisms, this Act could be useful in checking any contamination of diseases as a result of field use of living modified organisms.

In relation to environmental control, the most important legislation would have to be the Environmental Quality Act 1974. The Act however deals with waste and pollution control and has little to do with biotechnology. To supplant this, the

Bio Safety Act 2007 was passed. The Bio Safety Act 2007 regulates two main activities involving Living Modified Organisms namely:

- release and import activities
- contained use activities

For both activities, there is a need for 'blessing from the Board'. For contained use, notification is sufficient but for release and import activities, approval from the Board is necessary.

The Act is however several decades behind technology as its main concern is mainly living modified organisms. This does not reflect the current developments of health and medical biotechnology in Malaysia that has gone beyond LMOs into more nascent technology such as tissues, cellular based products and stem cells.

The Act's main concern is safety and efficacy of use of LMOs, particularly on plant, animal and human health. The second concern is its potential impact on the environment and potential loss of biodiversity.

The provisions on release of LMOS is ahead of time as Malaysia is not yet conducting field trials on genetically modified crops, but is already importing LMOs for animal feed as well as food for humans.

Even in relation to LMOs, the Act does not go beyond the R & D stage into product development and commercialisation of the finished products. The limited scope of the terminology means that it is unclear whether the Act covers research on transgenic animals or the genetic modification of animals. The Act is also silent on human cells, tissues and cellular and tissue based products.

The Bio Safety Act imposes the requirement of labeling. The Regulation is however silent on the details; there is thus no requirement that recombinant drugs such as recombinant proteins, bio markers and the like be labeled in Malaysia.

Under the Bio Safety Act, enforcement will be on sectoral basis. For example, the Ministries of Agriculture would be relying on Pesticides Act 1974, Plant Quarantine Act 1976 and the Food Act in ensuring that the obligations under the Bio Safety Act are complied with.

However these Acts are outdated and have not been expanded to cover genetically modified crops.

There is also concern that the Bio Safety Act is over broad. Unlike the Cartagena Protocol on Bio-safety which only regulates GMOs released into the environment via planting and field trials, the Bio Safety Act includes LMOs meant for food, feed and processing. It has also been said that the Bio Safety Act extends to products of LMOS which may possibly include for example, flour.

The GMAC guidelines, which were drafted earlier than the Bio Safety Act 2007, contain general recommendations for the commercialisation of GMOs. The main weakness of GMAC guidelines is that compliance is not mandatory but voluntary. Another apparent set back is that the Guidelines do not deal with the socio-economic impacts of risks and the potential adverse effects on biotechnology.

For the commercialisation of biotechnology products, several processes could be involved. These range from drug approval process, environmental control, breeder's right and industry standards. The approval process for biological based products is still being developed, as a result of which recombinant vaccines are treated the same as any other new medication. Special labeling of GMO products is also being developed, as well as industry standards such as halal certification. In relation to environmental control over the commercialisation of products containing GMOs, the Bio Safety Act 2007 is of little use. However, in relation to the creation of new varieties through genetic modification, the Protection of New Plant Varieties Act 2007 would be relevant. The Act extends to the production of GM crops for health reasons such as golden rice with increased levels of beta carotene which is beneficial for people with vitamin A deficiency and also bananas with vaccines.

Table 1
An Overview of the Regulatory Framework of Biotechnology Research in Malaysia

Legislation	*Issues*	*Constraints*
Biosafety Act, 2007	Relates to import and export of human, plant, animal health and environmental biodiversity. Covers two activities involving Living Modified Organisms (a. release and import activities b. contained use activities) Setting up of GMAC that provides licence and approval for genetic modification. Requires risk Assessment Reports, Emergency Response Plan, etc.	Does not deal with labeling, product development and commercialization. Covers only living modified organisms. Not certain whether covers transgenic animals. Does not cover human cells, tissues and cellular and tissue based products.
Pathology Laboratory Act 2007	This Act deals with regulation and control of pathology laboratories and for matters connected therewith. Sets up a licensing system for the setting up of Pathology Laboratory.	Confines the services of pathology to registered medical practitioner. With molecular biotechnology, it is possible that screening is done by a molecular biologist; i.e. a scientist and not necessarily by a medical practitioner.
Customs (Prohibition of Imports) Order 1998: 4th Schedule	Bans the importation of certain animals into Malaysia including pests and invertebrate animals. Pests include any invertebrate or vertebrate animal, fungus, bacterium, virus, viroid, mycroplasma like organisms, weeds, or other organisms which is capable of being injurious to plants and including any dangerous pest. Any invertebrate animal (including the eggs of such animals) fungus, bacterium, virus, or any other organism which is beneficial to agriculture and which is not capable of being injurious to plants.	Does not deal with the importation of animal and human tissues, cells, blood samples, genes, embryos, cellular and tissue-based products etc.Position of pathogen and bioremediation is not clarified.
Human Tissue Act 1974	Deals with human body parts from deceased persons for therapeutic purposes and for purposes of medical education and research.	Outdated. Does not cover human tissues, genes and gene samples. Does not reflect current technology where tissue sample can be taken from live patients.

Contd.

Legislation	*Issues*	*Constraints*
Pesticides Act, 1974	Sets up a Board to process the manufacture and registration of pesticides that have effects on plants, animals and fruits in Malaysia.	Does not set out the process for the approval for the field use of GMOs.
Sarawak Biodiversity Regulation, 2004 (made pursuant to Sarawak Biodiversity Centre Ordinance 1997)	Covers the collection, taking and removal of biological resources from the state land forest, protected forest, land reserve, national park, or wild life sanctuary. Sets up a mechanism for approval of research permit. Deals with access and benefit sharing. Right to IPR over discoveries from research in accordance with terms of agreement between the parties and provision for payment of royalty, fees and other considerations on use of discovery not covered by agreement. Regulates ethno-biological research approval, IPR and access benefit sharing with indigenous people. The Act empowers the Council to maintain an inventory of genetic resources.	Only state ordinance. No equivalent regulatory framework at Federal level. In compliance with the Convention of Biological Diversity. Does not extend to humans. Would it cover marine and coastal areas?
Act 549 Standards of Malaysia Act 1996	Establish the framework for the establishment of standards to promote industrial efficiency anddevelopment, and for consumer protection, through standardisation activities	Future development of standards on GMO products or non GMOs?
Fisheries Act 1985Act 317	This Act relates generally to fisheries (including the conservation, management and development ofmaritime and estuarine fishing and fisheries, in Malaysian fisheries waters), turtles and riverine fishing in Malaysia. Deals with optimum utilization of fishery resources, consistent with sound conservation and management principles and with the avoidance of over-fishing, and in accordance with the overall national policies, development plans and programmes.	Applicable only to Federal Territory (not to state land). Deals with fishing not bio-prospecting of marine resources.

Contd.

Legislation	*Issues*	*Constraints*
Environmental Quality Act 1974	The Act sets up a mechanism to protect and maintain quality of environment; coordinating activities relating to the discharge of wastes, and general control of the environment.	Sets the general standards in relation to environmental quality. Applicability to grey biotechnology?
Plant Quarantine Act 1976	Deals with the use, control, import and export of pests, beneficialorganisms, plants and soil present in Malaysia. Introduced to control dangerous pest or noxious plant	Does not deal with GMOs.
Trade Descriptions Act 1972	Deals with false trade descriptions in the course of a trade or business. Creates criminal offence for applying false description to any goods or to supply or offer to supply any goods to which false trade description has been applied.	Could be extended to false labeling of products containing GMOs - if such requirement is set by law. The definition of 'trade description' is wide enough to cover such instances.
Animals Act 1953	This Act deals with the prevention of diseases of animals, cruelty to animals, and control of the movement of animals and promotes conservation and general welfare of animals.	Does not deal with genetic modification of animals and animal experimentation.
Protection Of New Plant Varieties Act 2004	The Act provides for the protection of the rights of breeders of new plant varieties, recognition and protection of contribution made by farmers, local communities and indigenous people. It establishes a Plant Varieties Board with regulatory powers. It sets the threshold for registration new plant varieties. Requires disclosure of the source of the geneticmaterial or the immediate parental lines of the plant variety and prior informed consent from local community or the indigenous people in cases where the plant variety is developed from traditional varieties;Requires documents relating to compliance with	Overlaps with patents in relation to genetically modified plants. Clashes with patent law on requirements for prior informed consent and access and benefit sharing for genetically modified plants.

Contd.

Legislation	*Issues*	*Constraints*
	any law regulating access to genetic or biological resources; Requires compliance with any law regulating activities involving genetically modified organisms in cases where the development of the plant variety involves genetic modification Sets a generous exception for: (d) any act of propagation by small farmers using the harvested material of the registered plant variety planted on theirown holdings; (e)any exchange of reasonable amounts of propagating materials among small farmers.	

Experience of the Stakeholders and Industry Players on the Current Legal and Regulatory Framework

The relevance of regulation in business practices cannot be over-emphasised. Generally, it serves to create an orderly atmosphere and may, if properly designed, facilitate business activities and guarantee the interests of players. Conversely, regulation results in agony and frustration for businesses where it is either inadequate or poorly enforced. Reasons are simply that while regulations are made pursuant to the vision of legislators and policymakers, the acts of operators give actual effects to the words of such regulations. Thus, an effective assessment of regulation or policy must take account of the operators' experience. Stakeholders' contributions were obtained on a range of issues especially those touching on regulation of biotechnology practices including research and development as well as commercialisation. This section provides an analysis of the views of the stakeholders regarding the regulatory environment for biotechnology development in Malaysia.

Research and Development

Biotechnology is a product of human efforts and innovation and can only develop in a condition with solid scientific and technological background. Although Malaysia has been classified as a medium developing country according to the size of her research institutions to generate biotechnology invention[84], lack of critical scientific mass is a major set-back in the industry. The critical scientific mass needed to drive the industry is in short supply, probably due to decline in the study of life sciences. In addition, researches conducted by the universities and research institutions, which form a substantial part of the Malaysian science base, fail to generate the critical basic biotechnology inventions as a result of lack of coordination between research activities and policy goals.[85] Moreover, there is apparent lack of asset consciousness (in research outcomes) on the part of researchers, in academic institutions, whose mentality is shaped by the publication syndrome. It was thus suggested that public funding of research may need to insist on stage by stage review to determine the worth and prospect of research projects, especially as academic institutions undertake the largest R&D funded by government.[86] It appears that the situation extends to the private sector too, in view of the fact that there is general decline in the studies of life sciences.

There is however a notable exception in the case of SIRIM Bhd[87] which, with well over two decades of experience in biotechnology research, has made major contribution to biotechnology research and development in Malaysia. It is well staffed with knowledge workers and considers capacity building as a priority. Its focus area consists of:

- Development of herbal based cosmetic products formulation and manufacturing process
- Production of industrial enzymes and fine chemicals through microbial fermentation
- Development of environmental processes such as bioremediation and recycling technology
- Providing environmental toxicity assessment and evolution services
- Development of biosensor and sampling devices
- Development of biotechnology measurement standards

Ethics, morality and public order trail science and researchers generally refrain from projects that may attract public or religious outrage. Hence, laws and regulations often provide unequivocal guide regarding comfort zones for research activities. Respondents are unanimous that regulations are insufficient to provide the usual pathways for biotechnology research in the country.

However, according to one respondent, the Bio Safety Act 2007, the only Federal legislation consciously enacted to deal with biotechnology related issues, has made significant impact in the industry. It must however be added that the scope of the Act is generally limited to human and environmental safety matters. In that regard, the Sarawak Biodiversity Centre Ordinance appears to provide a clearer picture of what is expected of a researcher intending to make use of materials from the centre. The frustration is more apparent in the expression of one respondent who stated as follows:

"... there is no national guideline or legal regulation that one is required to observe in the conduct of R&D in Malaysia. There are no rules relating to the use of cell based therapy, biologics and handling of data, like Data Exclusivity, or privacy. At most there may be some self imposed ethical guidelines like what obtains in UKM hospital. Here, there are institutional guidelines that researchers are obliged to observe on matters touching on confidentiality, access to data, consent, tissue transfer, etc. Truly, the Human Tissue Act is in existence but it has become obsolete and does not even cover such issues as transfer of tissue overseas. Ideally, overseas transfer of tissues should only be permitted under certain environmental conditions e.g. absence of required technology locally etc. The Ministry of Health should develop guidelines for R&D; it is ripe for bio-banking to be introduced at the national level and it appears that Pathologists have to champion that course."[88]

Absence of a national standard on the issue of informed consent of owners of bio-tissues aroused concern of respondents. According to this view, institutions are free to adopt a convenient approach when obtaining patients' consent to experimental use of their tissues. Approach to consent may either be generic or specific. The disadvantage of specific consent is that consent is limited to the specific purpose for which it was obtained. The tissue samples cannot be used for other purpose(s) without further recourse to the donor and once he dies the collection cannot serve any future purpose to which he did not consent. Since the other option is allowable some institutions including UKM practise the generic consent approach. As such, tissues collected may be used for future research but the practice is to keep them under anonymous names (i.e. coded) and so they can be seen but not linked to any names.

Opinion is divided in the industry on the question of regulatory approvals for R&D. Some operators believe that internal approval of institutions' board only need to be obtained to conduct R&D especially in health institutions or at most of the Ministry of Health, and the result of the exercise is to be verified by a Pathologist under the Pathology Laboratory Act 2007. Views from other sectors of the industry state that different regulatory approvals are required especially in the states. Particularly, in the context of bio-prospecting as land falls within the jurisdiction of states. Different states practice different procedures for the approval of permits to collect samples for research. Thus, it is not surprising that different players face multiple regulatory environments in order to comply with different rules when prescribed by various government authorities empowered to grant permission for use of resources. Added to that, the state authorities' policies over usage of forest resources also differ.

However, opinions appear to agree that approval of the National Drug Council is not required to research and development in the area of health biotechnology and the nutraceutical[89]. The views of the regulators are that multiple approvals should not be a problem but the real challenge lies in lack of co-ordination between approving authorities. Meanwhile, there are initiatives on the part of the regulatory authorities to mitigate problems caused by such lack of coordination and examples of such initiative is the formation of a cluster working group, a framework for information sharing and the Biotech Policy Implementation Council through which the BiotechCorp[90] provides coordination for the industry.[91]

Access to Advanced Technology

Acquisition of or access to advanced technology is a key factor driving biotechnology development in the major biotechnology countries of the world. Generally, different strategies are adopted towards gaining access to advanced technology. They include encouragement of foreign investments, acquisition of new technologies and building capacities of local firms and workers to undertake new inventions. The government has initiated several programmes through Biotechcorp aimed at providing incentives to core investors in the biotechnology business. Part of it is the Bio Nexus status offered to companies that fulfill certain criteria. Recent reports indicate that the programme worked well in attracting investors as the required target was promptly achieved. It is however too early to begin to assess the performance of such companies at this time.

Moreover, Biotechcorp and a number of other government institutions play an important role in facilitating access to technology. For instance, SIRIM maintains a patents database for public access. In addition, it routinely organises technology fairs, including the 2006 technology fair to enable industry players to buy technology so as to complement existing technology. In fact this function is one of the core responsibilities of Biotechcorp, a profile of its performance in this regard is the subject of another section of this report. Respondents confirmed the use of cluster or collaboration as a mode of tapping from the competences of others. For instance, the respondent from SIRIM confirmed that the Institute tapped from the experience of FRIM in the area of traditional knowledge to work on Tongkat Ali, pagaga, (megoshi, guava), and Kacip Fatima, through collaboration with Massachusetts Institute of Technology (MIT)[92]. Universities and research institutions are provided with funds to conduct research in niche areas, although these collaborative efforts appear to isolate the private sector for, as noted one respondent, his organisation "lacks enough information about the ability of the private sector participants".[93] Thus, some public sector participants hold the view that research in Malaysia has not reached the level of getting technology from outside and that in the meantime, they make do with materials sourced from within Malaysia.

Intellectual Property Rights ('IPR') Portfolio

The role of IPRs in the development of biotechnology is widely appreciated and practitioners in the market consider IP portfolio as an important business asset. The profile of IP assets in the industry does not appear to be bad as practitioners take advantage of the well known rights especially patent and trademarks. Some organisations have a unit on IPR which perform functions like IPR management, training and IP consultancy. In addition for instance, SIRIM produces biotechnology related services, IP management, registration, and valuation. However, with the increase exposure to IP related issues, there is a growing dissent to the expansion of IPRs particularly in life forms, especially in relation to the policy to be adopted on GMOs and the possibility of accession to the Budapest Treaty[94]. However, while they are not opposed generally to IPR, some respondents advised caution on its use to protect scientific discoveries. In particular, Professor Rahman believes that scientific discoveries ought not to be patentable. He provided a basis for the argument as follows:

"When genetic properties or solutions are discovered, they are not inventions. If it is allowed that such discovery is patented what becomes of the Patients right to his tissues – remember the US case in Re: John Moore. Oncology's tissue should be non-profit, charges should relate only to process. Similar arguments go for bio-markers or genome discovery except where the researchers convert the tissue to diagnostic chips, then that may amount to inventions".

Most respondents expressed pleasure about the mode of operation in the IPR offices but some insist that IPRs enforcement in Malaysia was less than effective[95]. In addition, IP assets management (from the point of discovery to the point of comercialisation) is underdeveloped in Malaysia.

Capacity Building

Different methods are adopted in the industry for capacity building. For instance, one respondent stated that in his organisation, the IP and Knowledge management department contributes to capacity building by organising trainings and promoting the participation of workers in conferences and workshops. As a strategy to make knowledge available, his organization has a database of papers from workshops attended by staff that other staff can access for their benefit. Approach in some organisations include providing encouragement to staff to pursue higher degrees.

Commercialisation

Commercialisation experience in the industry is almost zero. Hence, respondents could not offer precise opinions on this area. The little experience there is relates to the cases of labeling, concerning ingredients and *halal* marking and in case of goods meant for export to EU countries which are required to carry ECO labeling as well as HACCP (Hazzard Analysis and Critical Control Points)[96]. In the views of some respondents, the general requirement for developing products for commercialisation is the compliance with rules of standard like Good Laboratory Practice (GLP), Good Manufacturing Practice (GMP), Good Clinical Practice (GCP) and GRP, etc. and even the Halal standards.

Further, the prospect of commercialisation of inventions by the researcher in public institutions with the help of spin-off companies is good. However, researchers in the public institutions express uncertainty as to the extent of rights available to them in respect of inventions made by them especially when spin-off companies are involved. At present they adopt the wait and see attitude until there is clarification on questions like whether they are entitled to hold equity in spin-off companies given their positions as government servants, or hold board positions like being the CEO of such company.

In sum, the challenges that were faced by the industry players could be represented in the following diagram.

Table 2
Challenges at Research Level

Absence of national guidelines on ethics, thus institutional research board decides based on internal policies
Absence of regulation on bio-banking
No rules relating to cell based therapy, biologics
No rules on handling of personal data, access to data, sharing of data
No national guidelines on the handling of tissue transfer
Absence of national guidelines/uniform standards on informed consent uncertainty whether guidelines drafted by the Ministry of Health would govern R & D institutes that fall under the jurisdiction of the Ministry of Education
Absence of regulation to control novel and emerging therapies
Lack of expertise on bio-ethics
Abuse of DNA sample
Lack of proper infrastructure
Lack of skilled manpower
Absence of rules on bio-prospecting. Permit obtained at state levels. Requirements vary from state to state. Some states requires multiple approvals. Some process too onerous
Absence of rules on benefit sharing
Absence of rules on traditional knowledge

Table 3
Challenges at Product Development

Absence of rules on good laboratory practices and good manufacturing practices.
Absence of rules on pre clinical trials of biotechnology based products on human and animals
Absence of rules on privacy

Table 4
Challenges at Commercialisation Level

The process of registration of IP is lengthy, complicated and slow
Uncertainties on the strategy to be adopted for commercialisation
Lack of clarity on whether academics could hold top position in spin off companies
Uncertainties on the kind of access and benefit sharing mechanism

Contd.

Hard to comply with bio-safety measures
Lack of funding in developing new technologies
Absence of guidelines on bio-similars, biologics.
Absence of halal standards for biotechnology based drugs. So far, products produced are neutraceuticals which do not require approval from the National Drug Council.

The Gap Between the Regulatory and Legal Framework and the Needs of the Biotechnology Health R & D Institutes

Respondents report of several gaps between the regulatory and legal framework and the needs of the biotechnology health R & D institutes. Firstly, there is an absence of uniform standards on bioethical principles in Malaysia. Other countries set a National Bioethics Committee to advise on ethical issues as mandated by the Universal Declaration on Bioethics and Human Rights. In Malaysia, all R & D institutes decide ethical issues on an ad hoc basis and based on ethical standards drawn by their own institutions. The Ministry of Health and the Malaysian Medical Council also have ethics committees on various aspects of biomedical research. However, enforcement of the ethical guidelines drafted by the Ministry of Health and MMC suffers from lack of rigorous enforcement and existence of stringent penalty.

For agricultural biotechnology, certain bodies such as MARDI are also concerned with safety issues. However decision is made based on in house policies. Although they do have policies on bio-diagnostics and bio safety, decision is made at product level, not at R & D level.

Religious guidance from the religious bodies on various aspects of biomedical research is very much lacking. Fatwa issued by the National Fatwa Committee is based on request/ complaints and thus are sporadic and case specific.

Privacy issues are a critical factor in biomedical R & D. Yet the absence of legislation on privacy leads to differing practices among biomedical research institutes. Where consent is obtained for the use of samples for research, emphasis is more on consent on individuals involved in R & D. There is little regard on beneficence (i.e. procedure not necessarily beneficial to the patient); there is no clear demarcation between patient care and research, and there is no guarantee of justice (i.e. not everybody have access to the latest biomedical products).

Conclusion and Suggestions for Reform

Despite all the aspirations and initiatives in spearheading the biotechnology initiatives, Malaysia still lacks the necessary legal and regulatory framework. The only statute that has been passed specifically for biotechnology is the Bio Safety Act 2007. Several other legislations currently in place have relevance to the biotechnology industry and could be fine tuned to extend to the biotechnology industry but have yet to be done. These legislations are crucial to support the three stages of the biotechnology industry; i.e. research, product development and commercialisation.

Interviews with relevant stakeholders have also endorsed this position. From their estimation, many of the usual processes routinely done in research labs either for research purposes or for purposes of product development for commercialisation are yet to be regulated properly. Some of them even lamented that the Bio Safety Act 2007 is several decades behind the current technology. The Act which is framed to cover living modified organisms is yet to be tailored to cover cell based therapy, genetics and other emerging therapies which are at the frontiers in medical and health biotechnology. There is still no clear approach in issues such as bio-ethics, bio-banking, privacy, handling of tissue transfer, bio-prospecting, benefit sharing and traditional knowledge.

All in all, this research proves that a lot needs to be done to improve the current legal and regulatory framework surrounding legal and medical biotechnology research in Malaysia.

Footnotes

1. As amended 2003 and the accompanying regulations; the Sarawak Biodiversity Regulations, 2004.

2. Section 2 of the Pesticides Act 1974 defines "pest" to include bacteria, virus, fungi, weeds, insects, rodents, birds, or any other plant or animal that adversely affects or attacks animals, plants, fruits or property;
3. "pesticide" means, subject to subsection (2) –
   (a) any substance that contains an active ingredient; or
   (b) any preparation, mixture or material that contains any one or more of the active ingredients as one of its constituents, but does not include contaminated food or any article listed in the Second Schedule;
4. MOH-Malaysian Code of Practice and Guidelines for Assisted Reproductive Techniques (ART) Centres, 2002
5. Para 9 on Storage and Disposal of Gametes and Embryos
6. Para 14 on Prohibited/Unacceptable Practices
7. Para 10.4 on Prohibitions
8. Para 10.5
9. Ministry of Health, June 2007.
10. National Organ, Tissue and Cell Transplantation Policy, Ministry of Health, June 2007.
11. Majlis Fatwa Kebangsaan ke 66; 22 February 2005.
12. These views are based on the presentation by the author and Majdah Zawawi entitled "The Legal Position of Research on Human Embryo: A Comparative Study on Selected Jurisdictions" at the Workshop on Guidelines on Stem Cell Research and Transplant, Kementerian Kesihatan Malaysia, Hyatt Regency Hotel, 22 April 2007. According to a clarification from of the officers of the Malaysian Fatwa Council, the first statement in relation to therapeutic cloning was referring to the practice of PGD with particular reference to the case of Zain Hashmi.
13. Section 15 of the Fisheries Act 1985.
14. Section 15(2) of the Fisheries Act 1985.
15. Section 37 of the Fisheries Act 1985.
16. Section 2 of the Fisheries Act 1985 defines "fish" to mean any aquatic animal or plant life, sedentary or not, and includes all species of finfish, crustacea, mollusca, aquatic mammals, or their eggs or spawn, fry, fingerling, spat or young, but does not include any species of otters, turtles or their eggs.
17. "A Look at the Science: How Transgenic Fish Are Created and Examples of Current Research." Washington, D.C.: Pew Initiative on Food and Biotechnology, January 2003. 9 February 2005 <http://pewagbiotech.org/research/fish/trifold.pdf>. cited in "Transgenic Fish, Policy Issues package", State Environmental Resource Centre, available at ww.serconline.org/transFish/fact.html
18. Section 43 of the Fisheries Act 1985.
19. Section 35 of the National Forestry Act 1984.
20. The circumstances are:
    (a) the taking of such forest produce is incidental to or necessary for the purpose for which the use permit is issued; or

(b) such forest produce is, under the use permit, allowed to be grown by the holder thereof.

21. Section 40 of the National Forestry Act 1984.
22. Under the second schedule, the major forest produce comprises the following:
    (a) Round timber
    (b) Poles
    (c) Fuelwood
    (d) Charcoal
    (e) All types of rattan.
23. See my earlier work on this, Intellectual Property Aspects of Biological Resources–the Malaysian Perspective, Perspectives on Intellectual Property: Intellectual Property Aspects of Ethnobiology, vol. 6, (1999), Sweet & Maxwell, London.
24. Order 3.
25. Order 4.
26. Order 5.
27. Second Schedule of the Order.
28. Third Schedule of the Order.
29. "Biodiversity" means biological diversity, being the variability among living organisms from all sources, including plant materials, terrestrial, marine and other aquatic ecosystems and the ecological complexes of which they are part, and the diversity within species, between species and ecosystem, and includes biological resources.
30. "Biological resources" means genetic resources or materials of plant, animal or microbial origin or any other biotic components of ecosystems, with actual or potential use or value for humanity."
31. Section 3 (1) of the Regulations provides: No person shall enter and collect or take away any biological resources from a State land forest, forest reserve, protected forest, national part, nature reserve or Wild Life Sanctuary without a permit issues by the Director or the Controller under the Forests Ordinance, the National Parks and Nature Reserve Ordinance, or the Wild Life Protection Ordinance, 1998, as the case may be.
32. Section 4 of the Regulations.
33. Section 21 of the Regulations.
34. Section 24 (2) of the Regulation.
35 "derivative" in relation to biological resources, includes their genetic and genomic form or materials".
36. Rule 19(2) of the Regulations.
37. Rule 32(2) of the Regulations.
38. Section 3 of the Sarawak Biodiversity Centre (Amendments) Ordinance, 2003 amending Section 5 (b) of the principal Ordinance.
39. Section 6 of the Sarawak Biodiversity Centre (Amendments) Ordinance, 2003 substituting sections 21 and 22 of the principal Ordinance.
40. Section 3 of the Act.
41. Section 2 of the Act.

42. A "registered medical practitioner" means any person who is registered as such under the Medical Act 1971 and who holds a valid practising certificate. See section 2 of the Act.
43. Section 2 of the Act.
44. Section 2 of the Prevention and Control of Infectious Diseases Act, 1988 (Act 342).
45. Section 4 of the Act.
46. Section 10 of the Act.
47. This Act was gazetted on 20th August 2007.
48. "Modern biotechnology" means the application of-
    (a) In vitro nucleic acid techniques, including recombinant deoxyribonucleic acid (DNA) and direct injection of the nucleic acid into cells or organelles, or
    (b) Fusion of cells beyond the taxonomic family that overcome natural physiological reproductive or recombination barriers and that are not techniques used in traditional breeding and selection.
49. "Living modified organism" means any living organism that possesses a novel combination of genetic material obtained through the use of modern biotechnology.
50. "Products of such organisms" means any product derived from a living modified organism or part of a living modified organism-
    (a) If the product contains detectable recombinant deoxyribonucleic acid (DNA): or
    (b) Where the profile, characteristics or properties of the product is or are no longer equivalent to its conventional counterpart irrespective of the presence of the recombinant deoxyribonucleic acid (DNA)
51. LMOs are living modified organisms, which include those organisms which are still alive and can propagate themselves. GMOs include all, even like crushed corn seed, which are not capable of propagation.
52. "release activity" means any intentional introduction of living modified organisms or products of such organisms into the environment.
53. "biological diversity" means the variability among living organisms from all sources including, inter alia, terrestrial, marine and other aquatic ecosystems and the ecological complexes of which they are part; and includes diversity within species, between species and of ecosystems."
54. GMAC consists of a group of scientists and the Secretariat of the GMAC is in MoSTE.
55. Transgenic refers to organism that contains genetic materials introduced through recombinant DNA techniques.
56. See generally, Poison Act, 1952 (Revised 1989), Dangerous Drugs Act 1952 (Revised 1980), Sales of Drugs Act 1952 and Medicine (Advertisement & Sale) Act 1956.
57. See section 2, Sale of Drugs Act 1952 (Revised 1989).
58. See section 2, Sale of Drugs Act 1952 (Revised 1989).
59. See section 26(1), Sale of Drugs Act 1952 (Revised 1989).
60. Control of Drugs and Cosmetics Regulations 1984 (P.U.(A) 223/84) (gazetted in June 1984), as amended by Control of Drugs and Cosmetics

(Amendment) Regulations 2001 (P.U.(A) 186/2001), Control of Drugs and Cosmetics (Amendment) Regulations 2002 (P.U.(A) 291/2002), Control of Drugs and Cosmetics (Amendment) Regulations 2006 (P.U. (A) 336/2006 and Control of Drugs and Cosmetics (Amendment) Regulations 2008 (P.U.(A) 342/2008).

61. See Drug Registration Guidance Document (Malaysia), section 1, para 1.1.
62. Note that although section 3 of the Sale of Drugs Act 1952 defines "drug" sufficiently wide to include herbal remedy, under Regulation 2, the term "drug" has been defined not to include a herbal remedy.
    The term herbal remedy is defined in Regulation 2 to mean any drug consisting of a substance or a mixture of substances produced by drying, crushing or comminuting, but without subjecting to any other process, a natural substance or substances of plant, animal or mineral origin, or any part of such substance or substances.
63. See Regulation 7(1). Control of Drugs and Cosmetics Regulations 1984, as amended by Am. P.U.(A) 186/2001 and Am. P.U.(A) 336/2006).
64. See Regulation 2, Control of Drugs and Cosmetics Regulations 1984 as substituted by P.U. (A) 336/2006.
65. Note that section 27 of the Sale of Drugs Act provides that "The provisions of this Act so far as they are applicable may be extended by regulations made under this Act to apply to tobacco, cigars, cigarettes, snuff, soap, cosmetics and toilet preparations in like manner as the said provisions apply to drugs".
66. See also Ames Gross and Rachel Weintaub, Drug, Device and Cosmetic Regulations in Malaysia: 2005 Update, Pacific Bridge Medical, July 2005, available at www.pacificbridgemedical.com/.../malaysia/2005_drug_device_and_cosmetic, last accessed June 2009.
67. See Drug Registration Guidance Document (Malaysia), section 1, para 3.1. (Available at http://www.bpfk.gov.my)
68. See Drug Registration Guidance Document (Malaysia), section 1, para 3.1 - a generic product is a product that is essentially similar to a currently registered product in Malaysia. The term generic is not applicable to biological and biotechnology products.
69. See Drug Registration Guidance Document (Malaysia), section 1, para 3.1-antiseptics/skin disinfectants; lozenges/pastilles; dietary supple ments; topical analgesics/counter-irritants; emollients/demulcents; keratolytic; topical nasal decongestants.
70. See Drug Registration Guidance Document (Malaysia), section 1, para 3.2.
71. Note: See Drug Registration Guidance Document (Malaysia), section 1, para 13.7 - With the increasing availability of generic products, a mechanism is established to ensure that such products are therapeutically equivalent to the innovators products and are clinically interchangeable. Therefore, demonstration of bioequivalence (BE) is accepted as the most appropriate method of substantiating therapeutic equivalence between medicinal products. A list of drug substances, which, when formulated

in oral solid dosage forms, require BE data as a prerequisite for registration, has been established by the DCA. This list is updated based on requirements.

72. See Drug Registration Guidance Document (Malaysia), section 1, para 5.1.
73. See Regulation 8(6), Control of Drugs and Cosmetics Regulations 1984.
74. See Regulation 8(7), Control of Drugs and Cosmetics Regulations 1984.
75. See Regulation 12, Control of Drugs and Cosmetics Regulations 1984.
76. Note that by Regulation 15(5), products which are not registered with the Drug Control Authority and are intended to be manufactured locally for the purpose of clinical trial shall require clinical trial exemption (CTX) from the DCA.
77. A variety is defined as to mean " a plant grouping within a single botanical taxonomy of the lowest known rank-
    (a) Which can be defined by the expression of the characteristics resulting from a given genotype or a combination of genotypes;
    (b) Which can be distinguished from any other plant grouping by the expression of at least one of such characteristics; and
    (c) Which can be considered as a unit with regard to its suitability for being propagated unchanged and includes propagating material and harvested material of the plant variety.
78. Section 12(1)(h) of the Protection of New Plant Varieties Act 2004.
79. Section 12(1)(g) of the Protection of New Plant Varieties Act 2004.
80. Section 10 of the Protection of New Plant Varieties Act 2004.
81. Section 23 (1) of the Protection of New Plant Varieties Act 2004.
82. Pathogen refers to any organism capable of producing disease.
83. Bioremediation refers to the use of living organisms (e.g. bacteria, plants) to remove environmental contaminants from soils and water.
84. M.R. Bhagavan, "Introduction", in New Generic Technologies in the Developing Countries, edited by M.R. Bhagavan, (Basingstoke: Macmillan, 1997), pp. 3-4. Also cited in Graham Dutfield, "Literature survey on intellectual property rights and sustainable human development", (Geneva, 2003), 44-55.
85. Mr. Razif Aziz, Vice President, Legal and Regulatory Affairs, Biotechcorp, interview granted on June 10, 2008.
86. *Ibid.*
87. Standard and Industrialization Research Institute Malaysia is a wholly-owned company of the Government is the largest provider of technical and standards services. Further information on SIRIM could be obtained from www.sirim.gov.my
88. Prof. Abdul Rahman A Jamal, UKM Medical Molecular Biology Institute (UMBI), UKM, interviewed on 10/6/2008.
89. Nutraceutical is a portmanteau of nutrition and pharmaceutical, and refers to extracts of foods claimed to have a medicinal effect on human health. The nutraceutical is usually contained in a medicinal format such as a capsule, tablet or powder in a prescribed dose. See http://en.wikipedia.org/wiki/Nutraceutical

90. Biotechcorp is the corporation responsible for overseeing activities in the industries. Researches conducted under this body is inspired by a number of factor which include public needs determined through survey, contractual request by a player in the industry, international commission jobs and participation in cluster programs.
91. The interview with Mr. Razif Aziz, Vice President, Legal and Regulatory Affairs, Biotechcorp, ibid.
92. Through an interview with Mr Ong Chui Koon, the section head of Intellectual Property Services and Technical Information, SIRIM, on the 21st July, 2008.
93. Through an interview with Assoc. Prof. Dr. Zilfalil b. Alwi, the Director of the Human Genome Centre, Universiti Sains Malaysia, Kubang Kerian, Kelantan.
94. The Budapest Treaty on the International Recognition of the Deposit of Microorganisms for the Purposes of Patent Procedure. This Treaty is concluded at Budapest on April 28, 1977 and amended on September 26, 1980. The Treaty sets up a mechanism for the deposit of micro-organism for the purpose of patent application.
95. Through personal interview with Mr. Ong Chui Koon at SIRIM, ibid.
96. Hazard Analysis and Critical Control Points (HACCP) is a systematic preventive approach to food and pharmaceutical safety that addresses physical, chemical, and biological hazards as a means of prevention rather than finished product inspection. HACCP is used in the food industry to identify potential food safety hazards, so that key actions, known as Critical Control Points (CCP's) can be taken to reduce or eliminate the risk of the hazards being realized. See http://en.wikipedia.org/wiki/HACCP

7

Conclusion

What are the lessons to be learnt from the Malaysian experience? Like many other developing countries rich in biological resources, Malaysia has identified biotechnology as a new economic impetus. To enable this, industrial policies have been introduced since 2005 in the form of the National Biotechnology Policy. The Policy has been instrumental in shaping and guiding the development of the biotechnology industries in Malaysia. Are these policies supported by suitable legislative framework as well? This chapter represents the key findings of the case study on Malaysia.

Agricultural Biotechnology

Malaysia's Agricultural Policy and its efforts to enhance the agricultural sector in the country by boosting the agricultural biotechnology research and development is movement in the right direction. In fact, these efforts will help fulfill the future food needs of the country and will become a means to generate profit. However, funds allocated to the biotechnology sector are relatively low as compared to some of the ASEAN countries. It is, therefore, suggested that the biotechnology sector should get more financial support from the government in order to aptly conduct both basic and advanced and applied researches. It is notable here that as biotechnology is a one of the priorities of the 9th Malaysia Plan and the Malaysian government is encouraging researchers to apply for grants for their research proposals, especially under the e-science scheme. There is resentment among researchers that many of their research proposals are rejected without satisfactory reasons given. In view of this, it is suggested that the allocation of various funds for research proposals should be transparent.

Third world countries, including Malaysia, suffer from lack of competent man power. In view of this it is suggested that collaborative research efforts should be encouraged. It would be desirable if collaborations are made between research institutions or educational institutions of developed or biotechnologically advanced countries and developing and least developed and biotechnologically less advanced countries. These collaborations should clearly specify all the facets of proposed researches and utility as well as sharing of end products. Collaborations within Malaysia among institutions like the Malaysian Agricultural Research (MARDI), Forest Research Institute Malaysia (FRIM), Palm Oil Research (PORIM), other biotechnology industries and educational institutions are also imperatively warranted.

In the whole scenario, capacity building is the most essential requirement. It will be better if ASEAN takes up the issue of capacity building among ASEAN countries. Since capacity building includes scientific and technical training, training for enhancing the capability in the area of risk assessment and risk management, and improvement of technological and institutional biotechnology skills, including bio-safety skills, ASEAN will have to develop a mechanism suitable for the member states with the help of biotechnology experts and financial resources from some international institutions, including Asian Development Bank, which is keen on extending financial support in this area. We have the example of Latin American countries, especially Chile, Peru and Colombia. In these countries, the Organization of American States with the help of government agencies and independent NGOs and with the fund provided by some international financial agencies, especially the International Development Research Centre and Canadian International Development Agency has done a remarkable job. The *modus operandi* was to develop the competence of these countries through transfer of technology for risk assessment and risk management, by increasing the competence of biotechnology companies in safety testing, bringing about consciousness among the people about the probable impact of LMOs and GMOs on the human health, and the environment, and establishing cooperation mechanisms among these countries and other countries. Cooperation is also warranted in the area of developing a viable bio safety legal and institutional framework.

Malaysia has three important sectors that need support from biotechnology researches, for example in palm oil, rubber and subsistence farming. Presently, there are a few innovative researches in all the three areas, but there is a need to further augment them in order to compete with the technology giants of the world so that the country could earn money by exporting GMOs and LMOs. But to secure overseas markets, the issues of safety and environmental effects needs to be addressed. As noted above, there are two international legal instruments in this area, the Agreement on the Application of Sanitary and Phyto-sanitary Measures (hereinafter SPS Agreement) under the WTO, and the Cartagena Protocol on Bio-safety under the Convention of Biological Diversity (hereinafter Cartagena Protocol). These two legal instruments are not co-extensive and co-existent. This is because the primary objects of both of them are different. One has been made to protect unnecessary obstruction of international trade of GMOs if they are safe to human, plant and animal health; whereas, the Cartagena Protocol has as its object to protect the environment and human health. However, both require risk assessments. Many ASEAN countries are members of the SPS Agreement and the Cartagena Protocol. It is necessary to have a critical appraisal of these legal instruments and discuss the area of conflict among them and to offer suggestions to make them compatible with each other.

After a critical appraisal of the two legal instruments and cases decided under them, we conclude that the Cartagena Protocol, which has its prime object to conserve the environment, provides a viable mechanism for trans-boundary movement of GMOs. In view of the five exclusions, its scope is limited to seeds and LMOs. Movement of LMOs depends on the AIA mechanisms, which has the basis of the risk assessment. Risk assessment is generally done by the producing country before it allows commercialization of any LMO. It is also done by the importing country if it intends to impose an import ban of any LMO. It has been observed that in some cases, risk assessment was done by the biotechnology company which was later accepted without any reservations by the importing state. This is a wrong practice.

Once a state has imposed import ban with respect to any LMO, it has to review it in view of any new scientific information or circumstances. It is different from the precautionary measure taken under the SPS Agreement. The Agreement requires review of the provisional SPS measure taken by a Member state within a reasonable period of time. The authors are of the opinion that under the Protocol, the period of review may be longer, which might prove to be more restrictive to international trade. But for the sake of a greater degree of protection of the biodiversity, which includes all living entities, the application of the precautionary principle in the Protocol is better than the provisional measure taken under Article 5.7 of the SPS Agreement. However, it is suggested that the in both the legal regimes, application of measure, which requires scientific experimentation, must not only depend on laboratory findings. On the ground actual effects tests must also be performed.

In order to ensure safety imperative repeated lab testing is an essential requirement. This is incumbent upon both exporting and importing countries. Any LMO or GMO developed by a country should not be commercially introduced without conducting repeated safety researches, intensive contained field testing and followed by testing on human beings. Introducing something in the haste with a predominant motivation of making profit might result in an irreparable loss. Terminator seeds and Bt. Cotton are examples. Malaysia should develop its own mechanisms for these. It should not rely on the testing carried out by a private company that has developed certain biotech species.

Right to information is one of the rights of the people. It is the right of the people to know what they are consuming or going to consume. This right can be ensured by adopting an amicable labeling mechanism. In order to ensure the enforcement of such a mechanism, testing should be carried out by an appropriate body from time to time.

Medical and Health Biotechnology

Despite the fiscal and economic initiatives, it is found that many key issues are yet to be dealt with. In relation to the existing legal and regulatory framework, the following general observations could be made.

In many areas, there do not exist any satisfactory rules to regulated research and development activities. At the level of research and development, the activities include, cell base therapy, handling of personal data, access to data, sharing of data, bio-banking, handling of DNA sample. There is thus a need to develop national guidelines on the handling of tissue transfer, informed consent and how to deal with novel and emerging therapies. There exists uncertainty whether guidelines drafted by the Ministry of Health would govern R & D institutes that fall under the jurisdiction of the Ministry of Education.

Bio-safety measures are set under the Bio-Safety Act 2007. However, these research institutes' main challenge is that it is difficult to comply with the bio-safety measures set under the Bio Safety Act, 2007.

Tissue collection is routinely done in research institutes and hospitals. Yet there is no proper law on privacy. Most research institutes develop institutional based ethics, which leads to a divergence of practices on privacy issues. There is a fear that there might be a possibility of abuse of DNA sample as currently there is no law that criminalises the wrongful use of human tissue. Emphasis is more on consent of individuals involved in R & D. There is little regard for beneficence (procedure not necessarily beneficial to the patient; no clear demarcation between patient care and research), and justice (not everybody have access to the latest biomedical products).

In Malaysia, for product development to take place effectively, there must be proper rules on pre clinical trials of biotechnology based products on human and animals. At the level of manufacturing, producing bio-technology based products or biologics requires standardized rules on good laboratory practices and good manufacturing practices.

Natural resources remain the main important source materials for biotechnology research in Malaysia. For effective utilization of biological resources to take place there must be proper rules on bio-prospecting. There remains an absence of rules on bio-prospecting. Permits are obtained at state levels. Requirements vary from state to state. Some states require multiple approvals and require documentation which may too onerous. There is, as yet, no federal based legislation on benefit sharing. Traditional knowledge plays a big role in the identification of herbal plants useful for medicinal properties. Yet there is no law regulating the use of traditional knowledge.

The compliance of biotechnology based products with *halal* requirement is a major concern in Malaysia. Currently, there is no *halal* standard for biotechnology based drugs.

A number of obstacles have been identified at commercialization level. The process of registration of Intellectual Property has been said to be too lengthy, complicated and slow. There is uncertainty on the patentability of human materials. There is lack of guidance on the strategy to be adopted for commercialization. There is a lack of clarity on whether academics could hold top position in spin off companies.

Observations and Findings

Agricultural Biotechnology

There are three critical areas that need to be addressed. The first is in relation to animal welfare in terms of the usage of GMO in animal feed. Under the present Animal Act, 1953, animal welfare only relates to any physical harm towards the animal. It does not cover any safety requirements in terms of animal feed. The second is in terms of transportation of GMOs. The Bio-safety Act 2007 did not explicitly regulate the issue of transportation of living modified organisms or products containing LMOs. It is suggested that Malaysia adopts the Cartagena Protocol as regards the transportation procedure. Thirdly, the labeling requirement under section 61 of the Bio-safety Act 2007 merely mandates that all living modified organisms, items containing LMOs and the products of such organisms be labeled. However, the authors suggest detailed labeling requirements for products containing GMOs and LMOs.

Consumer Protection and Environment

There are several areas where no proper attention has been given. In relation to safety issues, concerns have been raised in relation to the conclusiveness of the present method of testing the safety of GMO products. Currently, there are two main methods adopted in establishing bio-safety, i.e. lab testing and field testing. However, the current practice is that all the testing is commissioned by the GMO producers. It remains to be seen whether the testing has been done impartially with no influence from the GMO producers. Secondly, it is unclear whether Malaysia has adopted any standard operating procedures for field trials in testing the health risks of GMO products. Moreover, it is questionable whether Malaysia has the necessary expertise and facilities to conduct effective laboratory testing.

Health and Medical Biotechnology

The authors recognize the need to provide protection and reward to researchers but at the same time not disregarding the rights of the public. There are various prohibitions under the patent law that satisfies this basic objective. For example in relation to the prohibition in patenting plant or animal varieties, recent decision from the European Patent Courts seems to indicate a shift in approach whereby the patentability of a plant variety is now allowed as long as the word "variety" is not used in the claim. There is also a shift in examination standards for the basic criteria for patentability. The European Patent Office and the UK and the US courts have started to adopt a more stringent threshold for the patentability of biotechnological inventions on three issues, novelty, inventive step and industrial application.

The issue of the morality as a patent bar is also subject to varying interpretation from the European Patent Office. From the cases decided thus far there are three different standards for determining the morality of a patent application. The three tests are the balancing test, the acceptability test and the abhorrence test. In view of the differing interpretation as to what constitutes a moral or immoral exploitation of an invention, it is wise that the Malaysian Patent Office set up an ethics committee consisting of members of the scientific, religious, consumer, environmental and legal community to deliberate on moral issues.

Suggestions for Reform

Agricultural Biotechnology

1. There is a need to amend the Animal Act, 1953 to include the requirement of ensuring safe use of GMOs in animal feed;
2. In order to ensure consumers' protection the government should encourage the manufacturer to comply with sound labeling requirements for GMO products;
3. The Farm Accreditation Scheme Malaysia (SALM) is to ensure agricultural produce is safe for human consumption therefore it should be made mandatory by the Department of Agriculture for not only export market but also domestic market;
4. The government should lay down mandatory procedures for the transportation of GMO. Pending such legislation, adoption of Article 18 of the Cartagena Protocol on Biosafety should be made compulsory.
5. Ultimately, the government should adopt the international standards in field and laboratory testing of genetically modified products for safety reasons.

Health and Medical Biotechnology

1. There is a need to relook at all the enabling legislation on research and development of biotechnology based products to ensure that all the key areas are well supported in terms of legislative framework.
2. There is a need to develop national guidelines on the collection and handling of tissue sample, transfer of such sample, informed consent and privacy issues.
3. There is lack of guidance on emerging therapies such as cell based therapy and stem cell therapy. There is thus a need to examine novel legal issues arising from these emerging therapies.
4. There is a need to develop proper rules on pre clinical trials of biotechnology based products on human and animals.
5. There is a need to develop national standards on good laboratory practices and good manufacturing practices.
6. There is a need to develop a federal legislation on bio-prospecting. The current permit system that is manned by state authorities lead to divergence of practice. These divergent practices must be standardized, coordinated and centralized.
7. There is a need to develop federal legislation on benefit sharing.
8. There is a need to develop halal standards for biotechnology based products.
9. Biotechnology should not only benefit inventors and innovators, it should bring about a corresponding benefit to the public. So application by generic producers for marketing approval for biotech pharmaceutical patents, on expiry, should be reliance of data generated by the originator drug producer. This ensures that the relevant laws and regulation ultimately benefit the consumers.

Patent and Biotechnology

1. The restrictions against the patenting of plant and animal varieties should be removed.

2. In relation to the requirement of industrial application or utility, a more stringent approach should be adopted.
3. The required standard for novelty and inventive step should be raised to be in consonance with the higher level of expertise in relation to biotechnology related inventions.
4. To ensure humans are not patented, regulations should be made to specifically declare, *inter alia*, that processes for cloning human beings or processes for modifying the germ line genetic identity of human beings cannot be patented. Products of such processes should also be excluded.
5. In relation to morality, a committee should be formed consisting of people who are experienced in various disciplines of human endeavour to formulate guideline on morality which could be relied upon both by the examiners and the court.
6. Section 13(1)(b) of the Patents Act should be amended to ensure consistency in the use of terminology in this subsection.

Ethical Recommendations

1. There is a need to strengthen the existing framework whereby reliance is placed on ad hoc or institutional based Ethics Committees. This could be done by setting up a Bioethics Committee at the National level which will have responsibility for formulating a comprehensive Guide for all professional or institutional Ethics Committees;
2. The National Bioethics Committee must be given once established the mandate and power to scrutinize all research applications as well as hear and decide complaints touching on breach of ethics. It should also be given the power to impose some form of punishment where a case of unethical behaviour is established;
3. Reliance on the ad hoc and/or institutional Ethics Committees does not provide adequate safeguards. There is a need to properly legislate and regulate scientists and

all those involved in biotechnological research and production of goods stemming from these researches;

4. Ultimately, the government need to legislate specific areas of biotechnology according to the needs of the people and it must address the ethical concerns brought up by the use of biotechnology.
5. The Ministry of Health in conjunction with the Malaysian Medical Council also has ethics committee on various aspects of biomedical research
6. However enforcement of the ethical guidelines drafted by the Ministry of Health and Malaysian Medical Council suffers from lack of rigorous enforcement and existence of stringent penalty.

Bibliography

Aaron Cosby & Stas Burgeil (n.d.), The Cartagena Protocol on Biosaftety: An Analysis of Results, *IISD Briefing Note, IISD, Canada.* Available at http://www.iisd.org/pdf/biosafety.pdf.

Abdul Haseeb Ansari, Parveen Jamal & Maizatun Mustapha (2006), Meaning, Scope and Implementation of the Precautionary Principle: A Critical Appraisal. In Hunud Abia Kadouf and Sharifa Zubaidah Al Junid (eds.), *Land Use Planning and Environmental Sustainability in Malaysia: Policies and Trends,* Kuala Lumpur: International Islamic University Malaysia.

Anzfa (n.d.), *The Hon. Trish Worth, 4th Annual Food Composition and Labelling Standards.* Available at http://www.anzfa.gov.au/mediareleasepublications/speechs/speechthehont rishwor1539. cf>viewed on 18 June 2002, 2.

Asian Development Bank (2001), *Agricultural Biotechnology, Poverty Reduction, and Food Security.* Unpublished Working Paper, ADB, Manila.

Bondi Ogolla A. Markus & Xueman Wang (2003), International Biodiversity and the World Trade Organization: Relationship and Potential for Mutual Supportiveness. *Environmental Policy and Law, Vol.* 33(3-4). pp. 117-132.

Bruce Chassy (n.d.), *The Role of Agricultural Biotechnology in World Food Aid.* Available at http://usinfo.stste. gov/journals/ites/0903/ijee/chassy.htm.

Daniel C. Esty (2000), Environment and the Trading System: Picking up the Post Seattle Pieces. In J.J. Scott (ed.). *The wto after Seattle* (pp. 243-252). Washington: Institute for International Economics.

Darryl Macer (2000), Ethics and Assisted Human Reproduction. *Pathways: The Novartis Journal,* 1, 40–43. Available at <http://www.biol.tsukuba.ac.jp/~macer/Papers/View.htm>. October 15, 2004.

Ernst Young (n.d.), Beyond Borders: Global Biotechnology Report 2007. Available at a: www.ey.com/perspectives.

FAO (2000), Implementation and Development of Biotechnology. Paper delivered at the twenty-Fifth FAO Regional Conference for Asia and the Pacific, Yokohama, Japan, Aug/Sept.

FAO of the UN, Rome. The State of Food and Agriculture *2003-04* (Agricultural Biotechnology, Meeting the Needs of the Poor. Available at http://www.org/docrep2006/y5160E/Y5160E00. HTM.

Gary P. Sampson (2001), Effective Multilateral Environment Agreements and Why the WTO Needs them. *The World Economy*, Vol. 24(9).

Gilbert R. Winham (2003), International Regime Conflict in Trade and Environment: The Biosafety Protocol and the WTO. *World Trade Review*.

Hassan Mat Daud. The Current and Future Outlook of Agriculture Biotechnology in Malaysia, (Mardi: Kuala Lumpur).

Haloran J.H.M. (1998), *Why We Need Labeling of Genetically Engineered Food*. London: Consumer International, (pp 2-11), April.

Howard Mann (2000), The Cartagena Protocol on Biosafety: An Analysis. Paper presented at the ASEAN Workshop on International Trade in ASEAN Agreement and Forest Products and Measures to Align Trade and Environment, Bangkok, Thailand, June.

James Rachels (2000), Ethical Theory and Bioethics. In Helga Kuhse & Peter Singer (eds.), *Bioethics, an Anthology*. London: Blackwell Publishers.

James F. Childress (2000), A Principle-based Approach. In Helga Kuhse & Peter Singer (eds.), *Bioethics, an Anthology*. London: Blackwell Publishers.

Janssen, W. Falconi C.& Comen, J. (2000), The Role of National Agricultural Research Systems in providing Biotechnology Access to the Poor. In M. Qaim, A.F.

Frattinger & J. Von Brown (eds.), *Agricultural Biotechnology in Developing Countries: Towards Optimizing the Benefits for the Poor*. London: Kluwer Academic Publishers.

Javier Verastegui, Victor Martinez, Willey Roca, Myriam de Pena & Leonel Gil. (2004), The Multinational Biosafety Project of the

Organization of American States. *Electronic Journal of Biotechnology,* Vol. 7, No.1, April.

Jayapalan Kasipillai (2007), *A Comprehensive Guide to Malaysian Taxation*. Shah Alam: Mc Graw Hill.

Jgdish Bhagwati (2001), After Seattle: Free Trade and the WTO. *International Affairs,* Vol. 77(1).

Joel Kohen, John Komen & Jose Falck Zepeda. National Agricultural Biotechnology Research Capacity Building. *Working Paper 4-14, (FAO-ESA).* Available at http://ideas.repec.org/p/fao/0414. html.

John A. Robertson (2001), Human Embryonic Stem Cell Research: Ethical and Legal Issues. *Journal of Science and Society,* Vol. 2, 74, January.

Kathryn, Ms, Clements Gilje, Alexei Monsarrat (2000), *Labels* (Vol. 4, No.3). Minneapolis: Institute for Agriculture and Trade Policy for the Consumers Choice Council, May.

Ken Conca (2000), The WTO and Undermining of Global Environmental Governance. *Review of International Political Economy,* Vol. 7(3).

Leonarddus B.S Kardono (2005), *Indonesia Country Report: Programs and Activities on Biotechnology in Indonesia (2005).* Available at http://www.binasia.net/binesiaownload/downloadFile. asp?file.

Leslean Arshad (2008), Malaysia Concludes Five Biotechnology Pacts at Biosan diego, 2008. *Bernama,* June.

Looking Beyond the Label (2002), *The Star,* Section 2, p. 7., September 30.

Louis Marie Houdebine (n.d.), Food Safety Evaluation of Transgenic Animals. In *Transgenic Animals Generation and Use.* FDA, 21 CFR 501.4. *Available* http://www.fda.gov/cvm/january 98, Retrieved 5 Jan 2009.

Ministry of Science, Environment and Technology (1998), *Malaysia's National Policy on Biological Diversity.* Kuala Lumpur: Official declaration) Principles (xi), p.2., April 16.

Mark Philbrick (n.d.), *Disputed Hormones: Risk Assessment, the Cartagena Protocol, and the Legitimacy of WTO.* Available at http://are.berkley.edu/ courses/EEP131/old_files/notablestudent04/cartagena%20harmones%philbrick.pdf.

Mayeno, A.N. and G.J. Gleich (1994), Eosinophilia Myalgia Syndrome and Tryptophan Production: A Cautionary Tale. *TIBTECH*, at 346-352.

Michael Freeman (ed.) (2001), Ethics and Medical Decision-making. Aldershot: Ashgate Dartmouth.

Mitsuo Matsushita (2004), Governance of International Trade Under World Trade Organization Agreements-Relationship between WTO Agreements and Other Trade Agreements. *Journal of World Trade*, Vol. 38(2).

Mohd Hazim Shah (2004), A Tale of Two Scenarios in the Development of Science and Technology in Malaysia. In Mohd Hazim Shah and Phua Kai Lit (eds.), *Public policy, culture and the impact of globalisation in Malaysia*. Kuala Lumpur: Malaysian Social Science Association.

Ministry of Science, Technology and Innovation (2005), *Biotechnology for Wealth Creation and Social Well-being. The Way Forward*. Muslamah Johan. (2006, August 1). *The Star*, April 28.

Peel, J. (2005), *The Precautionary Principle in Practice–environment Decision*–making and Scientific Uncertainty.

Peel, J. (2006), Precautionary only in Name: Tensions between Precautions and Risk Assessment in the Australian GMO Regulation Framework. In E. Fisher, J. Jones & R.V. Schomberg (eds.), Implementing the precautionary principle (pp. 202-204).

Peter Timmer, C. (2003), Biotechnology and Food Systems in Developing Countries. The American Society for Nutritional Sciences, Vol.133: 3319-3322, November.

Pierre van der Eng (2004), Productivity and Comparative Advantage in Rice Agriculture in South-East Asia since 1870. 18 Asian Economic Journal.

Quijano, R.F. (2003), Elements of the Precautionary Principle. *Precaution, Environmental Science and Preventive Public Policy*, Vol. 21.

Raziah Hamzah (2008), Malaysia to Evolve as a Regional Biotechnology Hub. *Bernama*, July 3.

Rebecca J. Cook, Bernard M. Dickens & Mahmoud F. Fathalla (2003), Reproductive Health and Human Rights. *Integrating Medicine, Ethics and Law*. Oxford: Clarendon Press.

Robert E. Evension (2006), Status of Agricultural Biotechnology: An International Perspective. In Richard E. Just *et al,* (eds), *Status of Agricultural Biotechnology: An International Experience* (vol. 30). Regulating Agricultural Biotechnology: Economics and Policy. United States: Springer.

Runge C.F. and Ryan B. (2004), *The Global Diffusion of Plant Biotechnology: International Adoption and Research in 2004*. Report Prepared for Council of Biotechnology Information. Washington DC: Available at http:www.scidev.net/en/news/gm-boom-could-spell-economic-growth-for-poor-nati.htm

Sabrina Safrin (2002), Treaties in Collision? The Biosafety Protocol and the World Trade Organization Agreements. *The American Journal of International Law* (Vol. 96(3)).

Sakaridr Bhumiratana (2002), *Report on Biosafety Policy Options and Capacity* Building related to Genetically Modified Organisms in the Food Processing *Industry of ASEAN,* June.

Sampson, H.A., Mendelson, L., and J.P. Rosen (1992), Fatal and Near-fatal Anaphylactic Reactions to Food in Children and Adolescents. *The New England Journal of Medicine,* 327:380-384.

Sherley, J.L. (2008), The Importance of Valid Disclosures in the Human Embryonic Stem Cell Research Debate. *Cell Proliferation* (vol. 41, Suppl.1).

Sobolevsky, A, Moschini G.& Lapan, H. (2007), Genetically Modified Crops and Product Differentiation: Trade and Welfare Effects with Soybean Complex. *American Journal of Agricultural Economics* (Vol. 87).

Steven Suppan (n.d.), *EC Biotech Products: Ruling at the WTO and the Cartagena Protocol on Biosafety.* Available at http://www.save ourseeds.org/downloads/wto_ruling_cartagena.pdf.

Sufian Jusoh (2006), *Biotechnology Law and Regulations: The ASEAN Perspective.* Kuala Lumpur: Canron.

Tarish Kelly (2003), The WTO, the Environment and Health and Safety Standards. *The World Economy,* 26 (1), 131-151

Technical Consultation on Biological Risk Assessment in Food and Agriculture (2003), Bangkok, January.

The *Thailand's National Biotechnology Policy Framework 2004-2009.* Retrieve2d on: www.biotech.or.th

The World Trade Organization (2002), *WTO Agreement Series, Sanitary and Phytosanotary Measures*. Geneva: WTO.

Thomas R. McCormick (1998), Principles of Bioethics. *In Ethics in Medicine*. Washington: University of Washington School of Medicine. Available at October 14, 2004: <http://eduserv. hscer. washington.edu/bioethics/tools/princpl.html>

Tom L. Beauchamp & James F. (1994), *Childress, Principles of Biomedical Ethics (4th edn.)* New York: Oxford University Press.

Walter Glannon (2002), *Contemporary Readings in Biomedical Ethics*. Orlando: Harcourt College Publishers.

Winicoff. D. Jasanoff. S.. Busch, L White, R.G. & Wynne, B. (2005), Adjudicating the GM food Wars: Science, Risk and Democracy in the World Trade Law. *Yale Journal of International Law* (vol. 30, pp. 18-118).

The World Trade Organization (2008), *Recommended Procedures for Implementing the Transparency Obligation of the SPS Agreement (Article 7)*, G/SPS/W/215?Rev.2., April.

The World Trade Organization (2008), *Guidelines to further the Practical* Implication of Article 6 of the Agreement on the Application of Sanitary and *Phytosanitary Measures*. G/SPS/48.,May.

Index